THE
TIME

The Museum Time-Machine

Edited by Robert Lumley

Museums are an international growth industry. Not only are they increasing in numbers, but they are acquiring new functions in the organization of cultural activities. It is through museums that societies represent their relationship to their own history and to that of other cultures and peoples. Today, there are great differences and conflicts both inside and outside museums about how this should best be done, leading those concerned with running them to question the traditional concepts of what a museum is, what it can offer its public, and how history is conceived and presented. Although *The Museum Time-Machine* deals with recent public controversies, such as those over charges, sponsorship, and political interference, it is primarily concerned with broader cultural and social questions. Themes include the role of conservation in contemporary societies, the representation of women and working people, the impact of the media, and the relationship between museums and their publics. The debate is an international one, and *The Museum Time-Machine* contains contributions from France and Australia as well as Britain. Comparisons are also drawn with other western countries, such as the USA and Canada. The contributors include both museum professionals and academics, thus providing perspectives from both 'inside' and 'outside' the museum itself.

Students of leisure, culture, and museology, as well as museum professionals and the non-specialist museum-goer will find *The Museum Time-Machine* a provocative contribution to the current debate, as the museum reviews and redefines its role as representer of the past.

Robert Lumley is a Lecturer in the Department of Art History and Communication at Lanchester Polytechnic, Coventry.

THE
MUSEUM
TIME-MACHINE

Putting cultures
on display

Edited by
Robert Lumley

A COMEDIA book
published by ROUTLEDGE
London and New York

A Comedia book
First published in 1988 by
Routledge
11 New Fetter Lane, London EC4P 4EE

Reprinted 1990

Published in the USA by
Routledge
in association with Routledge, Chapman & Hall, Inc.
29 West 35th Street, New York NY 10001

© 1988 in the collection, Robert Lumley;
in the chapters, the individual contributors

Typeset by Scarborough Typesetting Services
Printed in England by Clays Ltd, St Ives plc

British Library Cataloguing in Publication Data
The museum time-machine. – (A Comedia book).
1. Museums
I. Lumley, Robert
069 AM5
ISBN 0–415–00651 1
ISBN 0–415–00652 X Pbk

Library of Congress Cataloging in Publication Data
The Museum time-machine: putting cultures on display
edited by Robert Lumley.
p. cm. (Comedia book)
ISBN 0–415–00651–1
ISBN 0–415–00652–X (pbk.)
1. Museums – Philosophy. I. Lumley, Robert, 1956–
AM7.M875 1988
069'.01 dc19 87–23085

Contents

v

Acknowledgements

All essays were written specifically for this book, apart from Philippe Hoyau's 'Heritage and "the conserver society": the French case', which first appeared as 'L'Année du patrimoine ou la société de conservation' in *Les Révoltes logiques* 12, summer, 1980. Bob West's 'The making of the English working past: a critical view of the Ironbridge Gorge Museum' is an adapted and shortened version of 'Danger! History at work: a critical consumer's guide to the Ironbridge Gorge Museum', an occasional paper, Centre for Contemporary Cultural Studies, Birmingham, 1985.

The editor and publishers would like to thank the following for their permission to reproduce the plates: (1) Shropshire Newspapers Ltd; (2) J. J. Sheridan; (3), (4), and (5) Beamish, North of England Open Air Museum; (6), (8) and (12) Roger Taylor; (7) *Daily Herald* Archive, National Museum of Photography, Film, and Television; (9) Charles Barker Lyons Ltd on behalf of Electrolux; (10) York Castle Museum; (11) George Woods and Hastings Museum and Art Gallery; (13) Women, Heritage, and Museums; (14) and (15) the Trustees of the British Museum; (16) Pitt Rivers Museum, Oxford; (17) Popperfoto.

Notes on the editor and contributors

Robert Lumley studied at the Centre for Contemporary Cultural Studies, University of Birmingham, from 1975 to 1979. He lectures in the Department of Art History and Communications at Coventry Polytechnic. His publications include articles on cultural theory and social movements with particular reference to the Italian experience.

Tony Bennett is an Associate Professor and Director of the Institute of Cultural Policy Studies in the School of Humanities at Griffith University (Australia). His previous publications include *Formalism and Marxism* and *Bond and Beyond: The Political Career of a Popular Hero*. He is currently working on Australian, British, and American museum and heritage policies.

Brian Durrans, Deputy Keeper of the Museum of Mankind (the Ethnography Department of the British Museum), is currently working on material culture and colonial relations in India and Sarawak, and is editor of a forthcoming book on national and international exhibitions, called *Making Exhibitions of Ourselves* (Scolar Press).

Nathalie Heinich did her postgraduate studies at the Ecole des Hautes Etudes en Sciences Sociales in Paris, and works as a sociologist and research fellow at the CNRS. She has worked extensively on the sociology and social history of artistic professions and cultural practices. Her publications include articles in reviews (notably *Actes de la recherche en science sociale*), collections, and in encyclopedias.

Notes on the contributors

Eilean Hooper-Greenhill lectures in the Department of Museum Studies, University of Leicester. Formerly she was Education Officer at the National Portrait Gallery in London, and art teacher at the Cockpit Arts Workshop and Holland Park School.

Philippe Hoyau is a journalist and former member of the *Les Révoltes Logiques* review collective. He is currently working on contemporary French philosophy and poetry.

Sue Kirby is Curator of the Welwyn–Hatfield Museum Service. She was Assistant for Social History at Carlisle Museums and Art Gallery from 1980 to 1986, and Secretary of the Social History Curators Group from 1983 to 1986.

Alan Morton is a curator at the Science Museum in London where he was involved in the exhibition 'Nuclear Physics and Nuclear Power', which opened in 1982, and has also worked at the Royal Scottish Museum and at the Smithsonian Institution, Washington DC.

Gaby Porter is a mother and feminist working at the National Museum of Photography, Film, and Television in Bradford. Her participation in the Manchester Women's History Group and, latterly, in the Women, Heritage, and Museums network has contributed greatly to her critique of museums.

Jeremy Silver is Head of Education, Publications, and Research at the British Library National Sound Archive. His current research interests include the relations between literature and sound broadcasting, and the development of community radio in the UK.

Chris Turner (MA, DPhil) is a co-founder of Material Word Ltd (Unit 53, 17 George Street, Birmingham B12 9RG, UK), a co-operative specializing in the translation of academic, literary, and political texts.

Bob West completed his PhD on English ruralism and nationalism at the Centre for Contemporary Cultural Studies, University of Birmingham, in 1987. He works as a part-time tutor-counsellor for the Open University.

Introduction

ROBERT LUMLEY

The museum is said to be undergoing a 'renaissance'. In Britain, new museums are being set up at the rate of one a fortnight. In France, the government museum-building programme initiated with the Pompidou Centre has included the Musée d'Orsay, an imaginative restoration and re-use of one of Paris's grandest railway stations, and the La Villette complex, an 'urban park' enclosing the 'world's largest science museum'. In West Germany, the Frankfurt city council is creating eleven museums along the River Maine by 1990. In Japan and the USA, the museum boom is on an even bigger scale. Attendance is likewise on the increase, symbolized by the queues for 'blockbuster' exhibitions such as the Vienna one at the Pompidou Centre, which was kept open until 2 am because of the demand.

The numbers quoted in the press reports, promotional literature, and speeches reflect the fashion for hyperbole in the guise of science. None the less, they also point to significant developments – the renewed desire on the part of governments, cities, and private individuals to invest in museums; the museum as architectural innovation and hub of urban redevelopment; the rise of the museum director as star. Furthermore, the museum itself has been changing. It has become a place for visiting exhibitions, eating, studying, conserving and restoring artefacts, listening to music, seeing films, holding discussions, and meeting people. In fact, often the museum is no longer a building at all, but a site, as in the case of open-air versions, and is found in the country as well as the town. Nor is the simple institutional definition able to account for references to a 'museum society', which, as the threatened introduction of a quota on visitors to Venice indicates, is an idea that is materializing under our eyes.

'Museum', therefore, is a word acquiring new significance as the twenty-first century gets nearer, and is likely to be a key term in the wider debate over what it means to live in an old continent.[1] Not the museum in the narrow sense of a particular building or institution, but as a potent social metaphor and as a means whereby societies represent their relationship to their own history and to that of other cultures. Museums, in this sense, map out geographies of taste and values, which is an especially difficult and controversial task when it is necessary radically to redraw the maps in response to major social change. Although some new museums are trying to develop a role for themselves which is future-oriented and promotes innovation, the past is still the main concern.

History, however, is less and less seen as synonymous with the work of professional historians and the realm of books. If that view has long been anachronistic, it is only relatively recently that the many ways in which 'history' is made and remade, from personal memories to rituals of remembrance, have been seriously studied.[2] These have shown that history is used as a political resource whereby national identities are constructed and forms of power and privilege justified and celebrated; alternatively, or additionally, they have pointed to the resistance and opposition expressed through recourse to other traditions. Museums, precisely because their function has been to present ideas to a wider public in three-dimensional and accessible forms, have become an important vehicle for representing the past, and, therefore, have been drawn into the debate.

A major reason for putting together this collection of essays is to participate in that debate, and provoke angry responses as well as friendly ones. Several contributors are highly critical of some museums, which they see as peddling myths about the past, and they are all 'opinionated' rather than 'balanced'. In other words, they have 'something to say', and were asked to contribute on that basis. The collection is not, therefore, designed to be representative or comprehensive. Instead, its purpose is to identify some of the major changes currently taking place in the museum world, to open them up to discussion, and to follow up criticism with constructive proposals. The brief to contributors was also to write for the non-specialist, because there is no shortage of publications on museums, but there is little that is both critical and interesting to a wider public. Whereas a lot of controversy and discussion surrounding television has involved professionals, politicians, academics, and even the 'general public', the debate on museums has tended to be limited both in its participants and subject matter. Usually it has concerned admission charges or saving a painting 'for the nation', while the bigger issue of what museums are and should be doing is discussed by the professionals within the four walls of their institutions.

A quick glance at the notes on contributors will show the reader a mixture of 'museum professionals' with curatorial or educational posts and researchers, most of whom are not exclusively concerned with museums. It is hoped that this combination provides perspectives from both the 'inside' and the 'outside'. Someone responsible for the diplomatic and financial as well as the collecting and exhibiting sides of acquiring, say, a North American Indian headdress, sees things differently from the outside observer. National museums, especially, are like icebergs because only the tip – the public face – is visible to everyone. At the same time, the outsider can criticize more freely, even questioning the premises which professionals take for granted, and can identify more with a visitor's point of view. The aim of providing different perspectives is, furthermore, reflected in the comparisons drawn with other countries (notably Australia, the USA, and Canada), and the inclusion of two pieces dealing specifically with French examples. The latter are especially valuable because they come out of a rich tradition of social history and sociology, and relate to an ongoing national debate on culture and politics.[3]

The organization of the book, in fact, echoes the division of labour between museum professionals and those studying the museum from the outside. The first and last parts are written entirely by the researchers looking in, while the central section contains essays by practioners in the field. It should be added, however, that such an allocation of roles was never conscious. The main idea was to group the essays according to the main debates taking place in and around museums. So Part 1 is primarily devoted to the representation of history through the idea of heritage; Part 2 covers a variety of issues that are specific to types of museums (for example science museums) and to museums as institutions, but also issues of wider significance (for example the status of the oral within our culture); Part 3 deals with the museum public.

These divisions should make it easier for the reader to identify the key problem areas, such as the part museums play in representing our history to us. However, they should not be taken as hard and fast, and the reader will find out interesting and unexpected convergences and divergences between contributions for him or herself. This introduction will simply point the way, therefore, by showing some of the main themes which recur through the book.

Heritage and nostalgia

Part 1, 'The landscape of nostalgia', focuses on the rise of the open-air museum, starting from the premise that the idea of heritage now embraces everything labelled 'historical evidence', which, in Hoyau's words, goes from 'miners' cottages or public wash-houses to the halls of Versailles'. In fact, Hoyau's essay examines the process whereby the definition of heritage has been expanded, showing a surprising convergence in the aims of the ethnohistory movement of the 1970s and the policies of the French government, which in 1979 set up a Commission for the Ethnological Heritage. He writes: 'This new project represents not so much a desire to preserve and celebrate the "monumental" academic past as an attempt to promote new values on the basis of a thoroughly transformed conception of tradition and the national heritage'. Hoyau has been criticized for underestimating the extent to which the transformation of the national past has been won by 'the people', and for overestimating the importance of official cultural policy in attributing meanings to the past.[4] None the less, his discussion of the search for utopias in the past rather than in the future is full of fascinating insights.

Bob West and Tony Bennett, meanwhile, explore parallel themes through case-studies. West examines the pioneering Ironbridge Gorge Museum as an instance of 'political economy'; he argues that 'the new museum business has helped transform popular perceptions of the past . . . innovate ways of representing history . . . and fundamentally altered the environments and economies of places like Ironbridge'. He is highly critical both of the Trust itself, and of the role of some labour historians in supporting the project, which is analysed in terms of the involvement of historical tourism in the history-making business. Bennett, in a similar vein, speaks of Beamish as exemplifying a British ability 'to transform industrialism from a set of ruptural events into a moment in the unfolding of harmonious relations between rulers and ruled'. In addition, however, he traces the history of the open-air museum back to Scandinavian and American forerunners, showing how radical impulses were replaced by conflict-free notions of the past. He also points to alternative ways of representing 'the people'; the People's Palace in Glasgow and contemporary museum practice in Australia are compared favourably with Beamish.

'Bias' revisited

Part 2, 'Museums in a changing world', contains a variety of essays in which the perspective is very much that of the curator or museum professional. Although many themes and preoccupations unite the authors of Parts 1 and 2, the feel and the insights the latter bring are the insider's. If the view 'from afar' is more sweeping and panoramic, the perceptions here are more aware of the constraints (including the need to get official clearance for publishing articles such as these), and of the task of translating ideas into the three-dimensional forms of objects to be collected and exhibited

A professional ethos, or aspiration to professional status, is expressed, in this case, in demands for autonomy from political interference, whether from left or right.[5] However, it also leads to a rejection of the corporate spirit, and the corresponding attachment to concepts of 'neutrality' and 'objectivity' associated with an older and more conservative generation. Most of the contributors from museums are members of the Museums Professional Group, Social History Curators Group, and Women, Heritage, and Museums (WHAM) which are radical pressure groups inside the museum world. There is probably also, as Brian Durrans suggests, a generational factor at work. A new, highly educated generation has entered the museums in the past decade and questioned the status quo, including, as Gaby Porter says, the dominance of men and male perspectives in the profession.

In her essay 'Policy and politics', Sue Kirby sets out the main public controversies over museums in recent years. She discusses not only the financial pressures put on museums by inflation and government meanness but also the principles put at stake when charges are introduced, collections sold, and sponsorship increasingly relied on. These are the questions that have traditionally occupied the profession, the press, and politicians. In the last few years, however, disputes have extended to the question of 'bias'. The accusation has particularly been levelled in cases said to involve financial or political interference. Sue Kirby cites the case of British Nuclear Fuel's pressure on the Science Museum which resulted in the exclusion of material on social and economic aspects of nuclear power, and refers to the way museums of labour history have been dependent on the local political situation.

The term 'bias', however, implies intentionality and assumes the yardstick of objectivity. It is more an index of controversy than a tool of analysis. So the reader will find that terms such as 'representations' or 'ideology', which refer to structures or patterns of thought and behaviour that individuals are often unaware of, are preferred by most authors. Gaby Porter, for example, in her piece on representations of domestic life, analyses how women have either been excluded or marginalized in museum accounts of history because of the way inequalities and ideologies are translated into museum language. It is not so much that individual male curators consciously discriminate against women, but that deeper processes of ordering reality are at work, leading to decisions such as the one at the Science Museum to place domestic appliances 'in the basement beside the schools' entrance and the children's gallery, a long way down from the technological achievements above'.

Alan Morton and Brian Durrans, dealing respectively with museums of science and ethnography, find their workplaces caught up in a sometimes bizarre relationship to time and change. The former fantasises about the paradox that science museums are 'almost the victims of the very progress they collectively applaud', imagining a 'museum of museums' as examples of 'late-nineteenth and twentieth-century follies marking the triumph of consumer society'. Brian Durrans, meanwhile, writes: 'Ethnographic museums are influenced by the time-machines we conventionally use to represent other people's societies'. In fact, a model of time as 'progress' or 'evolution', moving from lower to higher forms, underpins the philosophy of the late Victorian museum and its spatial organization. Moreover, imperialism, nationalism, and the ideas of a confident dominant class gave direction and purpose to the institutions. Both authors, therefore, make critiques of this legacy, which is far from superseded, despite the decline of empire and British competitivity.

If it is useful and necessary to show how museums are themselves the product of history, that does not resolve the problem of their future, unless, of course, they are simply abolished or allowed to die. It means inventing a new role for the museum, and developing the special properties of the medium. Thus, for Brian Durrans, the collections of unique artefacts are likely to hold an even greater fascination tomorrow than they do today, and 'there are formal qualities in physical objects that communicate values across cultural divides and by doing so confirm a shared human destiny'. The ethnographic museum, once the embodiment of imperialist ideas, now offers possibilities for cross-cultural comparison in a spirit of openness and exchange. However, making museums address the key issues and debates in contemporary societies, such as the relationship between the First and the Third World, or the use of science and technology for military purposes, risks the controversy they have traditionally avoided.

So far in this introduction reference has largely been made to 'objects' or the visual aspects of the museum, thereby reiterating what McLuhan has called the 'sensory bias' of the culture.[6] As Jeremy Silver writes about sound: 'The exclusion of the oral by the written has often accurately been perceived as reflecting the cultural and historical exclusion from documentation of the people least likely to contribute to printed publications'. Despite the fact that, in Marion Segaud's words, 'sound makes space comprehensible; it introduces time, rhythm, action, all of which are the active ingredients of daily life', this dimension of our experience is largely unexplored in museums. If anything, museums dedicate themselves to 'the qualities of stillness and quiet. . . . associated with "serious" learning processes'.

The situation is, however, changing. Jeremy Silver refers to the technical developments making it possible to store and, crucially, to get easier access to sound in archives, and to the pioneering work of oral historians and others in establishing the importance of sounds and voices in our culture. He examines the different uses sound is put to – from the music industry to radio and theme parks – and argues that 'suitable critical discourse' has yet to be developed enabling us to understand and explore sound more fully.

The public's point of view

In Part 3, 'Sociology of the museum public', the perspective shifts again as we peer in from the outside. This part analyses the composition and behaviour of visitors. Before moving on, however, it is worth noting that the public has already been interestingly brought into accounts in both Parts 1 and 2.

The contributors in Part 1 can legitimately be described as critical consumers. Bob West, in fact, is quite explicit about this role: 'Being a critical critic is the only way I can enjoy the Ironbridge

Gorge Museum, and I constantly eavesdrop in the hope of finding kindred spirits'. Living in the immediate vicinity of one of the sites of the open-air museum gives him special insights, which combine with those acquired in studying contemporary culture. Familiarity, ironically, makes the museum 'strange' in a way it is not for the outsider. Tony Bennett, who asks the reader to treat museums as 'texts', has a similar interest in deciphering the messages encoded in the very fabric of the historical surroundings. If we cannot change a Beamish, at least we can read it as a 'crash course in the bourgeois myths of history'.

The contributors in Part 2, on the other hand, are at the other end of the communicative chain. Their job entails, among other things, organizing displays. It is interesting, therefore, to find an inquisitiveness about and respect for visitors' opinions rare in a profession in which, in Eilean Hooper-Greenhill's words, the curator is firmly positioned as 'expert in "his" subject, and the visitor equally firmly as "below" this level of knowledge'. Brian Durrans, for instance, advocates a much greater involvement of the public than simply providing 'hands-on' experiences: 'Much more exciting is the idea of harnessing the imagination, insight, and experience of visitors via participation in organizing exhibitions, and even allowing non-professionals to mount displays.' Such strategies disclose the relative nature of curatorial or institutional knowledge, show the museum as a process rather than as a finished product, and encourage visitors to see themselves in an active role.

Part 3 contains essays more aware of the barriers dividing the public from museums and the scale of ignorance about who the visitors actually are. While curatorial attitudes have a part in determining the relationship of the museum to its visitors, they are one factor among many. The profession has, for instance, always attached great importance to free admissions, seeing it as a right. Yet, as Nathalie Heinich observes in relation to the Pompidou Centre, 'the (relative) absence of an entry charge, which may at one time have been seen as a key weapon in the battle to democratize culture, has little actual impact on visitor numbers, since the barriers to culture are themselves cultural not economic'.

Museum architecture provides a useful point of entry into the discussion of the visiting public because it stands metaphorically as well as physically for the structures that define the boundaries between 'inside' and 'outside'. Often the museum is a building laden with associations, many negative. For example Paul Valéry, no lover of institutions, wrote of going into a museum:

> My voice changes and finds a level that is a little louder than in a church but much quieter than it sounds in daily life. Soon I no longer know what I've come to do in this solitude, which has something about it of the temple and the salon, the cemetery and the school.[7]

Nor is this feeling entirely a hangover from the past; Eilean Hooper-Greenhill notes: 'in many cases the message of the building may be enough to deter those who don't know classical culture, who know about the power of the law and who have not found many images of the past that have served them well'. She goes on to describe how most buildings are designed for the objects they 'imprison' rather than for the public that visits them.

The opposite of this negative image is represented by new museums whose architecture is as much an attraction as their contents.[8] The most celebrated example is the Pompidou Centre in Paris, which, moreover, was conceived from the start as opening the door to those who would otherwise avoid museums as 'not for them'. It is therefore, especially valuable to have Nathalie Heinich's study of the Centre's public, which measures the success of the utopian project against the kinds of users and use the museum has achieved in its ten years of operation.

Usually research on audiences is happy to deal purely in numbers. On this count, the Pompidou Centre has been a startling success, with 7.3 million visitors a year – double that anticipated – and this is how the figures are normally presented. Nathalie Heinich, however, uses the statistics to show that 'popularity' cannot here be equated with visits by members of the 'popular classes', and that the beneficiaries are the educated sections of the middle class. She then looks at the use of the different spaces to see whether the architects' and organizers' plan of mixing publics that would otherwise go to separate places in order to encourage 'cross-overs' and experimentation has worked. The findings are a reminder that the most democratic intentions can have the opposite effects when the power and class relations in the production and consumption of culture are underestimated; 'the outward appearance of freedom . . . is likely to give rise to aimless wandering which itself becomes transformed into anxiety; the capacity to "drift" is not so easy to acquire as one might think'.

Eilean Hooper-Greenhill's essay surveys the work done on the museum-going public rather than focusing on an individual case. In particular, she refers to the research in Canada and the USA whose achievements are contrasted with the underdevelopment of studies in Britain. The American conception of the visitor as a consumer making a choice in the market-place is shown as positive when compared with the stuffy indifference of many curators on the other side of the Atlantic. None the less, she writes that there is still a shortage of qualitative studies which analyse the visitor's experience using interpretative or ethnomethodological approaches. In the absence of these, museum professionals have no way of judging what messages they are managing to get across to the public, and the tyranny of numbers goes uncontested. The ideal, of course, would involve studying the communicative chain, from the intentions of the exhibition organizers to the exhibition itself and the 'sense' made of it by the public (in turn analysed in terms of its social composition, 'cultural capital', and so on).[9]

Some of the themes running through the chapters, such as the role of the public, have already been remarked on, and the reader will, anyway, discover underlying patterns as well as points of disagreement. However, three broad areas of concern are worth pointing out: the 'commercialization' of museums, the pursuit of 'realism', and the impact of the media.

Commercialization

First, the question of 'commercialization'. It is perhaps symptomatic of the different national traditions that the French authors speak about the role of the state and politics in culture, whereas the British refer largely to the cultural market-place. In France, it has been the *dirigiste* state that has founded prestigious new museums and cultivated the national heritage, while in Britain charitable trusts have led the way. It could be said that in France the museum addresses the 'citizen' and in Britain the 'consumer'. If this is an exaggeration, the growth of market-led initiatives in Britain and the relative decline of the state's role are changing the balance of the museum world.

Bob West's assessment of Ironbridge Gorge museum is particularly critical of the free enterprise spirit. For him, this reconstruction of the Industrial Revolution *in situ* reproduces equivalent forms of exploitation and entrepreneurship by turning a manufacturing into a service industry, and gearing a whole locality to tourist consumption. Alan Morton writes of the competition in the leisure sector: 'The greater the success of malls and theme parks, the greater the pressure on museums . . . to mount spectacular and expensive displays (to compete with, say, the Disney organization's EPCOT in Florida) or even place a museum "shop" in a prominent site'. It is not just that the market is at the turnstiles, but that its values and methods (marketing, advertising, retailing) are seen to be taking over, so that an educational function is displaced by an entertainment orientation. In consequence, museum staff are increasingly divided between scholars and salesmen, museum professionals and experts brought in from outside, educationalists and marketing people.[10]

The majority of contributors (the professionals among whom, it has to be said, work in the national, not private sector, museums) argue in favour of a public service ideal, which, strangely perhaps, is seen as stronger in the USA than in Britain today. Alan Morton, for example, makes the case for maintaining the unique quality of public space which belongs to the citizen, while others note that the museum has to develop forms of accountability and participation if the public is really to feel that the institution belongs to them. Clearly in the British case, public service, whether in broadcasting or welfare, has come under attack from market-based provision.[11] Indeed, it is generally acknowledged that it is private initiatives that have forced the pace and attracted visitors. There is, therefore, an acceptance that there are lessons to be learnt and blessings to be found in commercial disguises. Brian Durrans sees a positive side in ethnographic museums being forced to purchase mundane and contemporary objects rather than older, rarer items made too expensive by the art market. The most sympathetic to the consumer-orientation, however, are those who adopt the user's point of view, as Eilean Hooper-Greenhill's essay shows.[12] Here, the act of 'consumption', which is not restricted to the aesthetic, has a democratizing potential denied by the enemies of 'commercialization'. If, as Pierre Bourdieu has suggested, the department store is 'the poor man's art gallery' because it 'presents objects that are familiar . . . but more especially because there, people feel free to judge in the name of the legitimate arbitrariness of tastes and colours', then the introduction of museum shops, display techniques taken from window-dressing, and the juxaposition of everyday and 'art' objects can make museums more accessible.[13]

'Realism'

A second theme that recurs is 'realism'. The term is notoriously difficult to pin down. It has provoked celebrated debates, and continues to haunt discussions.[14] When Umberto Eco identified the pursuit of the 'real thing' (hyperreality) as an important tendency in contemporary American culture, as exemplified in the museums of the West Coast, he perhaps put his finger on a more general phenomenon.[15] The use of period dress, role-play, working exhibits, real locations, and smells, sounds, and 'experiences' has spread to Europe.[16] Whereas in the nineteenth century Europe exported its concept of the museum to the USA, in the late twentieth century, the balance of trade has been reversed. 'Colonial Williamsburg' – Revd Goodwin's 'reconstruction of an enchanted world where all is as it was two centuries ago' – is the model for our times, even though not in every detail.[17]

The open-air museum, however, as Tony Bennett shows, has its roots in a Scandinavian folk revival which was originally a 'progressive phenomenon' – 'a movement of revolt against the centre by the cultural periphery of Europe'. It is not the form itself, therefore, that is at issue, but the way it has been developed. A 'reality effect' has substituted an attempt to reveal historical processes. It is the problem of how to represent the latter that deeply concerns many of the authors of this book. On the one hand, they search to show what is omitted, excluded, or censored – the 'hidden history' of working-class women, the 'violence done to the producers and the environment', the oral culture;[18] on the other, they criticize what is displayed – the trappings and remains of the past that serve to put to sleep, not awaken, a sense of history. Gaby Porter, for example, argues that museums' 'reliance on history and social process to select material' has meant that an object-centred re-presentation of 'reality' has consigned the property-less to oblivion, whereas the march of technological progress has tended to leave women in particular behind; 'much of women's historical experience lies in areas where "change" measured in objects and technology is slow, and where women are seen as secondary, operators and consumers rather than inventors or producers'.

However, Bob West found himself caught out by his own pursuit of 'what it was really like' when faced with candle-making at the Ironbridge Museum:

This was an ill-lighted, pokey and miserable place, the air was heavy with the gagging vapour of quantities of melted wax . . .

two people in 'Victorian clothes' were busy making candles. . . . I felt personally confused by this particular aspect of my day out, as, on the one hand, it contradicted my criticism of the lack of authenticity, while drawing into hard relief the potentially unacceptable consequences of really reproducing a hazardous work environment.[19]

The paradox here, to paraphrase Eco, is that the only way to attain the real thing is by fabricating the absolute fake.[20]

It is not 'reality', though, that is the goal. A didactic, positivist 'realism', such as is found in Eastern European museums is as unacceptable as the Disneyland version of the past. Instead, the different essays emphasize how museums construct 'realities', and can do so only with the co-operation of the visitor. Gaby Porter criticizes the attempt to sustain the illusion of the display which claims 'this is how it was', leaving no room for questioning or doubt. The moment when the mask of role-play slips (or when the contemporary world breaks into the reconstructed past) is welcomed by both Tony Bennett and Bob West. Meanwhile, for Brian Durrans, ethnographic museums should be dealing with how societies change and compare, 'especially if contemporary mass culture becomes a legitimate form for collecting and exhibitions'. The tendency to fix 'reality' in a timeless moment makes it impossible to understand processes.

Self-consciousness, reflexivity, and awareness of classification are conditions of existence in the modern world. Kenneth Hudson has observed: 'With every year that passes it strikes me more and more how much of our lives are spent in inverted commas', and has gone on to suggest that museums too, especially those which present other cultures, have to build those inverted commas into their exhibitions.[21] To put it differently, the museum text needs also to manifest the metatext, so that the very ability to read and make sense, as well as the choices leading to a particular display, are visible to the public.[22] At this point, museums could free themselves of the taboos which make them avoid risky and controversial subjects in the name of their 'authority'. For example, as David Lowenthal has proposed, the British Museum could mount an exhibition on the Elgin Marbles which showed the different sides to the argument about restoring them to Greece rather than censoring all mention of the subject.[23] Museums might then become more part of the mainstream of cultural life and less a deep backwater.

The impact of the media

The impact of the media is the third theme which resurfaces in the essays. As a medium, the museum has advantages over printed forms like the encyclopedia, because it has another dimension and brings, in Alan Morton's words, 'the romance of seeing the "real" on display'. Yet, with the advent of television, the museum has often been said to have become redundant: television is better at giving access to faraway people and places; it is more 'realistic' and can record complex and lengthy processes.[24] For one eminent museum director, 'television has replaced the museum. It is an armchair culture presented in such a way that the thinking is done for the viewer, for a programme presupposes a commentary and interpretation'. He adds, however, that 'what the museum still does, which is crucial for our society, is to offer an *open*, as against a *closed* experience'.[25]

Talk of the death of the museum, however, tells us more about the crisis of a humanist tradition than about current developments taken as a whole. The rise of each medium has provoked hostile reaction, but has usually led to the subordination rather than extinction of predecessors; the newspaper, for example, lost its immediacy value to radio and television, and was forced to develop other functions.[26] Jeremy Silver's essay is especially helpful here in that he discusses the relationship of oral/aural culture to first writing and then to the technologies of sound recording, storage, and retrieval. If museums have long been silent places with a 'sensory bias' towards the visual, the increasing orality of culture has been affecting displays and entire museum environments. However, as Jeremy Silver insists, the new means of reproduction have a radical impact on conceptions of 'authenticity', 'naturalness', and cultural legitimacy. In fact the relationship between a picture and its reproduction, and between a 'live' performance and a recording, can no longer be understood in terms of 'reflection' or 'origins'. The museum is, therefore, part of a mass-mediated environment, and not simply in competition with television. The very notion of reference to 'the real', so fundamental to the received wisdom of museology, is put in question. According to Jean Baudrillard, 'simulation is no longer that of a territory, a referential being or substance. It is the generation by models of a real without origin or reality: a hyperreal'.[27] This indeed was the theme of a major exhibition at the Pompidou Centre in 1985.[28]

Introduction

Far from making the museum obsolete, the media environment has had two main effects: first, to push museums to do what *only* they can do; second, to give rise to a new generation of multi-media museums. The museums that have changed least are the fine art galleries, which are nearest to the model of the open text; the object is accompanied by the minimum of information, and visitors have to discover more for themselves via publications and so on if they so wish; otherwise, the painting or sculpture is meant to communicate in its own terms. Indeed, paradoxically, the very explosion of reproductions (postcards, posters, advertising, television programmes) has reinforced the aura of authenticity surrounding the original, and hence the particular value attached to seeing it in person.[29] The traditional museums with world masterpieces are, therefore, among the most visited, while the 'blockbuster' exhibitions are both cause and effect of extraordinary 'media events', in which the queue is an essential component.[30]

However, other museums, without this advantage, have been under greater pressure to win public interest by offering attractions. The notion of the museum as a collection for scholarly use has been largely replaced by the idea of the museum as a means of communication. In fact, many older ones have become curious hybrids, combining displays with cryptic labels and fairground-style interactive and participatory devices. Often opportunism rather than experimentation, based on a re-evaluation of the museum's cultural role, prevails; 'the conviction that the Museum is fundamentally an alienating institution and that somehow it must be made palatable to a larger, especially younger audience'.[31]

In the case of many open-air museums, the educative function has been almost entirely subordinated to the satisfaction of visitor expectations. The three-dimensional stage-sets, actors, story-lines, and so on can be seen as the result of an attempt to put television realism into museum form, with an extra 'experiential' dimension. So much so, that a leading British exponent of the open-air museum now finds that parts of Ironbridge and the whole of Beamish are trying to achieve what television could do better, and that a return to scholarship and collections of scientific value is needed.[32] However, within the museums themselves, the role of the scholar is in decline, whereas that of the marketing manager is growing in status and influence. The pursuit of 'hyperrealism', moreover, is backed by market forces, the philosophy of consumer sovereignty and trends in popular taste.

The foundation of new museums which are actually about twentieth-century media is a relatively recent but rapidly growing phenomenon. In Britain the opening of the National Museum of Photography, Film, and Television in Bradford and the Museum of the Moving Image (MOMI) in London are early examples of an international trend. The former is, in many ways, an extension of the repertoire of existing museum collecting and exhibiting; it is an outpost of the Science Museum, is housed in a converted theatre rather than purpose-built, concentrates on the technology of the media (photographic studio and television studio reconstructions), and celebrates British achievements (the new television gallery opened to coincide with the fiftieth anniversary of the first BBC broadcast). MOMI, on the other hand, is designed to mark a break with existing museum practice.

Since MOMI, at the time of writing, has yet to be opened, any comments are necessarily provisional. None the less, it is possible to outline how the projected museum represents some significant contemporary developments.[33] In many respects, MOMI is likely to be more traditional than intended; often the claim to be doing something absolutely new, especially when based on a caricature of the old, results in a failure to examine basic categories, and hence a repetition of existing formulae. At the same time, at least within a British context, the setting up of MOMI and the other new museum south of the river, the Design Museum, mark a shift in the museum scene in Britain. [34]

These new museums are 'high tech', futuristic, and would rather not be called 'museums' at all in so far as the word is associated with the past. They are largely funded by rich patrons (Sir Terence Conran, Sir Yue-Kong Pao, Paul Getty jun. and others) and by sponsorship, and plan to have admission charges.[35] They are designed to provide a service to industry, professionals, and students, and to have a primarily informational and educative function. Indeed, a sense of mission – establishing cultural recognition, developing visual literacy and critical awareness, bringing 'culture' and 'industry' together, making London a leader in the field – comes across in the literature promoting the projects. Anecdotes about the original brainwave, the plan, pride in being 'the first', and fears about others stealing ideas are further indicators of the excitement surrounding the foundation of an institution like MOMI. Founders have 'visions', whereas the directors who come afterwards have to work within a pre-existing structure.[36]

Introduction

The fact that MOMI is a museum of film and video also makes a difference, especially given the decision to use 'soft ware' and leave the collection and exhibition of 'hard ware' mainly to others. Instead of being object-centred and concerned about collection, the museum is going to be centred on images and temporary exhibitions. (Of course, the National Film Archive with its miles of film and plans to record millions of hours of television provides the back-up.) Importantly, MOMI stands at the point of intersection where images are endowed with 'aura' (the magic of the 'modern' represented by the laser 'tower' in the sky above Waterloo bridge, and the 'halo' of the old in the recreation of the peep-show), and where they are analysed and contextualized ('demystified' in the interests of education). This places it in an ideal position to address developments within the new media and contemporary culture more widely. If a new museum like MOMI is thereby able to play a critical role and to provoke debates beyond its confines, it could also have positive consequences in a museum world that has scarcely confronted what it means to live in a mass-mediated environment.

It is a curious feature of the present period that rapid change (the formation of the 'information' or 'post-industrial' society) is accompanied by two seemingly contradictory developments. On the one hand, there is the pursuit of 'authenticity' and the revival and recycling of the past; on the other, a fascination with modern technology and the science fictional future.[37] The two appear to belong to different worlds and different times. So, in museum terms, we have in Britain the 'great Northern experience' at Beamish, which recreates a 'historic' industrial landscape, and the 'high tech' museums of London, which are products and proponents of new technological developments. There is perhaps even a cruel irony in Labour councils planning to turn old industrial areas, like the Lower Don valley or the Black Country, into theme parks with museums ('for tourists'), while the successful entrepreneurs sponsor design or film and television museums ('for yuppies') in the metropolis.[38] However, the developments need to be understood as an interactive whole, not as separate and divergent.

The 'backward-looking' open-air museum is not in itself a relic; far from it. If anything, it has helped pioneer a more commercial approach to museum development, and, hence, to the redevelopment of entire localities. Its replacement of a manufacturing by a service industry and the re-use of sites for tourism anticipates radical changes in the countryside and rural economy. Moreover, the growth of nostalgia (both in the 'everyday life' of individuals and

17

groups, and in advertising imagery – the two should not be treated as the same) is provoked by the very transformations it laments.[39] On the other hand, the museums set up with the purpose of stimulating a culture based on current industrial and cultural innovation cannot escape the historicizing process inherent in the museum form itself.

The different kinds of museums emerging in the late twentieth-century are, therefore, equally faced with the problem of how to function as time-machines, whether they are historical or contemporary in their approach. So much so, that the surrealist idea for a new museum proposed by Eduardo Paolozzi seems more in keeping with the period than museums based on time-honoured classifications; Paolozzi writes:

> To counteract and perhaps contradict our tendency to isolate phenomena and impose a separateness of the object I proposed in a series of prints an idea for a new museum: where in an old building preferably an abandoned cathedral . . . a selection from the history of things the choice of material being an art form. The arrangement and juxaposition of objects and sculptures suggesting another philosophy, fakes combined with distinguished 're-productions' copies of masterpieces both in painting and engineering – the radial engine and a Leger painting, Bugatti wheels, cinema prints, crocodile skulls – all parts movable – an endless set of combinations, a new culture in which problems give way to possibilities.[40]

Paolozzi's 'Blue print' is an artist's view, and is not, therefore, concerned with many of the basic tasks of the museum curator (to collect, conserve, and so on). However, it suggests something very important, namely that museums can appeal to our sense of wonder *and* provoke us to thought; they can deal with past and present, and juxtapose European and non-European cultures to raise questions about the systems of classification we use. The museum, then, that feeds and feeds off recycled nostalgia is not just to be criticized for its political and social function, but for impoverishing the culture and, therefore, our sense of human possibilities. If museums are to have a cultural role as distinct from that of the theme park, it lies in helping us orient ourselves and make discoveries in a world in which inherited common-sense conceptions of time and place are increasingly redundant.

Acknowledgements

My thanks to David Morley, who first accepted the book proposal,

Introduction

and then gave invaluable support; to Alan Morton, whose help was vital, especially in the difficult early stages; to Patrick Wright, for ideas for Part 1; and finally, to all the contributors, who could hardly have made it easier for someone new to the editor's role. All errors are, of course, my own.

Notes and references

1 For the debate on this question, see Wright, P. (1985) *On Living in an Old Country*, London; and Lowenthal, D. (1985) *The Past is a Foreign Country*, Cambridge.
2 See Johnson, R., McLenon, G., Schwarz, W., and Sutton, D. (eds) (1982). *Making Histories*, London.
3 The key themes of the debate between the friends and enemies of museums go back to the French Revolution when aristocratic and religious 'relics' were first saved from political vandalism and then put on public display. For instance, the question of 'context' addressed by André Malraux (1949) in *Museums without Walls*, London, was, and has remained political: 'the museum did away with the significance of Palladium, of Saint or Saviour, ruled out associations of sanctity, qualities of adornment and possession'; see Francis Haskell (1985) 'Museums and their enemies', *Journal of Aesthetic Education*, summer: 13–23. Interestingly Pierre Bourdieu, a leading sociologist of culture in France today, argues that museums help to create an aesthetic disposition by removing an object's 'context' of use and function, and thereby reproduce 'aristocracies of taste': see Bourdieu, P. and Darbel, A. (1969) *L'Amour de l'art: les musées de l'art européens et leur publics*, Paris, p. 92.
4 Wright, P. (1985) *On Living in an Old Country*, London pp. 251–3; Patrick Wright is also appreciative of Hoyau, and, indeed, this essay was first included at his suggestion.
5 In Britain, curators have long wanted to consider themselves part of a profession, in the same way that teachers and doctors might. However, there is no formal entry requirement, and academic courses in museology have only recently been established.
6 For Marshall McLuhan on museums, see his (1969) *A Seminar: Museum of the City of New York*, New York.
7 Valéry, P. (1979) 'Le probléme des musées', in F. Dagognet (ed.) *Le Musée sans fin*, Paris (my translation).
8 A lucid account of recent tendencies in museum architecture is Montaner, J. and Oliveras, J. (1986) *The Museums of the Last Generation*, London.
9 For a pertinent discussion of the methodological problems in researching audiences, see Morley, D. (1980) *The Nationwide Audience*, London; and Morley, D. (1987) *Family Television*, London. In the museum field, the pioneering text is Bourdieu, P. and Darbel, A. (1969) *L'Amour de l'art: les musées de l'art européens et leur publics*, Paris.

10 See, for an British example, Pemberton, M. (1986) 'Talking shop: a guide to retailing in museums', *Museums Journal*, September. He writes:

> The enterprise and flair of the High St is diffusing in the world of museums. . . . Packaging means establishing a corporate identity. . . . Shopping is not just making a purchase, it is about the whole experience, including the ambiance of the shop, the style of the staff.

This approach is even more highly developed in the USA; see the special issue on marketing, advertising, and public relations in relation to museums of *Museum News*, August 1986. Contrast this to the thinking of a director of the old school: 'The basic philosophy of window-dressing is deception and seduction . . . the vulgarity which is such a prominent element in cut-throat competition is not only out of place in a museum, but destroys the very things the museum stands for'; Findlay, I. (1977) *Priceless Heritage: The Future of Museums*, London, p. 59.

11 For an interesting discussion of the origin and crisis of the idea of public service, Robins, K. and Webster, F. (1986) 'Broadcasting politics – communications and consumption', *Screen*, May–August: 30–46.

12 In Britain, Kenneth Hudson has for many years written in the name of the consumer. His (1980) *Good Museums Guide*, London, applies the principle of the *Good Food Guide* to the museum.

13 Bourdieu, P. (1980) 'The aristocracy of culture', *Media, Culture and Society* 2: 238, n. 15.

14 For example Williams, R. (1977) 'A lecture on realism', *Screen* 1: 61–74.

15 Eco, U. (1987) *Travels in Hyperreality*, London.

16 This phenomenon can be dismissed as gimmickry. On the other hand, one can ask whether it is symptomatic of a new 'historical poetics', and represents a further stage in realizing the nineteenth-century 'mythic aim of narrowing the gap between history as it happened, and history as it is written'; Bann, S. (1984) *The Clothing of Cleo: A Study of the Representation of History in 19th Century Britain and France*, Cambridge, p. 165.

17 See Bazin, G. *The Museum Age*, Brussels, pp. 256–7.

18 Criticism of dominant representations of 'reality' and the promotion of alternative 'myths' is a key theme of Horne, D. (1986) *The Public Culture*, London. See especially pp. 218–45 for the impact of ethnic cultural politics on museums. This is the cultural and political environment both parodied and celebrated in George C. Wolfe (1987) *The Colored Museum*, London; directions for staging include:

> THE CAST: An ensemble of five, two men and three women, all black, who perform all the characters that inhabit the exhibits.

> THE STAGE: White walls and recessed lighting. A starkness befitting a museum where the myths and madness of black/Negro/colored Americans are stored. Built into the walls are a series of small panels,

revolving walls and compartments from which actors can retrieve key props and make quick entrances . . .

The opening lines: 'Welcome aboad Celebrity Slaveship, departing the Gold Coast, and making short stops at Bahia, Port Au Prince and Havana, before our final destination of Savannah'.

19 West, B. (1985) 'Danger! History at work: a critical consumer's guide to the Ironbridge Gorge Museum', occasional paper, Centre for Contemporary Cultural Studies, Birmingham, p. 33. An abbreviated and adapted version of the original piece is published in this collection, Chapter 2.

20 Eco, U. (1987) *Travels in Hyperreality*, London.

21 Hudson, K. (1986) 'Problems in museum presentation of the westernisation of other cultures', a paper presented to the conference 'Making Exhibitions of Ourselves: the Limits of Objectivity in the Representation of Other Cultures', Museum of Mankind, January.

22 The catalogue of the exhibition 'Les Immatériaux' at the Pompidou Centre in Paris which reconstructs the planning of the event is symptomatic of this phenomenon as a conscious intellectual strategy; see *Les Immatériaux: album et inventaire* (1985), Centre Georges Pompidou, Paris. However, it can also be seen as an extension of the idea of taking people 'behind the scenes', or 'into the projecting box', which is increasingly common in museums.

23 David Lowenthal speaking at the Annual Study Weekend of the Museum Professionals Group, Exeter, September 1986. Transactions forthcoming.

24 See Hudson, K. (1977) *Museums for the 1980s*, London, pp. 78–9.

25 Strong, Sir Roy (1985) *Museums: Two Contributions towards the Debate*, London, p. 8. This line of argument assumes a credulous television viewer and a cultured museum visitor. Television, in brief, equals the negation of 'culture'.

26 Smith, A. (1980) *Goodbye Gutenberg: The Newspaper Revolution of the 1980's*, London, pp. 3–23.

27 Baudrillard, J. (1982) *Simulations*, New York, p. 3.

28 *Les Immatériaux: album et inventaire* (1985), Centre Georges Pompidou, Paris.

29 For the classic work on this phenomenon, see Benjamin, W. (1973) 'The work of art in the age of mechanical reproduction', *Illuminations*, London, pp. 219–53; for a critical assessment, Heinich, N. (1983) 'L'Aura de Walter Benjamin: note sur l'oeuvre d'art a l'ère de sa reproductibilité technique', *Actes de la recherche en science sociales* 49, September: 107–11.

30 For a recent debate of the 'blockbuster' in the USA, see the special issue of *Art in America*, June 1986; for Britain, Anscombe, I. (1986) 'Exhibition policy: serenity versus comprehension?', *National Art Collections Fund Magazine*, December: 4–9.

31 From a paper by David Elliot at the seminar, 'The Museum as Medium', organized by the Design Museum, 21 May 1987, roneo.

32 Referring to Beamish, the Black Country Museum, and Blists Hill, Neil Cossons has said: 'These museums are highly consumer-oriented, wildly popular with the public and capable of presenting a nostalgic, warm, and cosy picture of a past which was really bloody awful. . . . It seems we have taken the museum object and used the museum as a medium of communication, stretching it beyond its proper capacity to do the job' (from 'The Museum as Medium', a seminar organized by the Design Museum, 21 May 1987).

33 This part on MOMI is based on the museum's own pre-launch literature, press reports, and discussions with Anthony Smith, the director of the British Film Institute, and Philip Simpson, who is responsible for the educational side of the museum's activities. Unfortunately it was not possible to go into details about planned exhibitions, nor to interview the other main organizers of MOMI.

34 The Design Museum in London is due to open in May 1989. However, its foundation has been anticipated by the Boilerhouse based at the Victoria and Albert Museum, though independently run and financed by the Conran Foundation. The Boilerhouse, from 1982 to 1986, had the great merit of provoking discussions about contemporary design in a capital city with fewer exciting exhibitions in the area in a decade than held at the Centre de Création Industrielle at the Pompidou Centre in a year; see Bayley, S. (1985) 'Cars for cathedrals', *New Society*, 23 May: 274–7.

35 Fund-raising has been described as 'like fishing – you have to know where the fish lie, their feeding habits and so on'. It is easy to overlook the huge campaign that precedes the opening of a new capital-intensive museum, and the role of the big fish. For an analysis of contemporary forms of corporate patronage, see Wallis, B. (1986) 'The art of big business', *Art in America*, June: 28–33.

36 New museums are, therefore, often designed to be flexible, responsive to outside influences, and up to date with the latest ideas and information, rather than preoccupied with permanence and 'eternal values'. In this respect the Design Museum's projected tripartite division according to newspaper lay-out is exemplary: 'reference' (small permanent collection); 'features' (temporary thematized exhibitions); 'news and current affairs' ('up to the minute' coverage).

37 For a fascinating article on 'postmodernism', which begins with reflections on Disneyland, see Hebdige, D. (1986/7) 'A report from the Western Front: postmodernism and the "politics" of style', *Block*, winter: 4–26.

38 The development of 'leisure services' is booming, and it is not surprising if one thinks that the cost of creating one new job in tourism is £4,000 compared to £32,000 in manufacturing and £300,000 in mechanical engineering; for an interesting analysis of the connection between urban redevelopment, museums and appropriations of history, see Lunn, K. and Thomas, R. (1986) 'Portsmouth dockyards – The rerigging of a city's history', *History Workshop Journal* spring: 191–8.

39 Nostalgia is a problematic word, but it can be said that memories of 'how

things used to be' can provide a measure, however inadequate, for judging an unacceptable present.

40 Paolozzi, E. (1985) *Lost Magic Kingdoms*, London, pp. 7–8.

PART 1

The landscape of nostalgia

1

Heritage and 'the conserver society': the French case

PHILIPPE HOYAU
Translated by Chris Turner

Out of politeness the nobleman inspected their museum. He
repeated: 'Charming. Very good!' all the while tapping his lips
with the knob of his cane. For his own part, he thanked them for
saving these remains of the Middle Ages, age of religious faith
and knightly loyalty. He liked progress, and would, like them,
have given himself up to these interesting studies, but politics,
the local council, farming, a whole whirlwind of activity kept him
from it.

'In any case, after you, there would only be the gleanings;
because you will have taken all the curiosities in the *départ-
ment*.'

'Without conceit, that's what we think', said Pécuchet.

(Gustave Flaubert, *Bouvard and Pécuchet*)

'The past, there's our enemy. Humanity would be no worse off if we
burned down all the libraries and museums: in fact such an act
would bring it nothing but profit and glory', railed Jules Vallès
against the 'religion' of the old. He went on to say, 'There is a whole
clan of little men with their diplomas and distinctions of rank
beavering away to keep up this cult of things which though
magnificent in their own day are merely ridiculous and an encum-
brance in ours'.[1] This would certainly have put the cat among the
pigeons in the rue Valois,[2] when plans were being laid to propel us,
by means of 'Heritage Year' into a new cult of the past, albeit a very
different one from that denounced by Vallès. This new project in
fact represents not so much a desire to preserve and celebrate a
'monumental', academic past as an attempt to promote new values

27

on the basis of a thoroughly transformed conception of tradition and the national heritage.

The great inventory

Let us begin by rehearsing the facts. In November 1979 at the Arc-et-Senans salt-works, the then Minister of Culture, J.-P. Lecat, inaugurated 'Heritage Year' at a children's tea-party. A year earlier a Heritage Directorate had been set up at the Ministry of Culture and a Commission for the Ethnological Heritage had been formed, comprising civil servants and the leading lights of French ethnology. Shortly after this, Giscard d'Estaing laid down the terms of reference for the projected Museum of the Nineteenth Century, which was to be a 'pantheon' of modern and industrial art. In March 1980 an exhibition opened with the title 'Building in the Older Parts of Town'. Then came the announcement of the full Heritage Year programme, which turned out to be a real curiosity shop, ranging from the restoration of Vauban's fortifications to the creation of a museum of agricultural machinery, from the fostering of 'heritage awareness' in schools to the Monet exhibition, from the promotion of regional ethnology to collecting family photos. 'The notion of heritage has been expanded', observed the minister. 'The national heritage is no longer merely a matter of cold stones or of exhibits kept under glass in museum cabinets. It now includes the village wash-house, the little country church, local songs and forms of speech, crafts and skills.'[3]

The Commission for the Ethnological Heritage goes even further; it includes in the notion of 'Heritage' the specific modes of material existence and of the social organization of groups (both past and in process of formation), representations of the world, together, more generally, with the elements on which the unity of every social group is based, such as institutions, material and non-material goods, works virtual or actual, and so on. The Commission also argues that efforts must be directed towards the collection of all written or oral records, correspondence, files, written reminiscences, notebooks, and diaries and, moreover, that new 'objects' of study must be constituted, such as urban social and cultural forms, the economy and legal framework of pre-capitalist exchange, forms of popular knowledge collected and studied in the light of ethnobotany, ethnozoology, ethnolinguistics, ecology, and 'natural' medicine. Some of these projects start this year (and a 'File on the ethnological heritage' is already being assembled). They include studies of myth and cultural identity in the Nord-Pas-de-Calais coalfield, of life on the narrow boats on the canals of the Midi (focusing on work, on the boats both as 'tools' and as centres of family life, on demography, and on the formation of group identity), popular memory of the First World War, the constitution of a sound archive in Aubrac and in Aquitaine, an ethnological and cinematic record of life in an urban area and a village in the Bouches-du-Rhône, preservation and study of the world of Lyon weavers (in the Croix-Rousse quarter), the creation of *ecomuseums* (local and regional museums of 'ways of life' and work) of which there are already some thirty in Brittany, the constitution of oral archives of the Jewish community in Alsace, saving and promoting awareness of Brittany's sea-faring heritage, oral tradition in the Parisis, the Pays de France, and Vexin, an inventory of the first cinemas in the Ile de France area, a conference and exhibition on 'gardens lost and re-found' in the Languedoc, and, in the context of rural preservation, a study of a representative village in each of the fifteen districts of Haute Normandie.

The inventory of an 'industrial heritage' may seem novel and surprising, and yet industrial archaeology already has both its 'enthusiasts' and its experts;[4] for some years now it has spurred a new breed of archaeologists of factory-production to venture into the backyards of the industrial Nord *département*, along canal banks and into deserted factories. 'Just as a château or an old urban quarter are part of our cultural heritage', argues one of them, 'so the industrial plants of past centuries also have historic value for us today'.[5] This is the 'infrastructure' taking its revenge. By being assimilated into the nation's heritage, material production once again finds its place in the cultural landscape: efforts are made then to prevent the destruction of factories, industrial archaeology sight-seeing tours are organized, and children are initiated into the mysteries of hydraulic pumps.[6] At the same time, Bertrand Gille, our foremost historian of technology, calls on the heads of industry to preserve their companies' archives and worn-out machinery.

Curiously then, dead labour is restaged, with the violence done to the producers and the environment spirited away in a search for lived experience and past forms of social life. And if manufacturing architecture still exudes an atmosphere of suffering rather than one of harmony, it is none the less valid as testimony to an order which is 'real' because it once existed. As a result, once the notion of 'heritage' has been cut free from its attachment to beauty, anything can be part of it, from miners' cottages or public wash-houses to the halls of Versailles, so long as it is historical evidence. But it is, in fact, from the sheer extent of the inventory that this truth effect – and our identification with it – is sought. At the same time, though the introduction into the realm of 'conservation' of *patois* and popular knowledge on the one hand, and of technology, industrial architecture, and machinery on the other, forces a serious rethink upon the world of 'museology', its main effect is to offer much greater scope than before for the implementation of policies for the management, preservation, and valorization of the historical past.

The health of the community

The eclecticism of the programme, and the themes it mobilizes, in fact inflect these policies towards the 'plural'. 'Heritage Year' is a perfect reflection of this. Through these choices and the way they fit together, an imaginary object, the Past, seems to take shape. It forms around three major models: the family (the dwelling, rituals and customs, cooking and domestic production, and so on), conviviality (community life, festivals, production, and so on), and spirit of place (linguistic usage and *patois*, architecture, representations, techniques, cultural identity, ecology, and so on). Without prejudging the inherent interest of these themes, the evident investment in them both at the levels of scholarship and policy seems to us to produce several types of effects. We shall look at each of these in turn.

First, in so far as history and historical awareness is concerned, they allow the questioning and self-questioning history of concepts and criticism to be replaced by the illusion of colour, the magic of diversity, the detail of inventories, and an ecstatic contemplation of the Unchanging. At the same time, by combining these various models one with another, and moving from the local to the general, it becomes possible to build up a fictive totality called the Past. History is absorbed by and cancelled out in ethnology, while the elements of what we may call 'open' history – conflicts, interests, resistance, illusions, specific sequences of events – fade into the unchanging landscape and become fixed in a temporality which is one of repetition.[7] The pacified, neutralized 'past', divested of its residual burden of uncertainty may then be offered up for us collectively to identify with it. In our view, this seems to form the substance of the new discourse 'from above' (and not only from above) on history in France, in which the nation's greatness is seen as residing not so much in the magnificence of its Art as in the exquisite variety of its popular skills and the indestructible nature of its forms of social life, which have endured through so many social upheavals.

Second, this new orientation towards 'conservation' has given birth to a new discipline, 'ethnohistory'. Roughly speaking, its specific concern is with investigations of 'ways of life' and relations of production and representation both past and present, as they can be observed in a particular milieu or micro-milieu. As a fieldwork-based discipline, it is attentive to the minor, the everyday, and the trivial and it has taken as its horizon the life of the community or locality. It seems indeed to be not so much a specific branch of knowledge as a conjunction of different and yet convergent methods and sensibilities drawn from disciplines as diverse as anthropology geography, and the history of technology. Thus for example archaeology seeks to become more 'diversified', focused 'not simply on monuments, but on daily life, agrarian structures and indeed everything which makes up the substratum of a civilisation'.[8] Moreover the development of ethnohistory marks a redeployment of French ethnology, which, we are told, has been too long kept apart (by the burden of a colonial past) from its real source of inspiration which is the metropolis, where the archaic and the modern co-exist in a particularly rich blend. But its major achievement could prove to be that of adjusting ethnological and historical research to the 'ideological' imperatives of the day, and particularly of rationalizing nostalgia by providing it with 'real' content. More-over, by giving new value to what were formerly regarded as 'minor' forms of knowledge and objects that were previously scorned, ethnohistory affirms its spirit of openness and can therefore hope to have a very wide audience.

Third, the circulation of these widely accepted models allows a cultural consensus to emerge around the kind of stable values that modernity has failed to instill. But has perpetuity yet produced its response to the 'crisis' (which is, as so many are fond of telling us, ideological and political)? The *Report of the Working Party on the Ethnological Heritage* stresses that

There is a very great public interest today in the original elements which went to make up French society in the distant past. At the regional or local level, this interest is being trans-lated into a wide range of initiatives and a high level of vigorous social demands. It goes together with an increased desire on the part of citizens to gain control over how their own lives are organized and how the institutions with which they are most closely involved are run; they are seeking to acquire that control through increased participation in community activities. Lastly, it reveals a consciousness of problems of identity in which a preserved or re-found sense of difference plays a central role, a role that extends right into the organization of daily life as it is lived today.

Further on in the same document, we read:

In the last ten years or so, we have once again seen the emergence both in the countryside and the towns, in our larger cities and our new towns, and among the latest immigrant communities as well as in traditional areas, of a wide variety of groups which are becoming crucibles of new forms of social life and ethnic identifications, and of new cultural developments and mixes.

For his part, Georges-Henri Rivière, who has just received the 'National Heritage Prize', declares: 'People should take an interest. They should realize that these things (in the "minor" heritage) belong to them. This is what I call giving people back their identity, their local identity'.[9] Writing of the notion of 'community', in which, as they see it, 'ideally spatial unity, social unity and cultural coherence' should coincide, Daniel Fabre and Jacques Lacroix, have observed that in spite of 'the suspicion with which it is regarded by sociologists and politicians, the term evokes a potent image at the crossroads of history and utopia'[10]

From this point of view, nostalgia can now be seen as a prescriptive and prospective matter and 'Heritage Year' ushers in the age of its expanded reproduction. What is involved here is not so much the grand old dream of the 'good society' or a 'benign order', as an opportunity to renew the public's commitment to the political sphere and give fresh stimulus to local and regional allegiances; the leaders of a certain 'soft' socialism are already working towards this goal,[11] as are the uncritical advocates of a decentralized, self-governing, even 'ecological' society, which will somehow take over 'from below' at the end of the 'crisis'. Moreover, the report quoted above puts the emphasis on the solidarity linking 'benign' policies to ethnohistory and the preservation of the popular heritage:

This desire to take control of their own history reflects an ever-growing desire to participate in the management of their neighbourhood communities. In this regard, reforms tending to increase the responsibility of local collectivities will give an important boost to an ethnology policy.

In a certain sense, then, geography fills in where history seems to have no answers: as evidence of this, we need only think of all those people – 'intellectuals' and others – who, being unable to propose new values in the disenchanted post-1968 world, have turned instead to a religion of 'roots' and 'neighbourhood'. Yet, in subsuming politics in human relations, the warm unity of the Community and 'collective life', they have cut themselves off from that kind of history which can actually be made.

Cultural mobilization

With the 'minor heritage' rescued from oblivion, and with popular tradition now released from its subservience to 'Tradition' and recognized as being positively in the public interest, everybody can be enlisted in the cause:

> Heritage Year aims to be more than a mere collection of events. It is seeking to create a state of mind, to modify behaviour and ways of thinking . . . the measure of its success will be the extent to which it can create new interest among the general public to put their time, imagination, energy and money into the creation of that heritage which will be our contribution to posterity.[12]

This 'cultural service' is to take a variety of different forms, from simple policing measures ('We are speaking of a daily battle against indifference or vandalism, even unconscious vandalism on the part of visitors or ordinary citizens', writes *Le Monde*[13]), promotional events in schools (several hundred of these – both individual events and on-going projects – are planned for the whole of France) to organized leisure activities. History is then to be introduced into schools under cover of this notion of 'Heritage' at the very moment when its teaching has been severly hit in the secondary sector. At the same time, weekends are to be devoted to 'cultural tourism', to use the minister's phrase, the old idea of 'trips' having not lost every vestige of originality.[14] In both cases, however, the tourist route followed only succeeds in giving a spatial dimension to a mute, immobile history, all of which merely reproduces the old illusory goal Bergson spoke of, which consists in seeking to conceive time in spatial terms.

33

The Museum Time-Machine

It seems, then, that however much it is set about with scholarly pronouncements, the attempt to promote (or in the Ministry of Culture's terms, 'to inject dynamism into') this 'new heritage' could quite easily lead to the same boredom one sees in other museums. Will this 'enlarged' heritage, a shop-window of modern sensibilities, manage to avoid both the monotony which an evocation of a transparent, uncritically presented past might be expected to generate, and the rapid obsolescence built into policies and strategies dictated 'from above'? Who knows? For if the cult of the past denounced by Vallès drew its energy from the defence and illustration of (bourgeois and aristocratic) cultural privilege, the cult of the national Heritage '1980s style' seeks to derive its stimulus from the sense of disarray which characterizes the decade and to drawn its substance from the latest concerns of history, anthropology, and geography. It has already succeeded to some extent in doing this. This is a sign that a change is taking place, the effects of which will almost certainly be very far-reaching. A landscape has been laid out, the landscape of effective nostalgia.

Notes and references

1 *Le Nain jaune*, 24 February 1867.
2 Home of the Ministry of Culture in Paris.
3 *Culture et communication* 23, published by the Ministry of Culture.
4 Among those scholars are the group who are currently producing *L'Architecture industrielle dans la région lilloise 1830–1930*, of which two volumes have so far appeared.
5 Dumas, M. *L'Archéologie industrielle en France*.
6 There is an Industrial Archaeology Heritage Trail around Le Creusot.
7 In *La Mémoire longue, temps et histoire du village* (1980), François Zonabend writes

> Two perpetually interlocking types of memory ... mark out the rhythm of village life. The one, which is collective, reaches back to the early life of the community and is a story of origins whose traces can still be read in the native soil. The other, which is family-based, is the stuff of everyday conversation. The generations are its reference points, the extent of blood relations its measure, and it derives its rhythm from the major events in the villagers' lives. Both know nothing of that history which rules the life of the nation, the history taught in school. Together they weave a singular, immobile, stable time in which the group always finds itself as it was in spite of the upheavals of the modern world.

> This 'private' time of the community is clearly conceived as preservative time. It is a closed time which produces a memory of custom and habit, a 'long memory'.

8 Interview with the archaeologist Léon Pressouyre in *Culture et communication* 23, Ministry of Culture.
9 ibid.
10 *Communautés du sud, contributions à l'étude des collectivités rurales occitanes.*
11 See Borreil, J. 'Des politiques nostalgiques', *Révoltes logiques* 3.
12 *Culture et communication* 23, Ministry of Culture.
13 7 October 1978. This is an old question. A conception of the conservation of the heritage as being in the public interest dates back to the Revolution. It was initially a simple public order measure. The aim was to protect (religious and aristocratic) fortunes from being pillaged, destroyed, or dispersed either as part of a legacy or at public sales (after being seized as *émigré* property). The first such decree was promulgated on 18 October 1792 and created the *Commission des Monuments*. A report of 1792 notes:

> Amidst these necessary acts of destruction ordained by the love of liberty and equality, the monuments of science, art and letters must be preserved from the attacks which they might suffer at the hands of the over-zealous . . . they must be conserved in warehouses, to protect them from the wrath of fanatics.

14 Cultural and archaeological trails are to be marked out (in the Val de Seine for example); the National Geographical Institute is launching an *ad hoc* series of maps; 'Heritage Trails' have been developed by the French national ramblers' association; and activities are to be organized at many of France's historic monuments.

2

The making of the English working past: a critical view of the Ironbridge Gorge Museum[1]

BOB WEST

Introduction

In the autumn of 1982 we finally took possession of a late-nineteenth-century end-terrace house in Madeley, Shropshire. Madeley is a small town, but designated part of Telford, 'the birthplace of industry'. Nearby is the Ironbridge Gorge, one of many places in Britain that lays claim to being the very spot where, in 1709, 'the world's industrial revolution began'. For the past decade Ironbridge has been a regular haunt of ours for family outings from the West Midlands: a Bank Holiday mecca and the object of innumerable photographs in our household's collection. In one sense our interest in the area exactly reflects the most recent phase of the increasing lure of historical tourism in general, and in the West Midlands the gradual ascendancy of the Ironbridge Gorge Museum Trust (hereafter the Trust) in particular.

Therefore it should come as no surprise that our 'new', old house stands opposite one of the Trust's most popular sites, the Blists Hill Open Air Museum. From there noise and smoke and the clinking of money, all rumoured to be authentic symbols of nineteenth-century industrialism, pervade the valley. Built in the eighteenth century, our adjacent pub, the All Nations with the Union Jack to the fore on its appropriately rotted pub sign, has been the font of 'authentic' ale for a generation of intrepid CAMRA members. Everything here is old and the pub is the haunt of strange anachronisms from Blists Hill. Here at lunchtime one finds young men in sub-Victorian garb; heavy hobnail boots, plain serge trousers, and mock Halifax corduroy gathered at the waist with binder-twine, hauled up with wide braces and pulled too at the ankle with gaiters. Old jackets, dull, nondescript, but suggestively decrepit, open to reveal grubby collarless workingmen's shirts, or the occasional plain waistcoat perhaps with the stylish flourish of a watch fob and chain. Needless to say, these phantoms of the past-present quaff real ale, 'brewed traditionally', itself a sort of liquid history bearing silent witness against the present. Tending nineteenth-century machines at the museum is evidently enough to drive a man to drink down the nectar of the past.

The first time I stumbled upon this scene I had thoughts of an entrenched local conservatism, or of a place visited by Dr Who's Tardis, or even of a sinister sub-culture based upon the new brutalism of 'Victorian values'. On all counts I was not wrong of course, because after all what I had happened upon was simply history at work! However, if being nonplussed by these spectres was my response, precipitate careful research into past editions of *History Workshop Journal* might have forewarned me of their imminence. Some years ago that organ of 'socialist historians' found space for Barrie Trinder, the Trust's 'honorary historian', to set the scene. He said, 'In Ironbridge it is still possible to drink in some of the pubs where those who heaved into the place the ribs of the Iron Bridge must have refreshed themselves'.[2] Years have passed since this perspective was aired, years during which fantasy became prediction, years through which the historical imagination has taken its toll of young men and young women, just around the corner from the famous iron bridge. Yet I am not just referring to those who contract to 'dress up' to add a benign face to a particularly ruthless epoch, but to the countless coach-loads of schoolchildren and pleasure-seeking families as well, who are daily 'educated' into a very partial *imagined community* of 'the past'.

What is 'the past' with its sinister inverted commas? To me 'the past' is somewhere seen retrospectively in soft focus. It's a place viewed through a cottage window draped in Laura Ashley or William Morris curtains, back-lighted courtesy of Habitat, with the double-glazing polished by a Victorian worker on a Community Programme. Into 'the past' all manner of stories can be inserted; romantic blockbusters about the 'civilizing' role of Empire, fantastic tales of the English people and their boundless love for nation and monarch, industrial epics about the 'heroic' doings of good chaps like Abraham Darby, Thomas Telford, and Richard Trevithic. History, on the other hand, which is also invariably a work of some fiction, at least allows for the possibility of telling the past as a different story; a story perhaps to inform the present of progressive ideas and struggles against the old oppressions of class, race, and gender. If, however, a politics of the past was ever just a struggle between historians and the politically active in society, then the recent development of Britain as 'Ye Olde Leisure Park' requires some new thoughts and responses.

This article is an attempt to come to terms with some of the issues relating to historical tourism, the manufacture of museums and the role of the museum in terms of its local community. I am also concerned with the forms of history on offer in the Ironbridge Gorge Museum, but I have dealt with that subject elsewhere and at much greater length.[3] Therefore I want to begin by analysing the development of the Trust in terms of what I call its political economy. This means concentrating upon the ways in which the Trust was founded, then funded and run. I will discuss the Trust in terms of the development of historical tourism, arguing that it is deeply involved in the *history-making business*. I will examine the ways in which the museum develops its image, the process through which it legitimizes its view of 'the past', and its own sense of self-importance as educator and historian. This section concludes with a discussion of the Trust's philosophy of museum-making, and the kinds of interpretative assumptions it makes about history. The second, shorter section of my argument places the museum in terms of the locality and examines the impact of tourism on the local economy, and how a place like Ironbridge is used by the casual visitor. Finally, I want to locate the Trust's perception of 'the past' in terms of how it constructs 'community' and the turn-of-the-century labour process at the outdoor museum of Blists Hill. This will give me the opportunity to show how the working assumptions of the museum management and trustees are translated into historical representations.

The political economy of museum making

Capital and labour

In the early months of 1967 what was to become the Telford Development Corporation appointed a Working Party on Industrial Archaeology. This all-male working party was asked to assess the historical value of the Coalbrookdale, Ironbridge, and Blists Hill areas of East Shropshire. Infused with a sense of reverence for the past and an exaggerated sense of importance for the locality, the members began their historically self-conscious mission. Reading the *Final Report of the Working Party* gives an insight into the structure of feeling of this group. It appears to have developed its ideas at the interface of two forces; on the one hand, a sense of a vanishing 'great' industrial past, and on the other, a contemporary desire to conserve old buildings and machines from the 'ravishings' of time. This structure of feeling is one of the central concerns of dominant ideas of the National Heritage. Heritage centres upon a mega-story about the 'Island People', and the objects and institutions presumed to be of importance to them. Invariably these celebrate Empire, High Culture, and 'masculine' assessments of people and nation. Moreover, the threat of loss is felt to be more manifest and the act of *recovery* more urgent, if the artefacts of 'Heritage' are given world-historical significance. Consequently the working party adopted a form of historical megalomania; they became men emersed in 'one of the classic industrial regions of the world', quite convinced of the planetary significance of individual 'heroic' figures like Abraham Darby I, without whom 'the industrial revolution would have been impossible'.[4] With these assumptions in place the necessity to conserve the area was a foregone conclusion.

Apart from recognizing the central importance of the iron bridge itself, the aims of the working party concentrated upon two main areas. In the first instance they were concerned that the whole district could be developed to tell 'the history of British industry in a manner not attempted elsewhere in the country'.[5] This meant making Coalbrookdale what they called a 'living museum', a novel idea which in turn required that the county council designate part of the town a conservation area. Central to this part of the scheme was the transfer of Darby's old furnace and its associated museum of iron from Allied Iron Founders Ltd, who presently owned it and consented to the proposal. The overall scheme also meant developing Blists Hill as a 'public park', a place 'demonstrating an industrial story of unique interest in an almost ideal setting'. This they wanted on a long lease at a nominal rent from the Telford Development Corporation.[6]

The second aim of the working party was to propose a way of administering such a scheme and they suggested a public company, registered under the Companies Act, 1848, but limited by guarantee. This organization, which was to be named the Ironbridge Gorge Museum Trust Ltd, would be non-profit-making, and would attempt to register as a charity. Its main aims, apart from the desire for 'public participation', would be as follows:

> To secure the preservation, restoration, improvement, enhancement and maintenance of features and objects of historical, domestic and industrial interest in the area of Dawley New Town [now Telford] and the surrounding districts of East Shropshire, including the provision of museums and the organisation of meetings, exhibitions, lectures, publications and other forms of instruction relevant to the historical, domestic and industrial development of East Shropshire.[7]

The working party estimated that this ambitious programme required an equally ambitious capital sum of £500,000 and an estimated annual revenue expenditure of £15,000 after the initial period of growth. Both sums would soon be superseded.

The first problem of the nascent Trust was to find a way of raising large sums of money, while still remaining an 'independent museum'. Like many organizations before and since, the Trust prepared applications to the big charities like the Ford Foundation and the Gulbenkian Trust. However, given the Trust's emphasis upon industrial archaeology, letters were written to the chairmen of the largest British companies, and an *Appeals Brochure* was produced in 1969 to court industry 'for support in recording their own industrial heritage'. At this initial stage the British Steel Corporation made the largest donation, but over the years the Trust has received 'private' financial support from a broad range of business interests. On the local front money has come from the ironcasting firm of Glynwed Ltd, and the Midland brewers Mitchells and Butlers; nationalized industries and services like the Coal Board and British Rail have contributed; so too have local companies with huge national and international interests like Tarmac Ltd, the silo building contractors at Greenham Common Air Base. It is the intimacy between the Trust and the management structure of organizations like these, *and the assumptions they share*, that renders the Trust's idea of 'independence' a very relative one. What they all have in common is a professional-managerial view of the significance of history, and the museum faithfully reproduces this view in relics radically separated from their social relations of production and consumption.

The Trust could not survive on money from industry alone, nor could it simply rely on the wits of its trustees to raise funds. The task of fund-raising was given over to a separate body, the

1 World heritage championship team. From left to right: Environment Minister, William Waldegrave; ex-Tory MP for the Wrekin, Warren Hawksley; Councillor Bill Miller; and Director of the Museum, Stuart Smith. (Photo: Shropshire Newspapers Ltd)

Ironbridge Gorge Museum Trust, which would attempt to recruit financial support throughout Britain. Charitable status, money from charities, benefactors and Trust Presidents with big pockets, and independent fund-raising feasibility studies, all helped cash flow for the acquisition of new sites and historic objects throughout the 1970s. Another tier of support came from local and national government. All the local urban district councils have at one time contributed funds to the Trust, but by far the most important regional source of support has come from the Telford Development Corporation, which has initiated a number of projects to facilitate the general aims of the museum. Apart from the freehold leasing of sites, these works have mostly provided landscaping for the immediate vicinity of museum property. This adds to the general impression that the Trust is ever expanding its physical control of the area, and therefore the control of our lives.

National government has been generous too, with the Department of the Environment giving substantial lump sums and recently funding the museum through the National Heritage Memorial Fund, set up under the National Heritage Act, 1980. Moreover, with the iminent demise of the Telford Development Corporation in 1991, the government has made a capital endowment of £2 million to the Trust, and is likely to transfer the lease on a number of museum properties to government ownership.[8] Again, this level of commitment represents a set of shared assumptions, a view of 'the past' that rests on an idea of 'English Culture', now conveniently expanded to include the 'industrial heritage' as part of the nation *officially* sanctioned for public consumption.

The great irony of all this is that while the trustees were making friends in high places and influencing the 'chiefs of industry', the brunt of the fieldwork necessary to make the museum operative was done by volunteers or those for whom consent was not an issue. The 'Friends of the Ironbridge Gorge Museum' was formed in 1969 and their labour power, not to mention the annual subscription fee, has helped support the museum ever since. In the early days it was a case of volunteering to help clear sites and renovate old machinery, but more recently the Friends, especially at weekends, take on the role of 'interpretative guides' or fully costumed 'exhibit demonstrators'. It has been argued that this is an educational experience in its own right.

Everyone who becomes involved with a restoration project enters a learning situation, whether he is a skilled engineer re-assembling a steam engine, or one of a group of schoolboys digging mud out of a canal. Everyone who volunteers to guide visitors on a site, places himself in a situation where he has a great incentive to learn and to ask questions about history.[9]

Reading this description one could be excused for thinking that the restoration and interpretative work was carried out only by boys and men. Doubtless they tried to control things, but the male-centredness of this account belies the fact that the Friends has a large female membership, although its actual deployment, like its discursive absence here, often occurs within a pejorative male framework of what 'women's work' should be. At Blists Hill it's barmaids, sorry 'serving wenches', and the dispensers of Edwardian gob-stoppers, but not skilled workers or factory operatives.

The attractiveness of free labour makes the early Annual Reports of the Trust read like the roll-call at a military tattoo. Once the trustees had recognized that clearing scrub and debris could be called a 'training exercise', the military could hardly be expected to miss the challenge. Consequently the Royal Engineers and the Territorial and Army Volunteer Reserve helped prepare the ground for this cultural struggle over hearts and minds, while at the same time practising for more bloody manoeuvres. Other sources of labour were more obviously coercive. In 1972 the trustees assisted in a conference on 'Manpower and Museums' at which the Home Office, local authorities, and the Museum's Association were invited to discuss the use of prison labour in museum work. The Trust had already been using boys from the Stoke Heath Borstal Institute, and in 1973 it was offered a pilot scheme known as the Ironbridge Community Service Project under the Community Service Provision of the Criminal Justice Act, 1972.[10] 'Community Service' is a potentially progressive idea if only it weren't so coercive and the courts so prejudicial towards working-class youth, but doubtless the trustees have a strong sense of 'community' and such issues tend to evaporate.

This has become increasingly obvious with the inception of the Manpower Services Commission (MSC), and the unique opportunity it offers employers to appear to be benevolent to the unemployed on the one hand, while actually benefiting from exploiting cheap labour on the other. I know that the MSC has funded some politically innovative and popular projects like the Bradford Oral History Programme and the South Wales Miners'

Library, but the fact remains that this is part of a deeply insidious process. The MSC systematically institutes *low* wages as a *norm* and is rightly regarded with deep suspicion, especially by the young, who are often the ones prevailed upon to take up employment on such schemes. In the year 1976–7 when the Trust announced that £1 million had been raised on its behalf, the trustees successfully applied for eight projects under the MSC Job Creation Scheme.

Initially these jobs consisted of library cataloguing, bookbinding, painting and decorating, and general estate maintenance. As the MSC expanded its own sphere of influence with the Youth Opportunities Programme (YOP) and the Special Temporary Employment Programme (STEP), so the museum continued to develop its own interest in these schemes. With MSC money the Trust was able to set up the Jackfield Tile Workshop and Training Centre for the renovation of old tiles and the manufacturing of 'modern' tiles from old moulds. However, when MSC scrapped STEP the Trust was less than pleased, probably because this meant losing low-waged adult workers already socialized into work discipline, only to have them replaced by unsocialized, unskilled 16–19-year-olds on project-based work experience schemes.[11] Despite this the Trust has done well out of the MSC and the new Community Programme. By 1980 it had had access to £743,000 and currently relies on an annual subsidized labour force of approximately 200. In short, the museum has reaped the benefits and contributed towards the policing of the crisis of youth employment, and all this is a very long way from the blighted vision of 'public participation' set out in the *Final Report of the Working Party*.

Yet the topic of the political economy of museum-making is not reducible to the deployment of donated capital and the mobilization of free or cheap labour, partly because the museum could not function without the continuity provided by full-time staff. This was recognized early on in 1970 when the dream of a local history-making empire really began to take hold. The museum began with two full-time staff and has continued to grow, despite the occasional hiccup, until in the early 1980s it employed seventy-six full and part-time non-scheme staff.[12] Now there is considerable complexity in the employment structure of the museum. The work-force is deeply stratified and sometimes at odds within itself. This is inevitable in the different terms of employment and the hierarchies of the wage form, not forgetting the voluntary sector as well. MSC scheme employees and their supervisors often see

44

themselves inhabiting the lower ranks, the labouring classes. There is a definite *class* antagonism between them and the Friends of the Museum, who are mostly middle class and use their status in the museum as leisure. This is most obvious at weekends when the Scheme workers are displaced by the Friends, who have priority over them, and hence can *choose* which exhibits they wish to demonstrate to the public. At another level, some of the full-time site demonstrators show a tremendous antipathy towards management, speaking angrily about the apparently opulent 'wining and dining' that takes place to secure publicity, finance, and historical artefacts. Then there are the 'professionals' and the academic advisers, not to mention the white-collar, clerical, and secretarial staff. Each has its own structural position and doubtless its own opinions, although these are difficult to canvass as an outsider or visitor.

The history business

The success or failure of the museum depended upon the Trust's ability to negotiate and *develop* the terrain of historical tourism. Therefore it was not by coincidence that a recent job description for a senior research fellow, funded by Leverhulme, spoke of the museum as a 'brand leader'. It is clear that however else the management and trustees view themselves, as educators, as archivists, and restorers of 'the past', the museum has always been acutely aware of the market-place and the importance of packaging and selling history. In the very early years the Trust had 'open days', when visitors could examine the progress being made, especially at Blists Hill. The first of these in 1969 attracted 600 people and saw the earliest attempt to begin marketing the area, a process which has grown in tandem with the advertising of Telford New Town. Visitors could buy souvenirs like 'Brosely clay pipes, tea towels, prints of the iron bridge, pottery mugs and ashtrays'.[13] These attempts at selling were amateurish compared with what was to follow, as the museum became increasingly self-conscious about how to encourage and anticipate what was referred to as the 'visitor business'.[14] Having begun on the basis of casual opening hours, by 1974, with the first year of full-scale operations behind them, the museum had opened its doors to 100,000 visitors. Ironically this coincided with the beginnings of the oil crisis and the threat of petrol shortages, but this only increased the Trust's interest in the structure of the visitor market. Surveys of 'visitor origins' and 'visitor responses' were the outwards signs of a financially based inquisitiveness about the leisure and travelling habits of the public.[15] Slowly but surely as the gate receipts improved so the running costs increased and ticket prices climbed steadily, to mark the influence of inflation and changes in VAT assessment. All the time, however, the Trust kept a watchful eye on what it perceived to be its main competitor in the area, not the Black Country Museum at Dudley but the leisure park of Alton Towers, whose entrance prices it would not exceed.

The Trust's running costs were not just paid off with the money taken through gate receipts, but through the careful nurturing of the lucrative potential of a wide range of souvenirs. In 1973 45,000 museum guides were sold and by 1983 the museum produced its own *Publications List* containing over 150 items available in its shops and by mail order. Beyond the full range of museum guides, information sheets, and teaching aids, there are postcards, transparencies, posters, prints and books. This side of the operation became so significant that in February 1978 the Trust established the Ironbridge Gorge Trading Company Ltd, which is held in covenant to transfer all its profits to the Museum Trust every year. Clearly trustees and management admit to no conflict of interest between offering up 'the past' as a museum piece and selling 'the past' as a commodity. In an industrial capitalist society we could hardly expect there to be anything but this most intimate of relationships between industrial archaeology and commodity exchange. However, a more damning assessment is to see that what is identified as representative of 'the past', has been chosen on the basis that it lends itself to being profitably sold by the museum, and in some cases manufactured by them as well. Increasingly the commodity side of this museum business comes to dominate how 'the past' is made available to us. Hence, each museum site now has either a 'sales point' or a fully blown shop like those at the Coalbrookdale Museum of Iron and the Coalport China Museum; Blists Hill is a series of shops.

The process of marketing and the desire to control the visitor's experience has had two other consequences. You may recall that the initial aim of the working party for Blists Hill was for a 'public park' containing industrial artefacts. This rather amorphous idea for *public* access was quickly superseded although the date of the decision to renege on this was not recorded. By the early 1970s the Trust was pleased to accept the gift of some 'unclimbable fencing' for the site. This would stop 'unauthorized entry' and the area would be 'protected from trespass', therefore 'enabling visitor entry to be regulated and an entrance fee charged'. Having once been open to the public, this new move required an 'opening ceremony'.[16] In effect this was the moment of making public space *private*. The public would be actively encouraged to attend as if it *were* public space, but it was 'bourgeois public space' with its own constraints, preoccupations, and perceptions. Henceforward, and the process was implicit from the outset, Blists Hill and the rest of the museum would be organized, more or less, around the moral, political, economic (hegemonic) values of the middle classes, and their men in particular.[17]

The second consequence of wanting to define the visitor experience had more reflexive effects. We might call this effect *image control*, or that desire amongst those who seek to organize our pleasure, to fashion the spectacle in a uniform sort of way. The Trust began to develop this in 1972 with an 'integrated design image to be extended ... to embrace all interpretive facilities, publications, signposing, staff uniforms and all visual aspects of the Museum's work'.[18] What emerged were tasteful signs with white lettering on blue-black backgrounds, and the proliferation of a stylized Ironbridge logo that appeared on the backs of postcards, the fronts of books, and even on the road and motorway signs in the area. At regular intervals the signs go through a change of image. Now it's red on white, a bit more insistent but still managing to convey an idea of *good* taste. It's a kind of aesthetic morality, for surely it's no 'mere' promise of proletarian pleasure, nothing gaudy you understand, but a solid invitation to a 'respectable' day out, an 'improving' day out that is also 'educational'. In one sense this is evidently a self-image for the museum's policy-makers, but equally it's important to produce a successful aesthetic for a public increasingly exposed to the highly competitive, image-conscious world of advertising.

To be successful this museum image had to become known and not just locally. The Trust reckoned that the museum had become established and had 'acquired a national reputation' as early as 1973, largely due to the national press, BBC television, and the Open University.[19] Furthermore, the museum has become integrated into a number of networks that guarantee it representation in the public gaze like the English Tourist Board, the Heart of England Tourist Board, and recently through the television marketing of Wrekin District Council. Television advertisements for the area conjure the whole of Telford as a pleasurable family day out for shopping, leisure, and historical tourism. The Trust has also become involved in another local venture initiated to intervene in West Midland's tourism. The Wrekin Heritage Association represents the interests of the Trust as well as the Severn Valley Railway, Cosford Aerospace Museum, and the Midland Motor Museum at Bridgnorth. On their behalf the Wrekin Heritage Association has organized advertising exhibitions in major centres of population, sending out 'road shows' to Birmingham, Liverpool, Manchester, and Sheffield.[20]

An impressive cast list of trustees – for example the Earl of Plymouth, Lady Labourchere, and Sir Monty Finneston – cash flow, visitor numbers, and advertising all facilitate the process of legitimization. But, like a First Division football team, success in the museum business is marked by the size of the trophy cabinet in the director's office and the array of awards attached to the name of the club. Doubtless the Trust would claim First Division status and championship honours, from a run of success that began in 1973 with the British Tourist Authority's 'Come to Britain Trophy'. Then in European Architectural Heritage Year the museum won the Special Civic Trust Medallion, but the really major accolades followed in the latter half of the 1970s. In 1977 the Trust accepted the Museum of the Year Award, presented annually by National Heritage and sponsored by the *Illustrated London News*. In the following year came the greatest prize of all, the European Museum of the Year Award, a direct result of the previous year's success. Taken together, the Trust saw the two awards as placing 'Ironbridge firmly and irrevocably in the forefront of the nation's consciousness', and with the resulting increase in gate receipts estimated the joint value of the awards to be £20,000 or thereabouts.[21] Finally, in 1987 the museum became a 'World Heritage Site' complete with plaque, which left the trustees with only inter-galactic trophies to play for.

The process of legitimization has other networks, the greatest asset being the media-drenched monarchy. Any museum that can persuade part of the royal household to deign to visit, or bestow some award with due pomp, can simultaneously amplify its public image through a massive television, radio, and newspaper overkill, especially locally. When Prince Philip presented the museum with the Special Civic Trust Medallion he did so as a national-historical figure, located within a network of popular expectations about ceremony and pageantry. The real coup in this respect came in the bicentenary year of the iron bridge when the Prince of Wales became the central attraction of the festivities. The Executive Board's Annual Report captures exactly the sense of awe, reverence, and subjugation necessary to translate and retain the cultural capital that accrues from the visit of the heir to the throne.

> Undoubtedly the high point of the year, and indeed of the Museum's development so far, was the visit to the Ironbridge Gorge on 5th July 1979 of His Royal Highness the Prince of Wales. Coinciding almost to the day with the two hundredth anniversary of the completing of the arch of the Iron Bridge across the River Severn His Royal Highness' visit was a fitting and appropriate tribute to the great pioneers of the eighteenth century who built this outstanding symbol of the Industrial Revolution.[22]

This passage celebrated an ensemble of interests: the entrepreneurial spirit, the majesty of a prince, the work of the trustees, all for the most part 'great' men. One can almost feel the bridge straining under the ideological weight, more hefty even than the massed crowds watching the annual plastic duck race in 1985, which precipitated *real* cracks in the edifice. After his visit to a number of museum sites, the Prince responded in kind. He 'honoured the Trust and Development Trust by becoming their patron'. In the end, though, the success of the museum is not reducible to any one of these contributing factors and the situation has to be understood in all its complexity. Indeed, to raise a capital sum of £2.7 million in less than fifteen years, with a similar sum in the pipeline, was evidence enough of the ascendant rise of historical tourism as an area of popular culture, and of the growing status of this particularly persuasive Museum Trust.

Pedagogy and 'the past'

Apart from being successful at attracting the public, the museum is involved in organizing national-popular culture at an everyday level, as education, leisure, and pleasure. This aspect is bound up with what we might call the *philosophy* of museum-making, which in turn is an intimate cousin of the political economy of developing 'the past'. As I've already hinted, the political economy and the assumptions shared between the trustees and the 'chiefs of industry' prefigures the framing of the organization of the museum experience, by helping to structure the form and content of the history that is chosen to be displayed. The trustees, museum management, and the academic back-up claim the right to select and interpret history in this way, and to propagate their vision of 'the past' in a pedagogic style. The aims of the trust set out in the *Final Report of the Working Party* make this clear. Their perception of the Trust as a bona fide history teacher was inscribed in the fact that the museum was established as an *educational* Trust.

The museum has produced, with financial and ideological support from the educational wing of the multinational oil company BP, a *Teachers' Handbook*. This document gives teachers advice about how to organize school trips, what time will be necessary for each viewing, and which other museum publications will be the most suitable purchase as additional teaching aids. It describes the area as 'a superb open air classroom', 'a unique environment', 'for nowhere is it possible to study so many imposing monuments of this most significant period of our past in such a limited area'.[23] Over the years the Trust's capacity to attract school parties has been impressive. In the early years the majority of visitors to the Coalbrookdale Museum of Iron were schoolchildren, and by the mid-1970s the Trust was boasting of 40,000 visitors from educational institutions. From their research it was found that the majority of these came from within a forty-mile radius, although a significant number visited from Merseyside and a smaller number from even further afield: London, Cornwall, and Scotland.[24] By the 1980s, with the museum receiving nearly 200,000 visitors per annum, the number on educational visits was approximately half.[25]

Being an educator is only half of the museum's projected aim, as the Report of the Executive Board in 1974 made clear.

> The primary function of any museum is to conserve – to acquire and protect for posterity material of cultural value and importance. But in doing this it is essential that sight is not lost of the people for whom that material is being kept, the scholars and school children, overseas visitors and local residents whose heritage the Museum has the responsibility and privilege to guard.[26]

Here the emphasis was upon the self-evidently crucial significance of specific artefacts, on the role of the trustees to assess the value of what constituted material of 'cultural value and importance'. The catch-all about 'responsibility and privilege' was the deceptive remark of a paternal autocrat. Thus there is more than a suggestion of a lack of democracy in the process of ascribing meaning and value, where the process itself is hidden from the public gaze or informed by dominant codes of significance. These, unless stated

2 Paying their dues: schoolchildren visit the Ironbridge toll house. (Photo: J. J. Sheridan)

otherwise, invariably favour the privileged classes and anti-progressive accounts of history, with their blindness to class struggle, gender inequalities, and racist legacy of Empire. Equally such perceptions of history fetishize the artefact as 'Heritage', a hidden level of interpretation that forms its own kind of privileged knowledge, and creates popular symbols of the nation in almost mystical forms.

Historically the museum has cultivated a benign appearance, one of the other features of hailing oneself as the keeper of 'Heritage'. In the early years the museum's 'honorary historian' doubtless spoke with hand on heart, when he appeared to lay claim to the potential for a *critical* approach to British industrial history.

> It is equally important to consider how evidence is interpreted to the public. It is all too easy in a textbook or conventional indoor museum to portray innovations as the achievements of individual inventors or entrepreneurs, without regard for their effects on society. The advantage of far-reaching conservation schemes like those at . . . Ironbridge is that it is impossible in such settings to avoid asking a whole range of questions about the impact of innovations.[27]

This was written in the optimism of the mid-1970s, when radical history was just beginning to mop up the last of the progressive legacy of 1968, historiography being one of the final staid disciplines to crack, as it were. Consequently, viewed through rose-coloured spectacles and the kind of excitement that ushered in *History Workshop Journal*, the musuem could be perceived as being on the side of 'the people'.

However, a careful interrogation of Trinder's apparent progressive approach reveals a much older and more familiar inclination.

> The case for conserving buildings, processes and communities should not be that they aid one side or other in any of these debates [about the Industrial Revolution], but that they provide new levels of understanding of the issues involved.[28]

This is empiricism of the worst kind, predicated upon the illusion of 'objectivity' and 'fact'. Why not take sides? Why not be partial? How can we possibly understand the issues involved, when the whole point of history is being systematically denied? If historians like Trinder believe that the process of recovery is simply *academic* in the driest meaning of that term, they risk allowing the terrain of history to pass beyond the radical political imperative to challenge both past and present. Thinking that history is merely 'evidence' ignores the dominant framework into which 'evidence' passes. That framework, whether it be the relatively limited horizons of conservative historiography, or the sometimes totalizing claims of national-popular culture, sanitizes the past with the help of those like the Museum Trust who help organize everyday life. Question all you like, but putting one's faith in artefacts and technical processes is a *political* act, because it ignores the *social* relations of production and consumption which are never self-evident.

In its own terms the Trust is evidently concerned to produce 'clear historical messages',[29] which are said to be 'in response to a growing awareness of the significance of the Industrial Revolution in the history of this country and of the world'. This is the dominant framework being invoked, to which the Trust added the novelty of its own presentation of the historical experience. Evidently the museum is a symbol of

> a growing recognition that it is through field studies in places like the Ironbridge Gorge that a fuller understanding of the period can be gained, that meanings and relationships can be revealed through the use of original objects in an original landscape.[30]

The underlying assumption here is that the museum does provide a thoroughgoing critical analysis of the industrial revolution, and not merely a celebration with analytical overtones. In their own terms this view can be sustained only as long as the artefacts and sites remain inalienably 'authentic'. The claim of authenticity is a crucial one for the Trust, as it represents another facet of the process of legitimization, equally as important as the seal of approval given by royal patronage. Therefore to be found peddling something other than a rigorous account of the past, would tip the balance between commercialism and academic credibility in the direction of money for dreams. Even a cursory examination of the Open Air Museum at Blists Hill indicates that the costermonger has taken over the teaching. However, before I discuss that let me locate the museum in the context of the town of Ironbridge.

History-making and 'community'

Ironbridge: a museum town

It is almost impossible, as my introduction playfully implied, not to begin a description of Ironbridge, without making some grandiose claims for the area. This inference is so well established that, like a psychologist's word assocation test, the merest suggestion of the name Ironbridge brings forth the irresistable urge to utter superlatives of an historical kind. I'll avoid the temptation of stating, as others have done, that the iron bridge is the 'eighth wonder of the world'.[31] Instead I'll begin by saying that it's an impressive symbol of innovative manufacturing and engineering skills that stands as a monument to the emergent industrial bourgeoisie of the latter half of the eighteenth-century. I will also say that it represents exploited labour, a shift in work patterns, discipline, and time, and that it stands as a monument to manufacturing and commodity production. However, most of these meanings are not manifest in Ironbridge but remain latent and for the most part lost, in the technicist framework through which the bridge appears as *industrial archaeology*.

That the bridge represents the past as *technology* is undeniable, but its present appeal as a tourist attraction encourages a broader set of meanings. The bridge is a kind of promenading place, a pedestrian precinct that affords fine views of this always muddy and treacherous river, as it winds its way through the narrow wooded gorge. One of the over-arching effects of 'the past' as a representation of history is the extent to which once-industrial sites have become ruralized by design or neglect, or the shifting geographical movement of capital and productive industry. The same has happened here, and surely part of the appeal of Ironbridge is that its industry is countrified, another important aspect of the repertoire of English national-popular culture that helps the process of forgetfulness.

Tourists have been visiting this site for more than a century, and rural metaphor asserts that they come and go like the swifts and swallows that dart above their heads; just as seasonal, just as fleeting. It's a good place to eat ice-creams and gaze into the middle distance. It's somewhere, especially from its apex, where boys indulge in spitting competitions, or those with a horticultural eye inspect the tiny gardens of the bridge's neighbours. With so many visitors about, concentrated in the summer months, the bridge acts as an impromptu grandstand for the occasional raft race, or it substitutes for the village green as a suitable site for the dances of the morris men. These ancient fellows of yore, as 'traditional' as the real ale they slop and as 'ancient' as the most recent folk revival, add a degree of colour, incongruity, and male *bonhomie* to this bustling focal point. The bridge is undoubtedly the central attraction of the Trust's history-making colony on the banks of the River Severn, although clearly its present purpose is not primarily historical in the educational sense.

The town of Ironbridge is one of those places, like Hebden Bridge in West Yorkshire, that is caught in the contradiction between serving the local community with its transmuted bourgeois needs, and the transient expectations of the visitors. Just over ten years ago the overall feel of the place was one of dereliction, but the museum has changed all that and not entirely for the better. Post office, greengrocers, butchers, chemists, and small supermarkets, all somehow still impoverished, barely hold sway against the craft shops, antique shops, and endless knick-knack emporiums that all sell the very same glitzy junk. Added to this cafes, 'tea shoppes', and restaurants come and go like speculative butterflies, puffed up on the golden rays of summer when the visitors flit and cash registers chatter, only to spend the winter in fitful hibernation. Some die off, some return, others metamorphose into different dreams of an 'independent living'.

Yet the contradictions between changing but underlying local needs and the erratic 'outside' ones are concrete evidence of the danger of the *laissez-faire* effects of becoming the tertiary zone of the Trust's sphere of influence. Having once helped determine the seductive image of the area as a desirable place to visit and live, it begins to determine the structure of the local economy in a really unhealthy way. This is true of both the essential and the non-essential sectors, although in terms of the former the effect can be quite bizarre. Recently it was announced that Lloyds, the only bank in Ironbridge, was about to close, partly because of the seasonality of its business. Now the building is up for sale and visitors and residents have a two-mile trek to the nearest alternative bank. News of this was greeted locally with some anger and amazement, especially as Lloyds had recently donated £30,000 to the Museum Trust to build an 'old' bank at Blists Hill. For finance capital, it seems, it is more important to be represented in the museum world of the past-present and to accept one's place in antiquity, than to try to serve the modern world and the mundane needs of the everyday.

Meanwhile, the non-essential sector flourishes and its centre-piece is The Shop in the Square, run on the Trust's behalf by the Ironbridge Gorge Trading Company. The shop exudes its own plush comfort, striking a balance between the grossly expensive Coalport China, medium-priced items from the ludicrous 'Edwardian Kitchen Company', and cheap trinkets that the children can afford.

When Christmas comes it's the sort of shop you scour in desperation on 23 December for those last-minute useless items. It's the place for the presents you feel duty bound to purchase for neglected relatives, who respond with renewed bonds of familial intimacy. However, the precariousness of the other shops in Ironbridge is not only overshadowed by this shrine to 'good taste', but by the 'old' shops at Blists Hill.

Blists Hill: a 'community' at work?

This museum occupies a forty-two acre site on which the Trust has begun the lengthy renovation of a number of *in situ* buildings and artefacts. Here there is a coal-mine and headgear, blast furnaces, and a length of Shropshire Canal with its own impressive incline plane. These are all remnants of the days when this was a heaving, noisy, and dirty industrial region. However, the majority of buildings and machines to be found here have been imported, the Trust would say 'rescued', to go towards the construction of 'a working industrial community'.[32] The emphasis here is both on 'community' and 'work', although my perception of the validity of this venture is in stark contrast to that of the Trust. The idea of Blists Hill is to produce a 'community' in the physical sense, where historical space and 'authentic' activities can be represented, as a popular 'educational' spectacle. The *Blists Hill Open Air Museum Guide* informs the visitor of how to enjoy this past-present, and clearly it's intended to be a total bodily experience.

> You will see how people lived a hundred years ago, and where they worked. You can eat what they ate, smell what they could smell and drink what they drank. You can see how their candles, their shoes, their woodwork and their printed papers were made. And you will be surrounded by the evidence of two centuries of industrial activity.[33]

The 'community' of Blists Hill is fashioned from two illusions, one relating to the setting and the other to the selection process. In the first instance, as with the iron bridge itself, we are faced with the amnesia-inducing lure of a rural locality. The *Teachers' Handbook* puts it more favourably. 'The open wooded nature of Blists Hill has provided the Museum Trust with the opportunity to create an authentic industrial environment of the past',[34] but made more attractive by landscaping, so that the industrial past appears aesthetically or 'organically' tied to the countryside. The second illusion is one of typicality. What the visitor discovers is not a 'community' – with only three dwellings it could hardly be that – but a 'High Street' full of retailers and small business people. There is a chemist's shop, butcher's, printing shop, pub, sweet shop, cobbler's, plasterer's shop, and they all vie for your custom. If you can afford it, there are meat pies in the butcher's, posters in the printers, effigies in the plasterer's, candles in the candle-makers, humbugs and sugar-coated almonds in the sweet shop, and, of course, 'traditional' ale in the pub. For what we have here is a complete breakdown of the distinction between history-making and money-making. I don't wish to be purist about it, but there is a sense in which the educative function is almost entirely subordinated to the opportunism of commodity exchange, and to filling the coffers of the Trust.

Another aspect of Blists Hill that makes its 'community' decidedly an *imagined* one is the deployment of waged work as a spectacle in the museum's sawmill, candle-making shop, and iron foundry. This aspect, like the centrality of historical retailing, is another element of the museum that reflects the interests and assumptions of the trustees and management, and the capital flow from the 'chiefs of industry' and other business interests. However, the 'official' accounts of this have been quite different, as the 'honorary historian's' assessment of the value of Blists Hill shows. For him there were two crucial elements to the strategy of presenting working exhibits. First, that the public might gain an understanding of 'working conditions and of the reasons for particular practices', and second, such exhibits would raise a set of important questions about work routines and the structure of the labour market.[35] Once upon a time this might have been the overall aim of the Blists Hill project, but when I visited I felt wholly unconvinced by this argument.

Wandering through the sawmill I felt that the emphasis was heavily upon representing the antiquated labour-process as a *desirable* spectacle. In the woodworking shop men were making wheelbarrows and gates, a circular saw hummed through a piece of timber, while outside a large late-nineteenth-century horizontal saw was prepared to cut a 'flitch' from a slab of pine. Of course my eyes could feast upon the *means* of production; here was labour power, machinery, and raw materials. With eyes half closed and the historical imagination hard at work I might have been able to conjure some of the conditions of production, but how is this spectacle meant to convey any of the flavour of the *social relations* between labour and capital, or depict the deployment of 'masculinity' in the work-place?

I spent three of my most formative years working in family-run sawmills in the early 1970s, and this exhibit doesn't even begin to capture the essence of that contemporary experience, which was not wildly dissimilar to the more distant day-to-day practices of the sawmill. This exhibit didn't prompt questions bar those of a technical nature, and the exhibit demonstrators were not equipped to interpret the social relations of production associated with their 'historic' task. Believe me, this is no sawmill, but one of many places for the Blists Hill ghost town phantoms to inhabit. An actual sawmill is pervaded by the atmosphere of 'masculinity': risk, competition, aggressiveness, and sexual innuendo are lightened by humour and male friendships. There is real danger in a sawmill, the noise is deafening, and the sense of isolation acute. Accidents are common but men struggle not to show fear, castigating it in others; they minimize their injuries, and put a brave face on crushed hands and lost fingers.

Historically most sawmills have been small family businesses, with paternalistic, interfering bosses putting a kindly face on capitalism; your business is their business, and there's no place for trade unionism where wage deals are struck man to man. I went to work in the sawmills because I was desperate, the wage form was exploitation, every day was purgatory, but there was no other local alternative. How do you make a museum of an experience like that? What angered me about the sawmill and the woodworking shop was that the 'reality' it produced actively disorganized, and thus rendered illegitimate, any alternative account of what this experience of work amounts to. Up to a point I felt silenced by it and, in the absence of anything more relevant, felt drawn to identify with the tools, the noise and the smell. But isn't this what dominant memory always does? A museum like this with its professional-managerial assumptions provides a very partial framework for personal experience, and one which constantly threatens to compromise those visitors who want to sustain their own distinctive and opposed perspectives to the exploitation of waged work. Looking around this exhibit I felt demoralized, so I bought two ounces of Pontefract Cakes from the sweet shop to cheer myself up.

The candle-makers is on the opposite side of the 'High Street' from the woodworkers and here the museum seems to have got it right. In the gloom of an autumn afternoon this was an ill-lighted, pokey, and miserable place. Worse still, the air was heavy with the gagging vapour of quantities of melted wax that clung to clothes and made the room nauseous and claustrophobic. Two young people in period costume were busy making candles, employed by the Trust through an MSC scheme on a job-sharing basis that gives them four days' work one week and three the following week. One of them explained to me that being dressed in 'Victorian clothes' was one of the conditions of service (another MSC scheme makes the clothes), and that he was pleased to have a job, being fearful of when the scheme ended and his return to unemployment would be imminent. What struck me about this encounter was a deep irony. In the pursuit of authenticity the Trust had created a really hazardous and unhealthy work environment, apparently mindless of the health and safety of their employees. And, on top of this, these youngsters have to suffer the indignity of working for £50 a week. Victorian values indeed! The sawmill with its lack of authenticity, and the candle-making factory, with its seemingly genuine and certainly unhealthy atmosphere, should raise questions for everyone concerned with the representation and consumption of the past. I felt personally confused by this particular juxtaposition, although I do recognize a common denominator here. The professional-managerial perception of industrial history, at its most asinine, happily ignores the double exploitation of waged labour and the hazards of an unhealthy work environment.

Conclusion

It is important to see the modern practice of museum-making and the infrastructure of control at Ironbridge as having helped facilitate three interrelated outcomes. First, the new museum business has helped transform popular perceptions of the past; second, it has helped innovate ways of representing history, especially in *outdoor* museums; finally, it has fundamentally altered the environments and economies of places like Ironbridge. As a way of representing history the Trust has made a significant contribution to popularizing 'the past' as an available form of knowledge. Its contribution has been in the area of industrial archaeology, and recuperating capitalist industrialization as a *positive* moment of historical transformation. Locating industrial history in a rural setting, and as resulting from the inspiration of individual capitalists, is only as invidious as the parallel tendency to represent the labour process as a pleasurable spectacle and deny the presence of class struggle in the work-place.

These perceptions of history are those of the men of the professional-managerial classes, and consequently the political economy of the making of the Iron Bridge Gorge Museum is inscribed in each exhibit. This has increasingly been the case as the management and trustees become more confident, because *unchallenged*, in *their* perceptions and assumptions. Recently this was made abundantly clear when the museum began to blather about what it calls the 'Ironbridge spirit', an entrepreneurial variant of the Dunkirk variety. Apparently,

> examples of invention, innovation, energy and unwearied diligence on an heroic scale, and hardly to be evoked by as conventional a word as entrepreneurship, [sorry!] could be brought out further, and without straining the evidence could be made a source of inspiration for an age badly in need of it.[36]

Now the spectacle of Blists Hill falls into place. It represents *'the past' that worked*, in the double sense of being a successful one for capital *and* one where 'idle' hands were busy. The little Utopia of Blists Hill 'resolves' unemployment, the result of ancient and modern crises of capital, by appealing to 'the past' and by deploying the most vulnerable sectors of present-day society. The poorly paid MSC employee is forced to carry the burden of exploitation, in a historical process that changes just to remain the same, but where exploitation now is made to tell the story of harmony in the days of yore.

This version of 'the past' as a museum piece is the concrete proof of a lack of democracy in museum-making. The political economy of this Museum Trust, and the assumptions that consolidated themselves through the pursuit of funding and labour, have become merely a reflection of the larger conservative story of people and nation. However, the story-book is not closed and as readers of historical romance, we invariably don't believe *all* we read! The masses of visitors who idle across the iron bridge to reach the icecream van on the Brosely side, drink lager and Babycham instead of 'traditional ale', and visit Blists Hill because it's a nice place for the kids to run round, have different perceptions too. Historical tourism it may be, but is it primarily that? As critics of contemporary culture we might know where the historical message begins, but where does it end? For me it consolidates itself in opposition. Being a critical critic is the *only* way I can enjoy the Ironbridge Gorge Museum, and I constantly eavesdrop in the hope of finding kindred spirits. Most, I suspect, stay away. Consequently, if pressed to choose I would say that the Pleasure Beach at Blackpool or the amusements at Alton Towers are more my idea of a good day out. At least on the big dipper, having paid your money, everybody agrees that the pleasure is in being taken for a ride!

Notes and references

Museum sources

The *Final Report of the Working Party*, the *Appeals Brochure*, and the *Annual Reports and Accounts* (beginning in 1969) are all available on request from the Ironbridge Gorge Museum Trust. Other items used here, like the *Ironbridge Gorge Teachers' Handbook* and the *Blists Hill Open Air Museum Guide* (SJ693033) are stored at the museum library, or available from the museum shops!

1 Claims to individual authorship always present problems, and this is perhaps exaggerated on this occasion because the argument developed here borrows heavily from a collective project on narrative and nationalism, currently being written up by members of the Popular Memory Group at the Centre for Contemporary Cultural Studies, the University of Birmingham. I should like to thank all current and past members of the Popular Memory Group: Mariette Clare, Graham Dawson, Chris Glen, Richard Johnson, Pat McLernon, Laura Di Michelle, Jill Trott, and Michelle Weinroth. Additionally I should like to thank Lynne Sheridan and Tim Putnam for their valuable help in developing some of the arguments about the Ironbridge Gorge Museum Trust. I am also indebted to a number of people who made editorial suggestions or helped bring this piece to publication: thanks to Michael Green, Maureen McNeil, Bob Lumley, and Patrick Wright. Finally, despite my critical position on the Trust, I have received nothing but courtesy and open-handed help from the museum staff in public relations.
2 Trinder, B. (1976) 'Industrial conservation and industrial history: reflections on the Ironbridge Gorge Museum', *History Workshop Journal* (2) 175.
3 This article is a much shortened and amended version of my (1985) stencilled paper entitled 'Danger! History at work: a critical consumer's Guide to the Ironbridge Gorge Museum', Centre for Contemporary Cultural Studies, University of Birmingham. The original project was to write an article for *History Workshop Journal*, but the editors were divided over the 'tone' of my approach and one in particular threatened to resign from the editorial collective should my article appear. Democracy didn't prevail!

4 *Final Report of the Working Party*, p. 2 and p. 4.
5 ibid., p. 3.
6 ibid., p. 8.
7 ibid., p. 13.
8 *Guardian*, 6 May 1987. I was too busy rewriting this article to read the papers. Thanks to Lesley Whitehouse for this reference.
9 Trinder, B. (1976) 'Industrial conservation and industrial history: reflections on the Ironbridge Gorge Museum', *History Workshop Journal* 2: 175.
10 *Annual Report*, 1971–2 and 1972–3.
11 *Annual Report*, 1979–80.
12 *Annual Report*, 1982.
13 *Annual Report*, 1969–70.
14 *Annual Report*, 1981.
15 *Annual Report*, 1973–4 and 1974–5.
16 *Annual Report*, 1971–2 and 1972–3.
17 Bommes, M. and Wright, P. (1982) '"Charms of residence": the public and the past', in R. Johnson, G. McLenon, W. Schwarz, and D. Sutton (eds) *Making Histories*, London: Hutchinson pp. 225–64.
18 *Annual Report*, 1973–4.
19 *Annual Report*, 1972–3.
20 *Annual Report*, 1981.
21 *Annual Report*, 1977–8.
22 *Annual Report*, 1979–80.
23 *Ironbridge Gorge Teachers' Handbook* (nd), p. 3.
24 *Annual Report*, 1973–4.
25 These numbers fluctuate somewhat. Between 1983 and 1984, for example, there were 77,238 educational visitors. See *Annual Report*, 1984.
26 *Annual Report*, 1973–4.
27 Trinder, B. (1976) 'Industrial conservation and industrial history: reflections on the Ironbridge Gorge Museum', *History Workshop Journal* 2: 174.
28 ibid.
29 The Trust used this phrase in a 1984 job description for a senior research fellow funded by Leverhulme.
30 *Ironbridge Gorge Teachers' Handbook*, see the 'Foreword'.
31 This priceless item of knowledge occurs during the audio-visual presentation at the Severn Warehouse Visitor's Centre.
32 *Ironbridge Gorge Teachers' Handbook*, p. 10.
33 *Blists Hill Open Air Museum Guide* (nd), p. 4.
34 *Ironbridge Gorge Teachers' Handbook*, p. 10.
35 Trinder, B. (1976) 'Industrial conservation and industrial history: reflections on the Ironbridge Gorge Museum', *History Workshop Journal* 2: 174.
36 Text taken from the job description for a senior research fellow funded by Leverhulme.

3

Museums and 'the people'

TONY BENNETT

> One can say that until now folklore has been studied primarily as
> a 'picturesque' element. . . . Folklore should instead be studied as
> a 'conception of the world and life' implicit to a large degree in
> determinate (in time and space) strata of society and in opposi-
> tion (also for the most part implicit, mechanical and objective) to
> 'official' conceptions of the world.
>
> (Antonio Gramsci)[1]

The issue to which Gramsci points here – that of the political
seriousness attaching to the ways in which the cultures of subordinate classes are studied and represented – has assumed a particularly telling significance in connection with recent developments in
museum policy in Britain. Although somewhat belatedly compared
with Scandinavian countries and North America, the post-war
period has witnessed a flurry of new museum initiatives – folk
museums, open-air museums, living history farms – oriented
toward the collection, preservation, and display of artefacts relating to the daily lives, customs, rituals, and traditons of non-élite
social strata.

This development is, in its way, as significant as the legislative
and administrative reforms which, in the nineteenth century,
transformed museums from semi-private institutions restricted
largely to the ruling and professional classes into major organs of
the state dedicated to the instruction and edification of the general
public.[2] As a consequence of these changes, museums were
regarded by the end of the century as major vehicles for the
fulfilment of the state's new educative and moral role in relation to

the population as a whole. While late-nineteenth-century museums were thus intended *for* the people, they were certainly not *of* the people in the sense of displaying any interest in the lives, habits, and customs of either the contemporary working classes or the labouring classes of pre-industrial societies. If museums were regarded as providing object lessons in things, their central message was to materialize the power of the ruling classes (through the collections of imperialist plunder which found their way to the Victoria and Albert Museum, for example) in the interest of promoting a general acceptance of ruling-class cultural authority.

The extension of the social range of museum concerns in the post-war period, then, is a new departure. Yet while, in a relative sense, it is one to be welcomed, the consequence is often as Gramsci suggests: namely to represent the cultures of subordinate social classes not in their real complexity but 'as a "picturesque" element'. As a consequence, the terms in which the ways of life of such classes are represented are often so mortgaged to the dominant culture that 'the people' are encountered usually only in those massively idealized and deeply regressive forms which stalk the middle-class imagination. There are, of course, exceptions and I shall discuss some of these shortly. First, though, an example of the processes through which museums, in portraying 'the people', also sentimentalize them.

A countryside of the mind: Beamish

Visitors to the North of England Open Air Museum at Beamish, set in the heart of County Durham, are encouraged to make the Visitor Centre their first port of call. For there, the guidebook informs, they will find 'an introduction to the North East and its people, and an explanation of what Beamish is all about'.[3] This explanation takes the form of a tape-slide show which offers two interacting accounts of the region's origins. One strand of the narrative, organized in terms of geological time, traces the basis of the region's fortunes to the mineral deposits laid down in the volcanic period. A second strand, concerned with the human time of the region's inhabitants, tells the story of a tough and resilient people – retrospectively regionalized through cartoon sketches of, for example, cloth-capped Iron Age settlers who, in assimilating successive waves of invasion (Roman, Viking, Yorkshire), none the less remain the same throughout all ages, the embodiments of an undiluted and unchanging regional spirit. It is the convergence of these two strands of the narrative in the nineteenth century that purports to account for the north-east's unique history conceived as the product of a region blessed with plentiful mineral resources and with a people sufficiently tenacious, inventive, and, above all, canny enough to exploit its natural advantages.

A mythic story, then, and, on the face of it, a fairly innocuous one for it neither takes itself, nor asks to be taken, too seriously. Yet its significance consists as much in how it is told as what is said. In the early and concluding parts of the show, those which set the scene and define the terms in which the region's history is told, the commentary is carried by an impersonal narrator whose 'neutral' accent and carefully modulated tone clearly identify his voice as that of the home counties or the BBC. However, at a key point in the narrative, the point at which the region's people and its mineral resources come together in the nineteenth-century development of the north-east's mining industry, this narrative voice gives way to another voice – that of the region's working classes – as the story is picked up and developed in the thick Geordie accent of a fictional miner ('we call him Jonti') who tells the story of the region's industrial development as the result of 'me and me marrers' pulling together. The device is a familiar one from many television documentaries where the voice of the dominant culture is usually accorded the authoritative role while regional voices, often reduced to signs of some local quirkiness or eccentricity, occupy clearly subordinated positions. And so it is here. It is the voice of the south that is dominant in the narrative, deriving its authority not merely from its familiar BBC associations but also from its anonymity and the fact that the role accorded it is that of narrating the hard truths of geological time. It is, in short, simultaneously the voice of the dominant culture and that of impersonal truth. Jonti's voice, by contrast, is the voice of local experience. It embodies the people – but the people as envisaged within the dominant culture; as a regional folk which is as endlessly cheerful and good-natured as it is enterprising and industrious. The voice of Jonti – that of a cheeky and cheerful (jaunty) Geordie chappie – is that of the regional people as 'spoken' by the dominant culture in much the same way as the voice of the 'common man' is spoken by the popular press.

In this respect, the tape-slide show does indeed prepare the visitor for the museum proper where 'the people' of the north-east can be seen, and see themselves, only through the cracked looking-glass of the dominant culture. Beamish states its aim as being to exhibit the factors which 'influenced the life and work of the people

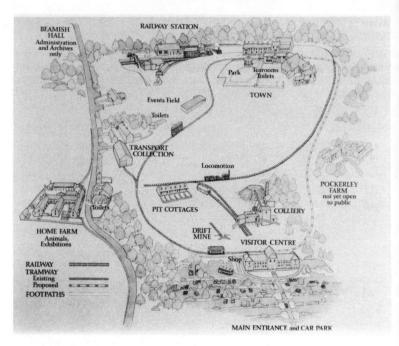

3 Map of Beamish, North of England Open Air Museum. (Photo: Beamish Museum)

of the region a century ago, when the North East was in the forefront of British industrial development'.[4] As such, it consists of a series of linked sites spanning the period from (roughly) the 1790s through to the 1930s, but with the greatest emphasis falling on the late Victorian and Edwardian periods. There is a model farm dating from the late eighteenth century but restored to an approximation of its mid-nineteenth-century lay-out and operating conditions; a colliery meant to represent the technology and working conditions in the mining industry on the eve of the First World War; a row of pit-cottages, their interiors designed and furnished to exhibit changes in the tastes and ways of life of mining families over the period from the 1890s through to 1938. The centre of a market town has also been reconstructed, complete with cobbled streets, a Co-op, pub, and bandstand – a slice of urban history from the 1830s through to the 1920s which abuts on to a country railway station restored to its 1910 condition. Archaic forms of transport (coach and

66

horses, a tramway) connect these sites while, within them, costumed museum workers act out their parts in this constructed past by displaying traditional industrial and domestic techniques.

Undoubtedly the significance of 'the Beamish experience' consists as much in what it excludes as what it includes. No museum can include everything, of course, but, at Beamish, there is a pattern to the exclusions which suggests that the museum embodies, indeed is committed to, an institutionalized mode of amnesia. One would be hard put, for example, to find any materials relating to the history of the region's labour and trade-union movements, and the activities of the women of the north-east in suffrage and feminist campaigns go entirely unremarked. In short, the conception of the regional people installed at Beamish is very much that of a people without a politics. Nor is this entirely a matter of the museum's absences. Many of the artefacts displayed might well have been exhibited in such a way as to suggest their associations with popular political movements. However, the tendency is for them to be severed of such associations and to serve, instead, as vehicles for the nostalgic remembrance of sentimentalized pasts. The premises of the Anfield Plain Industrial Co-operative Society, one of the major showpieces of the town centre, have thus been arranged so as to remind visitors of old pricing systems (pre-decimal), serving technologies (bacon slicers), and advertisements (the Fry's boys). No mention is made of the history of the co-operative movement, its aims and principles, or its relations to other socialist organizations. Similarly, the row of pit cottages, while showing shifts in interior decor and domestic technologies, represents these as solely concerning changes in taste rather than relating them to changing social relations within the home – changes in the sexual division of labour brought about by new domestic technologies or by shifts in the structure of the mining industry, for example.

None the less, important though such absences and omissions are, 'the Beamish experience' must ultimately be assessed in terms of what it *does* say rather than of what it leaves unsaid. Of crucial significance from this point of view are the respects in which the very conception of the museum as an embodiment of the region's history has been realized by bringing together buildings and artefacts from different areas of the north-east. The railway station, for example, has been reassembled from the components of a number of different disused stations dating from the period of the North Eastern Railway Company, while the town centre includes, in addition to the Co-op from Anfield Plain, a bandstand and a row of Georgian-style middle-class houses from Gateshead. Similarly, while the colliery buildings and much of the pit-head machinery are from the museum's immediate environs, the row of pit cottages has been brought to the site from Hetton-le-Hole, near Sunderland. It is only by severing these buildings from their particular and local histories and bringing them together on the same site that Beamish is able to organize that conception of the north-east as a distinctive region with a distinctive people whose interacting histories the museum then claims to realize.

Rather more significant, perhaps, is the fact that these diverse buildings and the artefacts they contain are also imagined as belonging to the same essential and unified time. And this in spite of the fact that the museum spans the period from the 1790s to the 1930s, with all the major exhibits being clearly dated. For the differentiation of times within this period impresses itself on the visitor with less force than the overwhelming sense of an undifferentiated time suggested by the museum's setting. At Beamish, everything – no matter how old it is – is frozen at the same point in time: the moment of transition from a rural to an industrial society. It matters little whether some parts of the town date from the 1830s and others from the 1920s, or whether the interiors of the pit cottages are meant to span the period from the 1890s to the 1930s; the very fact of reconstructing these earlier industrial technologies and associated forms of social organization in the heart of the countryside has the effect of installing the visitor in a twilight zone between the rural past and the fully industrialized present. At Beamish the processes of industrialization are represented on a human and manageable scale, taking the form of little islands of industrialism and urbanism which emerge from, and yet also harmonize with, the surrounding countryside.

Not just any countryside either. The museum is set in the grounds of Beamish Hall, family home of the Shafto family until 1952 and, before that, of such notable families as the Eden family in a line of ownership traceable to the period of the Norman conquest. Beamish Hall still stands, serving as the administrative centre of the museum and housing a further exhibition of local history artefacts. But it is also the museum's controlling ideological centre, a bourgeois country house under whose controlling gaze there is organized a harmonious set of relationships – between town and country, agriculture and industry, for example, as well as between classes which, in occupying separate zones (the middle classes dominate the town while the working classes live by the colliery), seem to live side-by-side and in harmony with one another, each accepting its allotted place. The consequence is that the story of industrial development in the north-east, rather than being told as one of ruptures, conflicts, and transformations, emerges as a process that is essentially continuous with the deeper and longer history of a countryside in which the power of the bourgeoisie has beome naturalized. It is, in this respect, similar to the Ironbridge Gorge Museum which, as Bob West puts it, 'ironically reconstitutes a sense of the industrial through an arcane idealisation of an organic ruralism'.[5]

Speaking of the ascendency, in the late Victorian period, of ruralized conceptions of the 'English way of life', Martin Wiener writes:

This countryside of the mind was everything industrial society was not – ancient, slow-moving, stable, cosy, and 'spiritual'. The English genius, it declared, was (despite appearances) not economic or technical, but social and spiritual; it did not lie in inventing, producing, or selling, but in preserving, harmonising, and moralising. The English character was not naturally progressive, but conservative; its greatest task – and achievement – lay in taming and 'civilising' the dangerous engines of progress it had unwittingly unleashed.[6]

Beamish may boast of the north-east's inventors, such as the Stephensons, and sing the virtues of its canny and industrious people. And it may claim that the north-east spearheaded the processes of industrialization, leading in areas where the rest of the country would only follow later. At the same time though, and outweighing this regionalist rhetoric, Beamish succeeds in taming 'the dangerous engines of progress' in seeming to materialize the countryside of the mind of which Wiener writes and, thereby, to make actual a purely imaginary history. And yet an imaginary history whose cultural power is very considerable. Why else might it be thought that the history of a century and more of large-scale industrialization and urbanization might be adequately represented by dismantling industrial structures from their original locations and reassembling them in such a country-house setting? How else might we account for Beamish's ability to attract visitors from Gateshead and Newcastle, where the ravages of industrialization are only too readily apparent, to this constructed idyll unless, to borrow from Michel Foucault's designation of history, we recognize it as 'a place of rest, certainty, reconciliation, a place of tranquillised sleep'.[7]

Peopling the past: Scandinavian and American forerunners

Much of this is not too surprising. As was noted earlier, Beamish forms a part of a more broadly based extension and democratization of the interests and concerns of British museums in the post-war period. Opened in the 1970s, it was the first open-air museum in England – but not in Britain: that title goes to the Welsh Folk Museum at St Fagan's which opened in 1946 – and, like most other such museums, has been deeply shaped and influenced by the earlier history of this museum form. The first such museum was opened by Artur Hazelius at Skansen, near Stockholm, in 1891. Consisting of reassembled farm buildings, a manor house, craft industries, a log church, stocks, whipping posts, and the like, the museum was staffed with guides dressed in folk costumes, with strolling musicians and folk dancers re-enacting traditonal customs. The popularity of the museum led to similar ones being established in other European countries in the late nineteenth and early twentieth centuries. The interest in folk culture, which developed earlier in Scandinavian societies than anywhere else, had originally been a progressive phenomenon, a part, as Peter Burke puts it, of 'a movement of revolt against the centre by the cultural periphery of Europe; part of a movement, among intellectuals, towards self-definition and liberation in regional or national terms'.[8] By the end of the century, however, Michael Wallace suggests that this interest in folk culture had degenerated into a form of a backward-looking romanticism:

> The Skansen movement blended romantic nostalgia with dismay at the emergence of capitalist social relations. As the new order had introduced mechanised mass production, a burgeoning working-class, and class conflict, these museums, often organised by aristocrats and professionals, set out to preserve and celebrate fast disappearing craft and rural traditions. What they commemorated, and in some degree fabricated, was the life of 'the folk', visualised as a harmonious population of peasants and craft workers.[9]

And worse was to come when, in the 1920s and 1930s, the open-air museum form was transplanted to American soil. Throughout the greater part of the nineteenth century, the USA's élites had displayed comparatively little interest in the development of museums or the preservation of historic sites. Moreover, such interest as there was came largely from representatives of the older American families whose wealth derived from inherited land, mercantile activities, or the early phases of industrial development. Indeed, many of the leading organizations in the preservationist lobby – the Daughters of the American Revolution (DAR), for example – explicitly required that their members be able to trace their descent to one of the early colonists.[10] If the representatives of corporate capital, the real driving force in the American economy in the late nineteenth century, displayed relatively little interest in questions of museum and heritage policy, this was partly because such matters had been colonized by the USA's patrician élites in ways which were clearly intended to exclude the vulgarity of the *nouveau riche*. But it was also because a disinterest in, even disdain for, the past could find strong support in those elements of the American republican tradition which contended that, just as the USA had been founded through a series of breaks with the past, so it could continue to be true to itself, to its own dynamic essence, only if it continually regarded the past as fit only for the rubbish dump of history rather than as something to be fetishized and memorialized. Nathaniel Hawthorne summarized this view nicely when, in 1862, he recorded his reflections prompted by a visit to the Warwickshire village of Witnash:

> Rather than the monotony of sluggish ages, loitering on a village green, toiling in hereditary fields, listening to the parson's drone lengthened through centuries in the grey Norman church, let us welcome whatever change may come – change of place, social customs, political institutions, modes of worship – trusting that . . . they will but make room for better systems, and for a higher type of man to clothe his life in them, and to fling them off in turn.[11]

Michael Wallace argues that the influence of this tradition declined appreciably in the aftermath of the First World War. So did the balance of influence within the preservationist lobby as, in the context of serious labour difficulties on the domestic front and the spectre of revolution in Europe, 'corporate capital moved to the forefront of the return to the past'.[12] It is one of the ironies of history that Henry Ford, who had earlier denounced history as bunk, was a prime mover in these developments and, in Greenfield Village, opened in 1929, was responsible for one of the first open-air museums in the USA – yet one which significantly transformed this hitherto exclusively European genre, just as it also embodied a break with the priorities of earlier American preservationist organizations. Wallace conveys something of this dual transformation of earlier museum forms effected by Greenfield Village in his discussion of the kind of 'peopling of the past' embodied in this imaginary township of yesteryear:

> Ford's Greenfield Village can best be understood as an Americanised Skansen. Ford celebrated not 'the folk' but the Common Man. He rejected the DAR's approach of exalting famous patriots and patrician élites. Indeed, he banished rich men's homes, lawyers' offices, and banks, from his village. This museum-hamlet paid homage to blacksmiths, machinists, the frontier farmers, celebrated craft skills and domestic labour, recalled old social customs like square dancing and folk fiddling, and praised the 'timeless and dateless' pioneer virtues of hard work, discipline, frugality, and self-reliance. It was a pre-capitalist Eden immune to modern ills, peopled with men and women of character.[13]

But it was an Eden destined to develop beyond itself, and for the better, inasmuch as the village also contained an Industrial Museum which, in celebrating the inventions of men of genius, supplied the mechanism of development through which the idyllic past embodied in the rest of the village had since been improved on. In this way, Wallace suggests, Greenfield Village had it both ways in offering a vision of 'the good old days' since when, due to capitalist progress, things have only got better. 'The two messages together', as Wallace puts it, '– life had been better in the old days and it had been getting better ever since – added up to a corporate employer's vision of history'.[14]

The message of Beamish is much the same, except that the engines of progress are attributed to the qualities of the region's people rather than being portrayed as the fruits of individual genius and, rather than being housed in a separate museum, are dispersed throughout the site, seeming to grow naturally out of the countryside. And this, as we have seen, is not just any countryside but that distinctively bourgeois countryside of the mind in which the present emerges uninterruptedly from a past in which the presence and leading role of the bourgeoisie is eternally naturalized. This ability to transform industrialism from a set of ruptural events into a mere moment in the unfolding of a set of harmonious

72

relations between rulers and people may well turn out to be a distinctively English contribution to the development of the open-air museum form.

In brief, then, there are grounds for caution regarding the effects of the more demotic and socially expansive orientation toward the past that has been evident in post-war museum policy. And this in spite of the arguments often advanced in its favour – that it has at least acknowledged the importance of the everyday lives of ordinary working people. For while *what* is shown in museums is important, the question of *how* museum artefacts get displayed and represented – and thus of what they are made to mean – is at least as significant. From this perspective, if Beamish is anything to go by, the development of museums concerned primarily with artefacts relating to the daily lives and customs of 'ordinary people' has resulted in a 'peopling of the past' in which the cultures and values of non-élite strata are subordinated to bourgeois culture and values just as effectively as they are in the great public museums which developed in the nineteenth century. However, this subordination is wrought rather differently, the result of a different ideological economy and one which, perhaps, has a greater capacity for organizing the visitor's experience precisely to the degree that it is more likely to pass unnoticed.

In the nineteenth-century museum the cultures of subordinate classes were – and largely still are – a simple absence, excluded not only as a matter of definition (the working classes were not regarded as having a culture worthy of preservation) but also as a matter of deliberate policy (of 'improving' the people by exposing them to the beneficial influence of middle-class culture). To visit institutions like the Victoria and Albert is, accordingly, to experience and witness the power of the ruling culture, a power which manifests itself precisely through its ability to exclude everything which, through its exclusion, is defined as other and subordinate. There is, as a consequence – at least for most of us – nothing familiar which might help us to relax and feel at home there. However, if we know that we are out of our place, we also know that this effect is not accidental, that we are in the midst of an object lesson in things which, in some measure, instructs through its capacity to intimidate.

Beamish by contrast, works on the ground of popular memory, and restyles it. In evoking past ways of life of which the visitor is likely to have had either direct or, through parents and grand-parents, indirect knowledge and experience, the overwhelming effect is one of an easy-going at-homeness and familiarity. At the same time, though, what one is at home with has, so to speak, been shifted elsewhere through the specific political and ideological associations which are lent to those remembered pasts by means of the rhetoric – the countryside of the mind – which governs the ways in which a past is selectively recalled and reconstructed. Of course, there is no reason to suppose that each and every visitor will consent to this restyling of popular memory, or experience it without some feeling of unease or contradiction. For the ground of popular memory – that is of the institutions which organize the terms in which the past is most commonly perceived and 'remembered' – is not an even one. If Beamish works along with certain dominant modes of styling a sentimentalized past (a visit to the museum is a bit like spending a day as an extra in an episode of *When the Boat Comes In*), the traditions of labour, trade-union, and feminist history provide resources which, if the visitor is so minded, might be called on to resist the lure of that past. Nor is the text of the museum entirely without contradictions of its own. It has its cracks, some of them occurring at the level of those practices which are least susceptible to planned control: the conduct of museum workers. For example, when I last visited Beamish the carefully contrived illusion of an authentic historical milieu was nicely undercut by a costumed museum worker who, in the midst of demonstrating traditional techniques of breadmaking in a carefully reproduced pit-cottage kitchen, chatted with a colleague on Dennis Norden's performance in the previous evening's episode of *It'll Be Alright on the Night*.

However, these are general points that might be made in relation to any museum or, indeed (for this is how I am suggesting we should regard museums), any text. And, however valid they might be, their implications are limited. No matter how true it might be that the ideal text of Beamish may be disrupted by its performers or that visitors may read against the grain of that text, it remains the case that the museum exemplifies a deeply conservative 'peopling of the past' in which the legacy of earlier moments in the development of the open-air museum form is readily apparent. Equally, though, this is not to suggest that the same result necessarily follows whenever and wherever museums concern themselves with the preservation and display of materials relating to the daily lives and customs of 'ordinary people'. While a conservative romanticism may be strongly associated with such practices historically, this connection is not an intrinsic or necessary one. It can be and, in

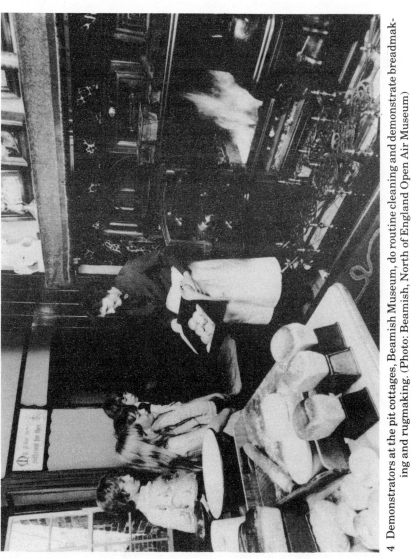

4 Demonstrators at the pit cottages, Beamish Museum, do routine cleaning and demonstrate breadmaking and rugmaking. (Photo: Beamish, North of England Open Air Museum)

view of the increasing popularity of 'museuming' as a leisure activity, needs to be broken.[15] The realization of such an objective on any significant scale would, of course, be dependent on changes in the structures of control over museums and a radical reorganization of their relations to different groups in the community. To pursue these questions properly would require another article. However, something of their significance can be gleaned from a brief consideration of two museums – Hyde Park Barracks in Sydney and People's Palace in Glasgow – which have been clearly committed to the project of producing other peoples and other pasts free from those socially dominant forms of the sentimentalization of the people which have plagued the development of open-air museums, folk museums, and the like.

Other peoples, other pasts

According to the official guide

> The Hyde Park Barracks presents a social history of New South Wales. Rather than a history of great individuals, it is a history of people's everyday lives and experiences. The exhibitions cover two centuries of Australian social life: people celebrating, immigrating, coming to town for the show, building homes, living in the Barracks.[16]

Like Beamish, then, a museum concerned with the everyday lives of ordinary people. Unlike Beamish, however, those people are not reduced, to recall Gramsci's terms, to being 'a picturesque element'. Located in the centre of Sydney, Hyde Park Barracks is concerned mainly to recall and commemorate moments in the popular history of that city. 'The people' represented in the museum is thus primarily an *urban people* and one that is in good measure defined in opposition to 'official conceptions of the world'.

This aspect of the museum is most conspicious in the display 'Sydney Celebrates' which, in exhibiting materials relating to the public celebrations through which the city's history is conventionally punctuated, systematically undercuts and disavows the consensualist rhetoric which formed a part of those celebrations and has governed the terms in which they have since been represented within official discourse. This is achieved partly by drawing attention to those groups which were excluded, or excluded themselves, from those celebrations. The text accompanying the materials relating to the celebrations in 1938 of the 150th anniversary of Australia's European settlement thus notes that floats depicting convict life or the activities of trade unions were banned from public parades in the city in the interests of presenting Australian history as a process free from bitterness and conflict. More tellingly, the text also informs us that 26 January 1938 – the anniversary of the founding of the first European settlement at Port Jackson – was also chosen as the date for a Day of Mourning Conference organized by Aboriginal leaders. Similarly the section of the display relating to the opening of Sydney Harbour Bridge in 1932 – a public celebration in which there was an unusually heightened degree of popular participation owing to the vital role the bridge's construction had played in the city's working-class economy – stresses the deep social divisions of the depression years. In further noting that the Labour government of New South Wales had declined to invite a representative of the royal family to open the bridge on the grounds that there were more pressing claims on the public purse, an anti-colonialist edge is lent to the pro-working-class sentiments which animate the display.

In these respects, then, the exhibition of artefacts relating to popular involvement in the city's public culture is informed by a conscious political didactic. The same is true of some of the other main displays. In the room devoted to the theme 'Bound for Botany Bay', for example, the story of successive waves of immigration to Australia is told by means of a series of individual narratives selected for their typicality and organized to promote critical reflection on the relations between past and present social conditions. Thus the story of the period of transportation is told so as to stress the similar relationships between unemployment and rising crime rates in nineteenth-century Britain and contemporary Australia.

In sum, Hyde Park Barracks not only differs from Beamish at the obvious level of its content, but also manifests and embodies a different way of conceiving and representing a people and their history. In part, no doubt, these differences reflect the different gestation periods for the two museums and, related to this, the different kinds of curatorial inputs which conditioned their development. The initial planning phase for Beamish occupied the period from 1958 to 1971 with the responsibility for collecting and arranging materials relating to the cultural lives of the popular classes being allocated to folk-life assistants at a time when, in Britain, the tradition of folk-life studies was (and remains) deeply influenced by romantic conceptions of the people as parts of a picturesque landscape.[17] Hyde Park Barracks, by contrast, was transformed into a museum over the period 1979–84, a period of renewed vigour in Australian historical scholarship owing to the challenges of important new work in labour, feminist, and Aboriginal history – intellectural currents which fed into the conception of and planning for the museum via the emphasis that was placed on social history as its main curatorial focus.

A fuller appreciation of the distinctiveness of Hyde Park Barracks and an assessment of its significance within the Australian context, however, requires that it be viewed in the light of both adjacent and earlier developments in Australian museum policy. For the fact that the museum is concerned with *Australian* social life is at least as significant as its orientation toward the everyday habits and customs of the ordinary citizen. Or rather, its significance consists in its combination of these two points of focus. For in being concerned with the everyday lives of ordinary people who, in being identified as Australian, are thereby also distinguished from and opposed to colonial conceptions of Australia as an outpost of the British empire, Hyde Park Barracks materializes and makes present what had been conspicuously absent from earlier Australian museums: the sense of a national people with an autonomous history.

This was commented on when, in the 1930s, the Carnegie Corporation commissioned a survey of Australian museums. The resulting report, published in 1933, drew particular attention to the relative lack of interest evinced by Australian museums in the collection and display of materials relating to the history of the continent's European settlement. Only three museums, it was observed, were given over entirely to aspects of post-settlement history – and one of these, the Australian War Memorial, was not officially opened until 1941. Nor was post-settlement history particularly well represented in other museums, and least of all those aspects of Australian history relating to the lives of ordinary Australians. The authors of the report thus remarked particularly on the fact that 'in no museum are there reproductions of the buildings occupied by the earlier settlers', regarding this as 'one of the most notable gaps in the whole of the existing museum collections'.[18] Yet museums had been established in Australia from as early as the 1820s and, by the 1930s, many of them had built up impressive geological and natural history collections as well as extensive collections of Aboriginal relics and cultural artefacts.[19]

Museums and 'the people'

Why, then, should the period since 1788 have seemed so devoid of interest to museums? A part of the answer consists in the disciplinary specialisms (usually geology or biology) of their curators. However, this in itself was merely a symptom of a deeper cultural problem: the perception, owing to the predominance of Eurocentric conceptions, that Australia, a fledgling among the nations of the world, had no history that was worthy of preservation, display, or commemoration. This was less true of the 1930s than it had been of the late nineteenth century when, at least to the members of the colonial bourgeoisie, it had seemed that the post-settlement period did not furnish the kind of raw materials out of which a past could be forged which could claim sufficient dignity and solemnity to vie with the European pasts which supplied their point of cultural reference in such matters.[20] Compared with the British national past – a past, as materialized in public ceremonials and museums, organized primarily around the deeds of monarchs, military heroes, and great statesmen – the activities of the early colonists (the convicts, the marines who policed them, later settlers, gold-diggers, bush-rangers) seemed lacking in substance of a similar kind.

It's not surprising, given this background, that the first museum to be conceived as a national institution and to devote itself entirely to the history of the post-settlement period should have been the Australian War Memorial. In its remembrance of the heroism of Australian troops in Europe and the Middle East (the theatres of 'real history'), this institution – intended as both a museum of the nation's military history and a shrine to its war dead – enabled there to be figured forth and materialized an Australian past which could claim the same status, weight, and dignity as the European pasts it so clearly sought to emulate and surpass.[21]

What is perhaps rather more surprising is the fact that the War Memorial is still the only fully national museum in Australia and will remain so until – and if, for its future is currently under review – the Museum of Australia opens. This will constitute a significant moment in the development of Australian museum policy, particularly as one of its three main galleries will be devoted to the post-settlement period. It is important, however, to view the development of this museum in a broader perspective. For its opening will constitute merely the culmination and most visible manifestation of a protracted phase in the development of Australian museum and, more generally, heritage policy, in which the earlier lack of interest in the preservation and display of materials relating to the post-settlement period has been significantly

reversed. Apart from the marked increase in the degree of importance accorded these overlapping areas of cultural policy, both have
manifested a similar commitment to the production and organization of a more clearly autonomized Australian past, one which, by
severing the ties of dependency through which (although always
with some degree of ambivalence and tension) the Australian past
had been earlier been associated with the longer past of the British
state, stands more clearly on its own.

The legislative peaks of these developments are soon summarized: the establishment of the Australian Council of National
Trusts in 1967; the establishment of a Committee of Inquiry into
the National Estate in 1973 leading, in 1976, to the enactment of
the Australian Heritage Bill and the subsequent compilation of a
register of protected properties; and, finally, the establishment, in
1974, of a Committee of Inquiry on Museums and National Collections with, as its most significant legislative outcome, the Museum
of Australia Act, 1980. This is, by any standards, a quite exception-
ally concentrated rush of legislative activity aimed at increasing
the scope of those spaces, buildings, and artefacts which are
officially zoned as belonging to the past while, at the same time,
nationalizing that past.

Moreover, and as distinct from the situation in Britain where the
politics of conservation and those of conservatism too often go hand
in hand, anathematizing both past and present alike, the greater
part of the impetus for these developments has been supplied by
Labour administrations. And by Labour administrations backed by
a fairly strong groundswell of popular support for their heritage
policies which, in general terms, evinced a clear commitment to
increasing the presence of the past within the public domain while
simultaneously nationalizing and democratizing its associations.
The inquiries referred to above were thus all inaugurated in the
Whitlam years and fuelled by the 'new nationalism' of that period.
Indeed the willingness of Labour administrations, state and federal, to preserve historic sites from threatened destruction by
developers served as a key emblem of this 'new nationalism' and its
commitment to representing the interests of 'all Australians'
against what were seen as the socially and environmentally
destructive activities of both international corporations and domestic élites. Nor was it merely at the level of governmental policies
that this rhetoric was enunciated and put into practice. The
campaigns, in the early 1970s, of residents' action groups to save
historic sites and buildings threatened by inner-city development

projects and the support offered those campaigns by the Builders Labourers Federation in banning work on the sites in dispute are the best indices of the degree to which the issue of conservation had acquired popular and democratic associations.[22]

It was against the immediate political context of these campaigns that the decision to transform Hyde Park Barracks into a museum of the city's social history was taken. Initially a convict dormitory from its opening in 1819 to 1848, when the era of transportation drew to a close, the building subsequently served a variety of functions (a reception centre for female immigrants and a lunatic asylum, for example) as well as housing a range of goverment offices (the Vaccine Institute and Inspector of Distilleries, for instance) until the 1960s when, together with the adjacent Royal Mint, it too was threatened with demolition as part of inner-city development schemes. The decision to preserve the building and open it to the public as a museum was clearly a response to both the campaigns of local resident action groups and the strong support these had received at the federal level.[23]

It would, however, be a mistake to posit too direct or immediate a connection between this originating political context and the orientation of the past that has since been materialized in the museum itself. There are too many intervening variables for this to be credible. Moreover, the text of the museum itself is an uneven and contradictory one. The influence of different curatorial visions is readily discernible as one moves from one room to another. While those I have briefly outlined manifest an intention to disrupt and call into question socially dominant conceptions of the past, there are others of which this is not true. The room devoted to changing styles in domestic architecture, for example, fails just as signally as do the pit-cottages at Beamish to suggest any critical perspectives on changing social relations within the home.

Perhaps the most disappointing aspect of the museum, however, consists in the degree to which it conceives and represents the social and cultural history of the city as something distinct from, and having no organic connections with, its political history. While thus evoking popular cultures and ways of life, these are not connected to any political traditions or constituencies. At least, not except as a movable feast. When the Barracks first opened as a museum, one of the temporary exhibition rooms was given over to a display of trade-union banners and other mementoes of the city's labour movement. The subsequent removal of this display and, to date, the failure to replace it with displays of an equivalent kind, has profoundly altered the whole ideological economy of the Barracks in depriving it of a point of political reference to which the representations of popular customs, traditions, and ways of life might be connected and thus be lifted above what often remains a level of purely anecdotal significance.

This point can be underlined by means of a brief contrast with the People's Palace in Glasgow, an institution which altogether justifies the claim of its present curator that there 'is no museum, gallery, arts or community centre quite like it anywhere else in the world'.[24] It was exceptional in its conception as housing under one roof a museum, picture gallery, winter garden, and musical hall, a place of both popular instruction and popular entertainment. It has been exceptional, as a museum, in having had the good fortune to be administered since its opening in 1898 by a city corporation with one of the longest and strongest traditions of municipal socialism in Europe. It is also exceptional in its location as the focal point of Glasgow Green, an important centre of Glasgow's popular culture – the place where the Glasgow Fair was held and where, now, the annual People's Marathon both starts and ends – as well as of its socialist and feminist political cultures (the place where Glasgow's trade-union movement began, where suffrage marches started from, where anti-conscription campaigns were launched). But it is perhaps most exceptional in the degree to which, as a museum of the city's history, it represents that history primarily in the form of a set of deeply interacting relations between, on the one hand, the ways of life and popular entertainments of ordinary Glaswegians and, on the other hand, their political traditions. Nor, moreover, is this done didactically by means, for instance, of separate rooms or displays devoted to the political history of the city. Rather, and more often than not in an understated way, political traditions and concerns are injected into the very tissue of everyday life, in the spheres of both work and leisure, by exhibiting artefacts relating to political campaigns side-by-side with those illustrating facets of the history of sport in the city or the development of different forms of domestic space.

There is, in other words, a clear attempt to connect a way of life to a way of politics, and in ways which suggest continuities between past and present political struggles. Displays of old-fashioned tobacconists and cinema foyers; the history of the local press; displays of tenement interiors depicting the history of housing conditions in the city; photographic displays of local strikes from the 1920s to the 1980s; an exhibition of local artists' depictions of the events, characters, and leaders of the 1984 miners' strike; pro-suffragette playing cards; accounts of the 1930s unemployment rallies side-by-side with salutes to local soccer heroes; exhibiting John MacLean's desk in the same room as Billy Connolly's banana boots – the juxtaposition of these different histories in such a way that their associations are carried over into one another conveys the suggestion of a radical political culture which grows out of and, in turn, suffuses the daily lives of ordinary Glaswegians. And of a political culture, moreover, which is – within the ideological economy of the museum – the dominant one. At the People's Palace, it is not 'the people' who are reduced to the level of the picturesque. Rather, it is ordinary Glaswegians – their culture and their politics – who supply the norm of humanity to which implicitly the museum addresses itself.

Questions of framework

The development of museums in the nineteenth century was governed by the view that it would be possible to achieve 'by the ordered display of selected artefacts a total representation of human reality and history'.[25] Museums, that is to say, were to arrange their displays to as to simulate the organization of the world – human and natural – outside the museum walls. This dream that the rational ordering of things might mirror the real order of things was soon revealed to be just that. Yet, both in the practices of museums and, as visitors, in our relations to them the illusion that they deal in the 'real stuff of history' persists. Few museums draw attention to the assumptions which have informed their choice of what to preserve or the principles which govern the organization of their exhibits. Few visitors have the time or inclination to look beyond what museums show them to ponder the significance of *how* they show what they show. Yet, as it has been my purpose to argue, this question of *how* is a critical one, sometimes bearing more consequentially on the visitor's experience than the actual objects displayed.

Indeed, to emphasize this point: there is relatively little difference between the types of objects displayed in the three museums I have considered, but there is a world of difference between the rhetorics governing the processes through which those objects have been assembled into particular display configurations with, as I have sought to show, significant consequences for the kinds of ideological meanings and associations likely to suggest themselves. If this calls attention to the political significance of the representational frameworks museums employ, this is not to suggest that there are not other aspects of museums equally in need of critical interrogation or that such representational issues should be considered in isolation. It's clear, for example, that the question of how things get displayed in museums cannot be divorced from questions concerning the training of curators or the structures of museum control and management – very material constraints which considerably limit the room for manoeuvre of radical museum workers.

However, these are not matters which can be readily influenced on a short-term basis. Nor are they ones which it lies within the visitor's power to do much about. But, if read in the right way – as a lesson in ruling-class rhetoric rather than as an object lesson in things – even the most conservatively organized museum can be put to good use. An afternoon at Beamish can be most instructive provided that it is looked to less as providing a lesson in industrial or regional history and more as a crash-course in the bourgeois myths of history.

Notes and references

1 Gramsci, A. (1985) *Selections from Cultural Writings*, London: Lawrence & Wishart, p. 189.
2 See, for useful surveys of these developments, Minihan, J. (1977) *The Nationalisation of Culture: The Development of State Subsidies to the Arts in Great Britain*, London: Hamish Hamilton; and Pearson, N., (1982) *The State and the Visual Arts*, Milton Keynes: Open University Press.
3 *Beamish: The Great Northern Experience*, souvenir guidebook (nd).
4 ibid.
5 West, B. (1985) 'Danger! History at work: a critical consumer's guide to the Ironbridge Gorge Museum', occasional paper, Centre for Contemporary Cultural Studies, Birmingham, p. 30.
6 Wiener, M. (1985) *English Culture and the Decline of the Industrial Spirit, 1850–1980*, Harmondsworth: Penguin, p. 6.
7 Foucault, M. (1972) *The Archaeology of Knowledge*, London: Tavistock, p. 14.
8 Burke, P. (1977) 'Popular culture in Norway and Sweden', *History Workshop* 3: 145.
9 Wallace, M. (1981) 'Visiting the past: history museums in the United States', *Radical History Review* 25: 72.
10 The most thorough survey of these matters is Hosmer, C. B., jun. (1965) *Presence of the Past: A History of the Preservation Movement in the United States before Williamsburg*, New York: G. P. Putnam's Sons.

11 Cited in Lowenthal, D. (1985) *The Past is a Foreign Country*, Cambridge University Press, p. 116.

12 Wallace, M. (1981) 'Visiting the past: history museums in the United States', *Radical History Review* 25: 68.

13 ibid., p. 72.

14 ibid., p. 73.

15 It has been estimated that, in Britain, a new museum was opened on average every two weeks throughout the 1970s when the number of visitors per annum also averaged out at 25 million. See Bassett, D. A. (1986) 'Museums and museum publications in Britain, 1975–85, part I: the range and nature of museums and their publications', *British Book News*, May.

16 *The Mint and the Hyde Park Barracks* (1985) Sydney: Trustees of the Museum of Applied Arts and Sciences, p. 16.

17 For further details, see *Beamish One. First Report of the North of England Open Air Museum Joint Committee* (1978) Beamish Hall, Stanley, County Durham.

18 Markham, S. F. and Richards, H. C. (1933) *A Report on the Museums and Art Galleries of Australia*, London: Museums Association, p. 44.

19 See Kohlstedt, S. G. (1983) 'Australian museums of natural history: public practices and scientific initiatives in the 19th century', *Historical Records of Australian Science* 5.

20 One of the best discussions of these questions is the penultimate chapter of Inglis, K. S. (1974) *The Australian Colonists: An Exploration of Social History 1788–1870*, Carlton: Melbourne University Press.

21 For the best account of the War Memorial, see Inglis, K. S. (1985) 'A sacred place: the making of the Australian War Memorial', *War and Society* 3 (2).

22 For a useful survey, see Nittim, Z. (1980) 'The coalition of resident action groups' in Roe, J. (ed.) *Twentieth Century Sydney: Studies in Urban and Social History*, Sydney: Hale Ironmonger.

23 For a brief history of the Barracks and its conversion, see Betteridge, M. (1982) 'The Mint and Hyde Park Barracks', *Kalori* (Museums Association of Australia), 59/60.

24 King, E. (1985) *The People's Palace and Glasgow Green*, Glasgow: Richard Drew.

25 Donato, E. (1979) 'The museum's furnace: notes toward a contextual reading of *Bouvard and Pecuchet*' in J. Harrari (ed.) *Textual Strategies: Perspectives in Post-Structuralist Criticism*, Ithaca and London: Cornell University Press, p. 221.

PART 2

Museums in a changing world

4

Policy and politics: charges, sponsorship, and bias

SUE KIRBY

Museums in Britain can be divided into two sectors, the public and the independent. Public sector museums are funded by either rates or taxes. The national museums are financed directly from central government funds and, since the National Heritage Act, 1983, are all under the supervision of boards of trustees. Local authorities have no mandatory duty to organize and administer museum services. There are merely permissive concurrent powers under the Libraries and Museums Act, 1964, as amended, for those which wish to run museums. The independent sector comprises a varied and fast-growing group of museums, many of which are both registered charities and limited liability companies. They raise funds from admission charges but also rely on grant-aid or annual payments from one or more public sources.[1]

At the same time as museums have taken on wider responsibilities in order to stimulate public interest they have been subject to increasing financial pressures. Public expenditure on the arts is very small – less than one-half of 1 per cent of total public expenditure according to one estimate.[2] Although total UK expenditure on museums has risen over the last five years and despite the fact that the number of visitors to museums shows a steady increase, both local and central government figures indicate that museums are losing ground in competition for funds with other arts activities.[3]

The fall has been sharpest in central government expenditure where the level of funding has come to a standstill despite the serious deterioration of museum buildings. Each year the modest increase in overall grant is cancelled out by higher percentage level wage settlements. Grants for new purchases have actually been reduced. The National Gallery's grant of £3.3 million for 1984 was reduced to £2.75 million for 1985 and held at that level for 1986 and 1987 to allow for repair and maintenance of the building. In real terms this is a cut of approximately 20 per cent at a time when prices for important works of art are soaring. Its inadequacy was clearly indicated by two well-publicized sales in December 1986 when Manet's 'La Rue Mosnier aux Paveurs' was sold at Christie's for £7.7 million and a Rembrandt fetched £7.26 million the following week. Drastic economies have also been made at the Victoria and Albert Museum. In 1976 Friday closing was introduced and the Circulating Exhibitions Department, which provided touring exhibitions for the provinces, shut down. In 1986 two incidents of flooding, attributed to inadequate building maintenance, damaged stored items destined for the Theatre Museum. Other nationals have building problems too. The British Museum needs £4 million to renew the floors and the National Gallery of Scotland has dry and wet rot. The situation is hardly brighter for local authority museums with the government aiming to reduce the real level of local authority spending. Inevitably those lobbying for museums have to compete with their colleagues in education, housing, health, and social services departments. As with the nationals the maintenance of buildings, often of historical interest in their own right, takes a large proportion of what funding is available while new display projects are shelved and staff posts frozen.

For and against museum charges

Faced with these constraints, museum authorities are being forced to look for additional sources of funding. There is particularly strong pressure for the introduction of admission charges. The idea of charging for admission to our national museums and galleries is not a new one. It was first suggested only thirty years after the opening of the British Museum, the world's first national museum, in the mid-eighteenth century, despite the wishes of its founding bene-factor Sir Hans Sloane that the collections should be available to the widest possible audience. The merits of charging were rejected then and on the subsequent occasions they were considered. The reason was summed up by Sir Frederick Kenyon, then Director of the British Museum, quoted in the Royal Commission Report of 1929:

> There is not the smallest doubt that the imposition of fees discourages attendances. The question therefore simply is

whether it is worthwhile to exclude the public (and especially of course the poorer members of the public) for the sake of pecuniary return to be expected from fees. The nation has a very large capital interest in the Museum and it is better to look for the return on it of educational advantages offered to the public than from a trivial taking of cash at the turnstiles.

So along with free education and free libraries there developed a tradition of free entry to museums and galleries associated with their role in the educational and academic world. But as the twentieth century has progressed this educational role has been challenged both by learning opportunities provided by television with its vastly greater resources and by the trend to see museums as part of the leisure and tourist industries. By the early 1970s the government had decided to risk the educational advantages for some cash at the turnstiles. One of the instigators of the plan to introduce charging at the nationals was Margaret Thatcher, then Secretary of State for Education and Science. The legislation was supposedly a measure to enable the trustees to charge at their discretion. Yet when pressed in Parliament to make the position clear, Mrs Thatcher told the Opposition, 'The Government require charges to be made', and concluded, 'I understood that the Trustees wanted an unequivocal statement. I trust that I have given them what they wanted'.[4]

The Conservative government ruled that from 1 January 1974 the national museums should introduce charges of 10p per adult rising to 20p in July and August. All income was to go to the Treasury. Within three weeks the scheme had been abandoned. Far from making a profit the exercise has been calculated to have cost the museums concerned over £34,000. The Heath government fell over the miners' strike and the incoming Labour administration withdrew charges.

Members of that government have lived to regret not removing the 1972 Act from the Statute Book. The Conservative governments of 1979 and 1983 were elected on the promise of liberalizing the economy by removing restraints, a factor underlying all Tory policies. Accordingly ministers have wanted to increase the opportunities for the national museums and galleries to run their own affairs and to raise money how they wished. The first to reintroduce charges was the National Maritime Museum in April 1984. The museum's director at that time, Neil Cossons, formerly of Ironbridge, an independent sector museum charging for admission, explained that charges would enable the museum to reopen on Mondays and to restore services lost as a result of the steady erosion of revenue since the start of the recession. He pointed out that by virtue of its location a visit to the National Maritime Museum is a deliberate outing rather than part of a general day's sight-seeing. Admission charges should not therefore mean too great a reduction in visitor numbers.[5] In fact attendances at the museum dropped by 36.6 per cent in 1986.[6] The implication behind Dr Cossons's statement was that the central London nationals would be hard hit by falling visitor rolls following any imposition of charges.

The warning has not gone unheeded: the British Museum and the National Galleries have come out firmly against charges. The Imperial War Museum has hedged its bets by putting up turnstiles but making charges discretionary and safeguarding income for museum use through a trust. Far more controversial are the voluntary charges at the Victoria and Albert Museum introduced in November 1985. Suggested donations are £2 per adult, £1 for students and pensioners. There is no reduction for unemployed people but children under 12 and Friends of the V and A are not asked to contribute. Over the first year of the scheme's operation admissions dropped by 40 per cent. Only 55 per cent of visitors actually made a contribution and the total amount raised was £100,000 short of the £500,000 expected. The Chairman of the Board of Trustees, Lord Carrington, blamed bad publicity and the drop in the number of American tourists to Britain.[7]

Equally contentious are the charges at the British Museum (Natural History). It faced a shortfall in funding of £1.5 million in 1986/7 and it has been predicted that this will have risen to £2.5 million by 1990. According to the museum's management, the aim of the charges introduced on 1 April 1987 is to avoid staff redundancies and gallery closures. The level of charges has been set to accommodate an expected 40 per cent drop in attendances. It is hoped that marketing initiatives and new exhibitions will eventually attract visitors back. It is not known what the Science Museum will do but its branch in York, the National Railway Museum, has introduced admission fees. Any scheme at South Kensington would have to involve the building of a separate entrance for the Wellcome medical science collection, donated on the condition that public access is free in perpetuity.

Changes at the nationals have meant that local authority curators have had to argue the case for retention of free admission to their own museums. Leaving aside the moral questions of access, charges are often rejected on economic grounds once the cost of employing extra staff to collect fees and the loss of both donations and sales are taken into account. Within the museums profession, a survey of members of the Museums Association published in March 1971 showed a clear majority against charges.[8] This has never been the official policy of the Association, representing as it does many museums which rely on charging, but it has agreed the following conditions: unwaged and low-waged people should be admitted at a reduced rate; there should be free admission for the equivalent of one day a week; and all funds raised should be used for the improvement of the museum's public service. In contrast the Museum Professionals Group has always been firmly opposed to the introduction of charges in national museums.[9] The Heath government's actions provoked an outcry amongst the general public. One result was the formation of National Heritage, the Museums Action Group, which in addition to campaigning on behalf of museums instituted the annual Museum of the Year awards. In the 1980s it is being argued that the climate of opinion has now changed. A MORI poll undertaken in January 1985 for the Royal Armouries revealed that 61 per cent of those interviewed believed that museums ought to raise some of their funds through admission charges rather than depending totally on government grants; 27 per cent were opposed to the idea. Yet opposition to charges has been well-aired in the correspondence columns of the serious national press and is still strong within the museums profession itself. A survey organized by the Museums Association in 1986 indicated that the membership overwhelmingly considers that there should be free access to the core collections of publicly-funded museums. But those in the independent sector are seen as an entirely different case and the great majority of those surveyed believe that each museum should be assessed independently.[10]

Civil service trade unions have also campaigned actively against the imposition of museum charges. Action has included mounting a picket and distributing leaflets outside the Victoria and Albert Museum when the voluntary donation scheme was first introduced. They have also supported the foundation of a national all-party grouping to protect the right of free access to the core collections of publicly funded museums, the Campaign for Free Access to Museums, launched in Edinburgh on 15 August 1986. The campaign has the support of the Museums Association and other museum organizations and is chaired by Mark Lazarowicz, Leader of Edinburgh District Council. It is circulating a national petition. Before the June 1987 General Election it secured a manifesto commitment to free admission from every political party represented in Parliament bar the Conservatives. Meanwhile a 35,000 signature petition has already been presented to the Trustees of the British Museum (Natural History). Earlier in 1986 Lord Jenkins introduced a Bill to ban admission charges at the nationals. It failed but the fight against charges goes on.

The sale of collections

From time to time museum authorities are tempted to raise money by the sale of collections. Sometimes this is done in a manner acceptable to the museums profession but it is always fraught with danger because such action serves to undermine public trust. In modern museum practice, once a donation from a member of the public has been accepted and registered the museum undertakes to look after it to the best of its ability in perpetuity. However, the situation may be different when items have been collected as the result of fieldwork, archaeological excavation, or purchase, and in these cases disposal or sale might be possible. There are also cases where parts of the collection now fall outside the collecting policy of the institution. This idea has its dangers – witness the wholesale dispersal and neglect of ethnographic and geological material seen after the war. Some of the specialist museum groups came into being in order to protect collections. But sometimes it is permissible. For example in 1977 and 1978 on the advice of its Keeper of Art, the London Borough of Southwark sold seven continental pictures at Christies for £8,000. These paintings were outside the collecting policy of the borough's gallery, the South London Art Gallery, Peckham, which collects Victorian works, paintings of local interest, and modern prints. Some of the proceeds were used to carry out urgently needed conservation on other paintings and the remainder went to supplement the gallery's meagre acquisition fund.

In contrast was the proposal in 1979 of Kirklees Metropolitan District Council to sell off works of art to offset a £1.25 million rate rise. The collections concerned had been built up over a number of years by the old boroughs of Huddersfield, Batley, and Dewsbury. Among the paintings considered for sale was a work by Francis Bacon, one of over thirty presented since the 1920s by the Contemporary Arts Society in the belief that they would be permanently available for public display. To make matters worse the professional officers responsible for the museum service were not consulted by the authority's Management and Finance Committee. Both the Contemporary Arts Society and the Museums Association objected strongly. The sales did not go ahead.

The Trafford collection, formed in 1974 from the collections of Altrincham, Sale, Stretford, and Urmston local authorities suffered a harsher fate. On 14 January 1984 a good number of paintings known to belong to the former Altrincham Museum and Stretford Art Gallery were sold at Sotheby's Chester salerooms. This event alerted a large number of museum groups and protests were made to Trafford which helped avert a further sale of natural history and Egyptian material on 15 June. Some of the natural history collections, the Egyptian, and the geological material have been placed on permanent loan to the Manchester Museum where they can easily be viewed by Trafford residents. Meanwhile other local and natural history collections remain in store.

Another sad case is the fate of the George Brown Collection. In 1985, without consultation of the University Museum Board, the Council of the University of Newcastle upon Tyne decided to sell this outstanding collection of material from the Western Pacific for £600,000 to the National Museum of Ethnography, Osaka, Japan. Put together by a nineteenth-century missionary, it was considered one of the most significant collections of ethnographic material in the UK from the point of view of its size, variety, and quality. The export licenses for nineteen items were suspended but before the hearing of the Reviewing Committee on the Export of Works of Art the bulk of the collection had been sold to Osaka. Four items were purchased by the British Museum in July 1986 but many museum people felt it would have been better if the collection had been kept together.

Paying the piper: sponsorship

Another source of funding for museums and galleries, and one that the present Thatcher government is keen to promote, is sponsorship. The Association for Business Sponsorship of the Arts (ABSA), founded in 1976, has organized seminars and made awards to encourage commercial backing of museums and gallery projects. In 1984 Lord Gowrie, then Minister for the Arts, gave ABSA the funding to appoint three sponsorship officers and announced the Business Sponsorship Initiative Scheme. Administered by ABSA on behalf of the Office for Arts and Libraries, this made available £1 million from central funds per annum to provide matching grants on a £3 to £1 basis for new sponsorship over a certain level. The amounts raised have delighted the government. In 1986 the requisite level of sponsorship was cut from £7,500 to £2,000 and grants were offered on a £1 for £1 basis for support over £1,000 from companies new to sponsorship. The upper limit of government contributions is £25,000 in any one case. In the same year an extra £250,000 was added to the fund. A further incentive was provided from 1 April when tax relief was granted for one-off gifts to charity avoiding the need for companies to enter on a four-year covenant. The way is now clear for sponsorship to rise to a level comparable to that in the USA.

Sponsorship is a mutually advantageous collaboration between business and the arts. The museum or gallery receives a much-needed injection of cash and possibly contact with new groups of people while the company enhances its image and receives good publicity. It is supported by the general public too, according to the MORI poll of January 1985, which indicated approval from 70 per cent even when corporate sponsorship means advertising within museums. But sponsorship is limited in its scope. To be an attractive business proposition it needs to be concerned with new developments. It is an addition rather than an alternative to basic finance and is unlikely to tackle nitty-gritty questions of bricks and mortar, storage and documentation, so often the biggest problems faced by museums.

There is a negative side to sponsorship too. Two situations need to be avoided – first, when the sponsor seeks to influence exhibition content and second, when the firm or organization has an interest in the subject matter. Perhaps the most invidious example is the Nuclear Physics/Nuclear Power Gallery opened at the Science Museum in 1982. The project received major sponsorship from the United Kingdom Atomic Energy Authority and smaller sums from both the Central Electricity Generating Board and British Nuclear Fuels Limited. These three organizations also loaned exhibits and the UKAEA provided three audio-visual programmes. However, when hidden costs such as staff time are taken into account, it can be seen that the museum itself made the largest contribution to the gallery. As is standard practice with exhibitions involving sponsorship at the Science Museum, a written agreement was drawn up giving final editorial control to the museum. At every stage, representatives of the industry scrutinized the texts prepared by museum staff. At the last minute, and without full consultation of all the curatorial staff involved, the then Museum Director, Dame Margaret Weston, agreed to changes to eight panels demanded by the industry. The end result is a gallery which fails to acknowledge adequately the controversial nature of its subject. Its main aim is to explain the technicalities of nuclear power. The wider social and economic implications are barely discussed. Although the common origins of nuclear weapons and nuclear power are shown, the post-1945 links between the civil and military uses of plutonium are not. Questions of safety are dismissed with reassuring phrases and the problems of transport and long-term disposal of nuclear waste merely mentioned. Also omitted is the growth of opposition to nuclear power and nuclear weapons. All this adds up to a strong case for a complementary display with input from anti-nuclear groups. At the very least there is a need to update the exhibition to include discussion of the health issues highlighted by recent research and of the 1986 Chernobyl disaster.

Until the expiry of its five-year lease in 1986, the Conran Foundation ran the Boilerhouse at the Victoria and Albert Museum to show modern industrial design. A precursor of the new Museum of Design, due to open in 1989, it hosted exhibitions for a number of manufacturers of consumer products. The danger is that such a project can become a mere showcase. Coca Cola's centenary show 'Designing a Megabrand' began with videos of American television advertisements and every visitor purchasing a catalogue got a free can of the sticky liquid. There was not one mention of the company's arch rivals Pepsi, a certain coyness about profit levels, and only the briefest hint of the reputed worldwide political influence of the company. This is distortion by omission.[11]

This type of bias is not restricted to national institutions. In 1985 Carlisle Museums and Art Gallery hosted the anniversary exhibition of a local textile firm now owned by a large retailing chain which subsidized the show to the tune of several thousand pounds. The company saw the event primarily as a public relations exercise. The text was written by the company archivist and the first draft ignored relevant research by museum staff. Later some of this was inserted but much information on pay and conditions was omitted. There was no mention of the harsh punishments meted out to workers convicted of stealing cloth in the company's early days. The term 'trade union' was replaced by 'craft association'. In the display of fabrics, samples showing key developments in design were jettisoned in favour of bread and butter lines. However, the same museum has had very happy experiences with sponsorship. When a local brewery subsidized an exhibition on the history of pubs in the city a final panel allowed discreet publicity for the firm while bringing the story of the eighteenth-century brewery up to date. Major exhibitions on the Cumbrian landscape (1982) and Carlisle railways (1986) attracted support from a variety of sources. In both cases the sponsors had no input into the content and were satisfied by a printed acknowledgement within the exhibition. The major sponsor for 'Carlisle: Railway City' was mentioned on publicity material and had a modest display stand outside the galleries for the duration of the exhibition.

Sponsorship needs to be handled with great care by museums. A distance should be kept between the sponsor and the product. This is already the case in television where the producers of a programme are actually forbidden to show the script of a programme to its sponsor.

The politics of bias

Problems of bias within museums are not restricted to temporary exhibitions. The large majority of museums are sponsored by a single body. There is an obvious danger when this is a commercial concern that the museum will be firmly relegated to public relations work. In the 1980s some local authorities are now demanding direct control over the content of displays. Edinburgh District Council views the museum as a tool for the pursuance of its wider policy objectives. It has mounted two exhibitions which, as the publicity makes clear in statements signed by councillors, set out to examine one side of contentious contemporary issues. 'Not Just Tea and Sandwiches' explores the role of the women's support groups in the 1984 Miners' Strike. 'No Easy Walk to Freedom' is 'an exhibition about the struggle for justice and equality in South Africa', part of the council's anti-apartheid campaign. In each case material included by museum staff but judged unsuitable by council members was removed. At a meeting on 'Bias in Museums' in September 1986 the Leader of Edinburgh District Council, Mark Lazarowicz, argued that local authorities are mandated to decide policy and that local government officers merely execute it.[12] Elected members, unlike museum curators, are at least directly accountable to the electorate. This issue caused more concern amongst the museum professionals attending the conference than any other.

Although such exhibitions are covered by the Museums Association's Code of Conduct for Museum Authorities, fear was expressed that they could undermine the independence of museums and alienate the trust of the public. It was felt that a situation might arise where the only views forwarded are those of the political party currently in power and every exhibition is scrutinized and censored by politicians.

It is still assumed in some quarters that museums are neutral environments and that museum activities – collecting, recording, researching, and exhibiting – can be carried out without bias. Some museum professionals see themselves as uniquely qualified to be objective. But museum curators are only human. They have their own political allegiances and religion or lack of faith. They may be blinkered by their class background, their race, or their sex. Specialisms and false academic boundaries often lead to a rather narrow view of a subject while self-censorship can come into play when controversy seems likely. In recent years there have been initiatives to tackle these issues. Inspired by the growth in women's history, Women, Heritage, and Museums (WHAM) was set up in 1984 to campaign for a more realistic portrayal of women in museums and to examine the experiences of women working in the profession. It has met with hostility from some sections of the museum world. Recent meetings and exhibitions have also explored the western presentation of other cultures. New ventures in museums such as the appointment by Leicestershire County Museums Service of an Assistant Keeper for Indian Arts and Crafts have involved local communities with the collection and exhibition of their own cultures.

Bias is also built into the structure and funding of museum and gallery services. Museum collections tend to reflect the taste, wealth, and concerns of the upper classes. Art has a large reading and spending public. Falling purchase grants make the headlines, the closure of another small local history museum does not. Nine out of ten major exhibitions can be classified as art and every large city has at least one art gallery. But it is a different story for other disciplines.

Social history provides a case in point. Although small local history museums abound they are often underfinanced and lack professional staff. Several large cities lack an adequate social history museum service. For example Glasgow Museums and Art Galleries employ only two local historians. There are thirteen others in the Archaeology, Ethnography, and History department, while thirty-five members of staff work in three sections dealing with the decorative and fine arts.[13] The City of Manchester has no social history museum at all. It is welcome news that the Greater Manchester Museum of Science and Industry is to expand its activities into the social history field so as to include the social and economic context of the magnificent machines at present displayed in splendid isolation.

Even where social history provision is good there is a reluctance to tackle political and social movements on a complex level. Plans to celebrate three anniversaries in 1988 show how social historians shy away from controversy. The defeat of the Spanish Armada can be commemorated without complications but the 1688 Glorious Revolution has an Irish dimension seen as too difficult to present. The anniversary will be a celebration of three centuries of Anglo-Dutch friendship. Even the County Councils Act, 1888, is seen as too controversial in the wake of the abolition of the metropolitan councils. Interestingly natural historians seem to welcome controversy, tackling difficult conservation and environmental issues in their exhibitions.

Some progress has been made in that a small number of museums exploring labour history have been developed in the last few years. But their continued existence is far from certain. A hung council in Tower Hamlets withdrew its grant from the National Museum of Labour History, forcing it to move from Limehouse Town Hall. Luckily the museum is to be rehoused in Salford and Manchester aided by the Association of Greater Manchester Authorities. In Liverpool the future of the Museum of Labour History was by no means clear when its sponsor Merseyside County Council was abolished. The new body, National Museums on Merseyside, administered by trustees, the majority of whom have no connection with Liverpool, has most interest in collections of national importance and the new Tate of the North. However the popularity of the museum looks to have saved it and there are even plans for its expansion.

The whole question of bias in museums is one which has only recently been acknowledged by the profession itself. It has not yet received much public attention. In contrast questions concerning museum financing, admission charges, and the sale of collections are old hat. The more these are discussed both in specialist museum publications and through the national media the greater the chance of increased public understanding of museums and of a museums service which has clear policies and direction. That will be a good thing for both museums and their public.

Notes and references

1 For a fuller discussion of the types of museums, see Robertson, I. (1985) 'Financing museums: the view of a professional', *Museums Journal* 85 (3), pp. 125–9.
2 Wilding, R. (1985) 'Financing museums: current and future trends', *Museums Journal* 85 (3), pp. 119–24.
3 Farnell, G. (1986) 'Picking up the crumbs', *Museum Professionals Group News* 22 spring, p. 2.
4 Cited by Norman Buchan MP (1985) 'What price the Arts?', *Admission Charges at National Museums*, Museum Professionals Group Transactions 21, p. 10.
5 'Admission charges to be introduced at the National Maritime Museum', *Museums Bulletin*, 23 (10) January 1984, p. 185.
6 Written reply to the Commons by Richard Luce, Arts Minister, 19 January 1987.
7 *Guardian*, 4 November 1986.
8 The Museums Association, founded in 1889 to represent the interests of museums and museum professionals, was incorporated as a company limited by guarantee in 1930 and is a registered charity. Its main aims are the promotion and development of museums and art galleries and the improvement in standards and training of museum staff.
9 The Museum Professionals Group, originally known as the Museum Assistants Group, was set up in the 1930s to provide a forum for museum professionals under Director level.
10 'Attitude survey', *Museums Bulletin* 26 (2) May 1986, p. 21. The survey attracted 650 replies from the 2,000 questionnaires issued. Of those replying, 74.7 per cent considered that there should be free access to the core collections of publicly funded museums, and 80.3 per cent believed that in the independent sector each museum's case should be considered individually.
11 Green, O. (1986) 'It's the real thing', *Museum Professionals Group News*, 23 summer, pp. 3–4.
12 Annual Study Weekend of the Museum Professionals Group, Exeter, September 1986. See 'Bias in Museums', *Museum Professionals Group Transactions* 22.
13 *Museums Yearbook* 1986. Springburn Council employs its own curator who works in the social history field.

5

Putting your house in order: representations of women and domestic life

GABY PORTER

The ideology embedded in form is the hardest of all to see. This is why it is important to emphasise process, as it undoes the fait accompli.

(Judith Williamson (1978) *Decoding Advertisements*, London: Marion Boyars)

European tourism is so patriarchal that to go on repeating the point would be tedious. With exceptions such as the Virgin Mary or Joan of Arc, women are simply not there. They make their appearances as dummies of sturdy peasant women in folk museum reconstructions of peasant kitchens, or in other useful supporting roles; they may be seen nude, or partly nude, created as an object for the male gaze.

(Donald Horne (1984) *The Great Museum*, London: Pluto)

Museums exert a powerful popular influence. Many people visit museums today as part of a general encounter through the media with their own and with everyday history. Museums have claimed this territory for themselves and for their visitors, with ambitious displays, reconstructions, and demonstrations. Beamish Museum, for example, offering 'simply acres of nostalgia', tells the visitor that 'this is how it was' in the reconstructions of street, home, pit, station, and farm.

Underneath the new veneer, however, curators still hold many of the attitudes of their predecessors: a concern for showing the quality of life in the past, in contrast to the shoddy and mass-produced culture of the present; a fascination with the way in which things work, rather than who works them, and to what end; a

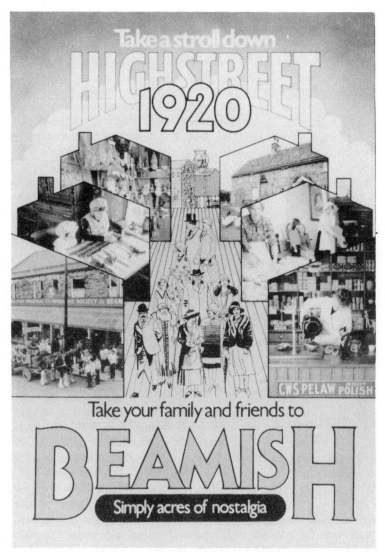

5 Leaflet publicizing 'simply acres of nostalgia' at Beamish Museum in 1986, when it won the Museum of the Year Award. (Photo: Beamish, North of England Open Air Museum)

preoccupation with the most varied, interesting, and differentiated aspects of the material culture, not with the full span of that culture; a desire to order human existence into neat hierarchical structures, determined by and also determining the content of museum collections, emulating the taxonomic orders of the natural sciences. These attitudes underlie – and often contradict – the emphasis presented in publicity leaflets, displays, and texts on the ordinary history of everyday people.

The curatorial approach is centred on the object, from which curators extrapolate a more general historical statement. They rarely reverse the process, to look at the whole material culture and to choose representative artefacts from it, relying instead on social process and material degradation to make selections. This is evident in the absence of a coherent approach to contemporary life, and of a strategy for collecting artefacts for the period in which we live. Employing such a specific selection, while at the same time claiming a general rather than a particular meaning, has profound consequences. For example less advantaged, affluent, and articulate groups – such as unskilled and casual workers, unemployed people, migrants, and travellers – are underrepresented or omitted from social and industrial museums.

The nature of the museum's service to its users on the one hand, and the immediate appeal, the physical and visible 'reality' of objects on the other, protect such prejudices from open acknowledgement or examination.[1] Contact between the curator and the user is mediated through the object and the display; the curator is distanced from his/her public, and is not immediately accountable in the same way as, for example, a teacher. General visitors to the museum do not 'read' what they see as the selection and interpretation of one person, or a group, from a range of possible 'meanings'; they have no access to alternative material, meanings, and arrangements. The process and the underlying principles of selection for display and collection are rarely discussed and shared with the public by individual curators or museums. The focus of any discussion, among professionals or with others, tends to be narrow, specific, and descriptive. While such communication is extremely important for a small, geographically dispersed, and fragmented profession, it fails to address broader issues. Thus museums have been slow to take up issues such as racism, class bias, and sex discrimination, either as employing institutions, or as a medium which propagates a particular and pervasive brand of history. This can be seen clearly in relation to women – both those working inside museums, and the representations of women offered in museum displays and collections.

Women working in museums

Women form 34 per cent of museum staff, according to a 1983 survey of 609 museums.[2] They are concentrated in particular areas: costume, arts, within the curatorial field; education; clerical, cleaning, and support grades. The directors, departmental heads, technical, and attendant staff of museums are overwhelmingly male (74, 64, 85, and 80 per cent respectively). Women at the professional level outnumber men only in the under-25 age group. The profession has grown significantly in the last two decades, and many more women are entering the professional levels of museum work, often through voluntary work – where women form the majority of volunteers – or by government sponsored temporary and/or part-time schemes.[3]

Museums appear to offer employment with flexibility and opportunities for advancement across a broad range of interests, skills, and levels of commitment. Yet museums expect an overriding commitment to museum work from staff at all levels. Evening lectures, weekend demonstrations, and holiday activities add to the working hours of professional staff. Professional isolation makes it difficult to share out work and to negotiate flexible working practices: there are virtually no job-sharing or other alternatives to full-time and overtime working for museum professionals. Staff at attendant levels do a large amount of weekend and shift-working. These patterns make museum work particularly difficult for those – mainly women – who work a double shift with childcare and responsibilities at home. Some women have felt that they could not sustain the expected level of commitment at work while rearing children; thus they have given up work in order to have children. Again, museum jobs are relatively sparse, and increasingly hard to find with cuts in local and central government funding. Thus those, mainly women, who decide to leave work for a period – to bring up children or to move to accommodate the career move of a partner – may have extreme difficulty in re-entering work, and may do so only at the cost of seniority and salary. Internal promotion to professional grades has formerly been an important way for women without formal qualifications to advance in museums, but professional career grades are increasingly rigid, and mobility is consequently reduced.

In 1983 a small group of women from museums and museum studies teaching met to plan a conference to discuss the representation of women in museum displays and collections, and the position of women working in museums.[4] This led to a weekend conference in April 1984, Women, Heritage, and Museums (WHAM), supported by the Equal Opportunities Commission and under the aegis of the Social History Curators Group. The conference was the first public platform for women's issues in museums and was attended by nearly a hundred people, mostly women. It led to the formation of an autonomous group, to act as a support and communication network for women working in, or with, museums, and also as a forum for discussion and action on specific aims. The group has fostered contact and dialogue with local teachers, women's history groups, and others working outside museums with an interest in women's history.

New organizing principles were embodied in WHAM from the beginning. Thus as the mother of a young baby I received payment for expenses and part-time childcare in order to act as conference organizer (most professional conferences are organized by curators in full-time work, who can take advantage of office facilities, while those out of work cannot afford to work without expenses). We were the first group to offer a crèche at a conference, and have tried to do so at subsequent meetings. The group is committed to working in a non-hierarchical way, networking through regional groups and offering expenses for those out of work, or on low pay through part-time and government-sponsored schemes, to attend planning meetings. These practical details seem banal, which in itself reflects the conservatism of normal patterns of working for museum personnel.

As with women's history, women working inside and outside museums were first drawn to WHAM through frustration with the representations of women which most museums offer, or with their invisibility in museum displays. From the cautious aim of 'putting women back' into history has grown a stronger campaign which recognizes that women can't simply be slotted in to the existing structure: we have to look at working practices across the whole spectrum of museum activity.

Material culture and invisibility

Entering museums to look at the history of men and women, the visitor will find that women are represented mainly – if not exclusively – in the home. In the social and local history museums which form the majority of all museums they are seated in the parlour, engaged in needlework, lacemaking, or other ladylike pursuits. Occasionally they can be found doing the laundry, or cooking in the kitchen, but household equipment is generally displayed as interesting and obsolete gadgetry rather than as a set of working tools. Women also appear as dummies in costume displays, which commonly use an upper- or middle-class domestic setting such as the parlour for a background. Women are absent from virtually every trade and craft workshop in small museums, and barely visible in the larger industrial museums. Except as domestic servants, shop assistants, and occasionally munitions workers, the museum visitor might be forgiven for thinking that women in the past did not work outside the home at all, and spent most of their time sitting at home sewing.

How does this extraordinary statement arise? How is the position of museums tenable in relation to current knowledge about women in history on the one hand and to the perception of museums as conveyors of 'truth' and 'reality' on the other? And how do we open up criticism and offer alternative and/or additional representations to shift the emphasis in museums and in museum practice generally?

The answer to the first of these questions is partly inherent in the material culture itself, and partly engendered by the attitudes and practices of curatorship.

Museum collecting, as I suggested earlier, relies on history and social process to select material. Objects are likely to survive through obsolescence and rapid technological change; superiority of materials and construction; relative prosperity and permanence of the owners; and through the actions and influence of certain individuals and groups who consider themselves and their possessions to be significant. Elsewhere, I have examined these influences across the whole spectrum of women's work.[5] Here I shall look closely at their operation in the domestic context to which so many women in museum representations are confined.

The Victorian parlour frequently displayed in museums arises from a material culture which was highly specialized and differentiated, well maintained and preserved. In the nineteenth century material possessions and furnishings were used by the middle classes as ranking devices, to confirm their social status.[6] Domestic life was increasingly separated from public life; housing, rooms, and furnishings became more specialized and separated from each other. Spatial and material specialization were complemented by domestic organization: the ordering of the household, the ordering of people within the household, the regimens of personal and

6 Photographs on an album page of the 1860s describe upper class wealth and leisure in the carefully managed park, gardens, house, and vehicle. The lady of the house is seen in her wheelchair, already an invalid. The servants – apart from the coachman – are discreetly hidden. (Photo: Roger Taylor)

domestic cleanliness helped to distinguish the middle classes from the working classes. Women were central in this social arrangement, as wives whose etiquette, household management, and conspicuous leisure established and maintained social position;

and as the vast majority of the servants who performed the ritual and manual functions required to support such a household.[7]

Museums and historic houses contain a wealth of material from this comfortable and comforting culture, and from both sides of the baize door. Thus the manual of household management, the servants' bells, the housemaid's cap and uniform, or the housekeeper's cupboard may have survived, along with the other paraphernalia of gentility – the visiting cards and cases, the gong, the cutlery for each course. Yet even here, a history based on objects in museum collections implies that most servants lived and worked with other servants in upper- or middle-class households. As Higgs remarks, 'this image has been widely disseminated by the media. . . . The world of "Upstairs, Downstairs" is now indelibly printed on the popular imagination'.[8]

However, according to census reports and recent research, most women worked in one-servant places as general servants or maids of all work, in small households, and for a short period only: servants were mainly young, unmarried women, working between leaving home and getting married.[9] These women scarcely had a separate material existence within the household, as the diaries of Hannah Cullwick, a general servant in London in the 1860s, show: her bed was in the kitchen, her food was broken victuals from the family table, and her 'uniform' for most of the day was a lilac cotton print dress covered by a heavy woollen apron.[10] Hannah cut her dresses down for patchwork quilts when they were no longer wearable, and probably used her aprons for cleaning cloths. The only, and exceptional, records of her working dress are the cartes-de-visite portraits taken by local studio photographers.[11]

Less than a quarter of the population even aspired to middle-class status at the period represented so frequently by the parlour display.[12] Most people lived in lodgings, rooms, or rented houses, and have left virtually no material evidence in museum or other collections. The shifting, precarious economy of such households and the life cycle of poverty of most working-class people have been well described by social historians and in recent autobiographies.[13] Under such conditions, material possessions and furnishings were sparse, simple and unspecialized, each item serving many functions. Thus a single table might serve for cooking and cleaning; for meals; for ironing; mending shoes and clothes, sewing; for reading; for paid homework; for treatment of family illnesses. Foodstuffs, furnishings, and clothing were worked and reworked until their uses were completely exhausted. Clothes were worn, handed on, and cut down until they wore out, when they would be used for quilts, rugs, or rags. Surplus items were pawned to make money and redeemed only if of great use or sentimental value. The material culture of these households has virtually worn away to nothing, leaving only the sentimental, ceremonial, and symbolic items – of little practical use – which have been treasured and preserved. Thus what remains for the museum to collect is unrepresentative of everyday existence.

Equally, records and illustrations are sparse for less prosperous households – and even for the middle classes themselves. Life in the majority of nineteenth-century households can be communicated – if at all – only through careful reconstruction from specific documents, photographs and engravings, memory and autobiography. Rooms, and items within them, were multifaceted, used in many different ways, difficult to express in a static display where visual interest is the key to engaging the viewer's attention. A small number of museums have attempted to overcome this: using definition and comparison at the Museum of Oxford (1975), where the living-room of a working-class dwelling is compared with the corner of a north Oxford drawing-room, and the members of each household are described; showing the life cycle, from cradle to workhouse and grave of a farm labourer's family at the Museum of Somerset Rural Life, Glastonbury (1977). Again, the sparse furnishings are brought to life when different functions and activities are demonstrated and acted out in educational and special activities in museums such as Beamish.

Confining categories

Curatorial practices also contribute to the invisibility of women in museums, or their relegation to the home in collections and displays. The key practices are identification and classification; fieldwork, recording, and collecting; interpretation and display. These procedures may be handled by one curator or by a number of different specialists depending on the size of the institution.

Classification is the system of grouping large collections of objects according to type, use, maker, process, or other relevant category. Most museums use a standard classification, which enables curators and users to locate and compare collections in more than one museum. The classification system is initially determined by the material in the museum collections – it is a tool for grouping and arranging that material – but it also, importantly, determines the way in which museums look at material. Themes chosen within museum displays tend to follow the same groupings as the classification system: for example, it's easier to mount an exhibition of portrait photographs on the studio photographers (mainly men) than on the sitters (men and women) if the collection is grouped according to photographer's name. The classification may also define the collecting intentions of the museum, by providing a 'shopping list' against which the museum can check its holdings, and set out to acquire the missing items in the sequence. Inevitably, therefore, shared classification systems bring shared prejudices and preferences to collecting and display.

The most prevalent classifications for social and local history museums are MERL, developed by the Museum of English Rural Life at Reading, and SHIC, the Social History and Industrial Classification, developed by a group of curators from different museums.[14] Both are hierarchical systems organized around spheres of use, and cutting vertically into activities within each sphere according to their special and distinctive artefacts, tools, skills, and products. The domestic sphere is separated from other spheres and in particular is set apart from, in antithesis to, working activity. Thus SHIC divides the classification into four main headings, 'covering all aspects of man's activity as a social animal':[15] community life, domestic and family life, personal life and working life.

The domestic category is divided into food and drink, cleaning, furnishings, hobbies. These divisions arise from actual, or anticipated, objects in the collections, especially in the proliferation of equipment and containers for preparing, cooking, serving, and storing food. It becomes almost impossible to look at the job of housework as a whole, at the range of tasks done by one person, including shopping and often childcare. Again, all activities within the home are assumed to be for consumption by the family: the classification makes no distinction between paid and unpaid work done at home, and locates productive work clearly outside the home.

Within any classification system, a single object may have more than one place. Thus every manufactured object can be viewed as an article of production or as an article of consumption or use: for example a patchwork quilt is the work of one woman or a group of women and is also a bedcover. Again, an object might have a number of uses: a needle might have been used for decorative needlework, for making functional items – clothing or furnishings – or for paid sewing at home or at work. The tools and equipment used

7 'The woman they call Mum . . . she is one of the world's hardest workers.'
Museums look at object-rich activities, such as cooking and serving, but
ignore laborious tasks like washing up. (Photo by Jarche in the *Daily Herald*,
23 November 1933, in H. V. Morton's series, 'Our Fellow Men'. *Daily Herald*
Archive, National Museum of Photography, Film, and Television.)

8 Running a stall at a garden fête to raise money for the First World War. From a family album – voluntary work was an important activity for many upper class women. (Photo: Roger Taylor)

by women working outside the home were generally few and unspecialized, their work was labour-intensive. Thus items relating to women's work are difficult to distinguish and locate without specific provenance or detailed historical information.

SHIC recommends that each object should have only one classification; the index guides the user to the relevant section heading(s). Here, the authors have chosen to treat women's work differently from men's. Thus where material is made by women, SHIC usually classifies the items according to use, so that details of makers and production are secondary. Also, items associated with women's work inside or outside the home – such as washing, cleaning, cooking – are almost exclusively placed in the domestic sphere, regardless of the fact that they might equally apply to work in industry or offices, while tools for home and general maintenance, for example, are cross-referenced to relevant categories in the working life section.

The slant of the classification may be offset by operating it differently to develop a dynamic model of the home, with multiple references which prompt the user to connect to the spheres of working life, community life, and personal life, and which suggest the comparison and interdependence of activities and interests in different spheres. More thorough recording and collecting, with emphasis on the provenance – the detailed history and context – of every object would itself extend or override the boundaries of the classification.

An alternative classification, used in Sweden and the USA, has greater flexibility than the systems commonly used in Britain, offering a wide range of functions within each sphere or 'pool' and linking common activities in different spheres.[16] The system has facilitated a major contemporary recording and collecting project in Sweden, with a number of museums co-operating in detailed recording and collecting. In the 'Homes Pool', for example, the project includes socializing; playing; working in the home (not housework); travel; buying and consuming.[17]

Homes without housework

In recent years, museum curators have placed a greater emphasis on context, on the particular and the authentic. The historic milieu of factory, street, or workshop is recorded with notes, photographs, film, and video and sound tapes. Such fieldwork illuminates the relationship between people and the objects around them, and shows the context and use of artefacts and materials. It informs the curator's process of selection, and may add to the understanding of material already in the museums's collection, as well as offering new acquisitions. It also gives detailed records for historical reconstruction, often applied to recreate craft workshops both in small museums and in large industrial museums such as Ironbridge Gorge or Kelham Island, Sheffield.

Fieldwork is a process which informs the observer of the alien, 'other' culture – in anthropology to look at other races and cultures, in sociology to look at other classes and lifestyles. In museum fieldwork the curator is introduced to an unfamiliar area of specific activity, beyond his/her personal or class experience and where printed sources are scarce of non-existent. (Over several years, I have learned the details of brickmaking, papermaking, hatmaking and hat block making, steelmaking and photojournalism in this way.)

However, curators do no fieldwork studies of housework, despite the large number of relevant and poorly documented artefacts in museum collections, and the almost universal displays of domestic settings in museums. The gadgetry of the home and of housework is recognized as historically finite and is widely displayed and collected, but there is no study of the home as work-place. Professional methodology and specialist knowledge are considered to be unnecessary because housework is assumed to be familiar, unhistorical. The home holds interest not in its own right, but as a counterpoint to the world of work and change outside the home which the museum constructs. It provides a passive background to the activities of the work-place, or, in science and technology displays, as familiar ground from which to launch into more difficult territory.

Curators assemble domestic displays entirely from printed sources on the one hand, and from their own experience and know-how on the other. The abundance of technical literature on the home in the form of advertising, magazine articles, mail order catalogues, promotional material, and maintenance leaflets, often well illustrated, contrasts with the lack of equivalent printed material for many other areas of museum activity and collecting. These are an attractively easy resource for the curator, and have become confused with and substituted for the history of usage in the home.

Displays of household applicances at the Castle Museum, York (1985), and at the Science Museum, South Kensington, have been assembled on this basis. The texts and images from advertising and technical literature inform the selection of objects, and supply the

at your service!

Electrolux model 62 instruction book

9 Advertisements recognize that the housewife carries out housework, but their imagery refutes it: laborious work is relieved by the use of the commodity, or the commodity itself appears to do the work. Museums rely heavily on such materials to 'explain' objects.

captions for labels, the illustrations and context for displays, replacing the users' experience on the one hand, or work studies on the other. Resembling promotional exhibitions, the displays present a truncated story of ambitions and preconceptions which is not complemented by usage and working context.

The message in both displays is the same, although in London it is implicit and in York it is explicit: machines in the home have reduced housework, they have laid off and liberated the worker: 'the exhibition . . . looks at the machines that have made home life easier, especially in our own century';[18] 'they give us time to relax and enjoy home entertainments'.[19] A joky leaflet for the York displays shows on one side a sooty and greasy-aproned housemaid fleeing from an onslaught of new appliances.[20] Overleaf a domestic servant sitting with her feet up on a chair, tools cast aside, holds in her hand a leaflet entitled 'Solution of the servant problem'.

These images are taken from early-twentieth-century advertisements by John Hassall, but they are not attributed or explained. The images and text together carry strong messages of class and sex in relation to housework and to technological change which continue in the exhibition but which are never discussed: they are offered not as opinion but as fact. They exemplify and reinforce the social denial of housework as real work: would we expect the same approach to other areas of work – a display on a recently obsolete local industry advertised by showing redundant workers in the unemployment office, for example? – though arguably it would be more true than in housework. Both displays beg the question of why, despite technological change, housework continues to absorb more hours of each working day for women, paid and unpaid, than most other occupations, and why housework time has not decreased although the hours of employed workers outside the home have.

By accepting the messages of manufacturers and advertisers, and substituting them for historical study, the displays fail to educate and inform the visitor about the particular features of domestic work in relation to period, locality, age, and class. Housework is divorced from relevant issues such as childcare, local housing conditions, sewage and utilities, alternative employment and local wage rates for women, control of sexuality and family size.

Neither display confronts the almost universal fact of housework as women's work; indeed the Science Museum fails to mention women in the texts throughout the main interpretative gallery.

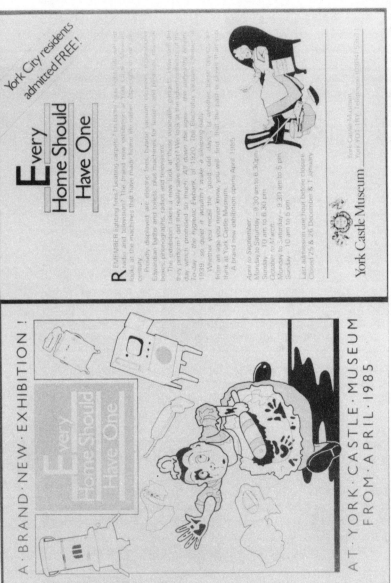

10 Publicity leaflet, York Castle Museum, April 1985. The images, adapted from early twentieth-century adverts, carry strong messages of class and sex in relation to housework and to technological change. (Photo: York Castle Museum)

Men are named as inventors and manufactures; women as operators are suggested by the brand names ('Housewife's Darling') and
the illustrations, but the labels refer to 'people' or 'servants'
operating the machines. Nowhere does the gallery state the fundamental difference between factory technology – which controls the
worker, the work process, and overall industrial organization – and
domestic technology where household organization remains the
same, and the housewife applies machines to particular tasks. The
status of domestic issues within science and technology is suggested by the location of the Science Museum's gallery in the
museum's basement, beside the schools' entrance and children's
gallery, but a long way down from the major technological achievements displayed above.

An alternative approach might usefully have drawn on recent
time/use surveys and research studies of housework and technology in the home.[21] These suggest that the proliferation of small
appliances has extended, rather than eliminated, household tasks:
the greatest number of appliances are in those households where
housework time is longest, and the housewife has no other employment. Appliances have transferred some tasks formerly seen as
men's work (emptying the rubbish, doing the washing up) to women
(using the sink disposal unit, filling the dishwasher), and have
transferred tasks from paid to unpaid workers, causing technological unemployment for laundresses and seamstresses, and replacing paid shopworkers with unpaid shoppers who collect,
transport, and store goods from centralized shopping centres.[22]
Conversely, many studies of work have pointed to the prevalence,
and recent increase, of homeworking,[23] and have stressed the
interdependence, as opposed to the separation, of home and work.[24]

Alternative representations

Returning to my earlier questions, how is the position of museums
tenable in relation to current knowledge about women in history on
the one hand and to the perception of museums as conveyors of
'truth' and 'reality' on the other? And how do we open up criticism
and offer alternative and/or additional representations?

Museums are anxious to avoid studies and inferences which they
see as political and propagandist: curators regard their own work
as factual, non-theoretical, working with the physical, the real.
Thus issues such as the (mis)representation of women are seen as
irrelevant or as inevitable, a side-effect of a straightforward,

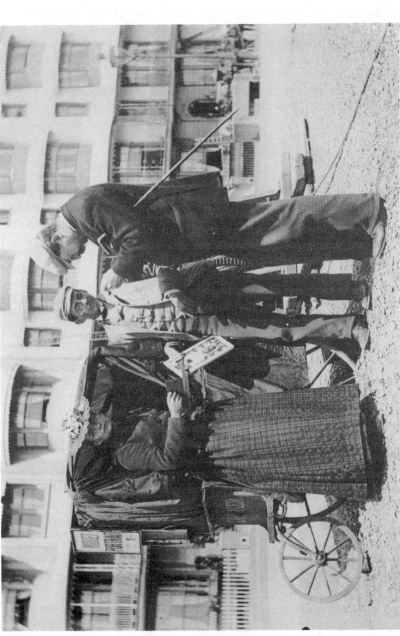

11 A man and woman at Brede's Race selling portraits to a client. As in other businesses, women worked in portrait photography but are rarely named on portrait cards or acknowledged in photographic history. (Photo: George Woods.

empiricist approach to history and to the material culture. The overtly political aims of WHAM challenge the cherished convention of objective and unbiased professionalism: the concern with women's representation is seen as a threat rather than a corrective to current practice.

As I have shown, the 'common-sense' approach betrays itself by its contradictions and its silences. Empiricism alone is no guarantee of objectivity. By claiming to have no position, it protects its working methods, and their consequent effects and prejudices, from examination. Curators must acknowledge that their own structures of thought and practice are instrumental in forming or re-presenting 'reality', not simply reflecting 'reality'.

Museums offer representations uncritically, adopting and reinforcing the norms and definitions current in other media. By selection, association, and interpretation, curators help to reinforce certain clusters of meanings and to ignore others. This is powerfully illustrated in the displays quoted above. As in advertising, women are identified almost entirely with home and family, and absent from the work-place and from public life, unless in portrayals which trivialize them, or treat them as threatening. Museums operate a fundamental divide between work and home, work and personal life, work and leisure. This conceals the *work* which women perform in the home to support the divide.[25] It also leads to a curious reticence about areas which cannot thus be divided, for instance in the persistence of paid cleaners in the home.

A tension exists for museums between looking at 'real life' on the one hand, and looking for visual and material richness and diversity in objects and displays, fun and entertainment for the visitors on the other. Where museums look at 'real life' they concentrate on those parts which have changed, and which thus offer contrast and fascination (as in the motive power galleries of industrial museums), or on exposing to public gaze processes which are usually hidden and unexplained. Much of women's historical experience lies in areas where 'change' measured by objects and technologies is slow, and where women are seen as secondary, operators or consumers, rather than inventors or producers. Again, they work on processes and in places which are taken for granted, assumed to be familiar.

One way in which museums can operate is to work consciously to present a broader spectrum of women's activities. The craft workshop and work-place displays might be extended to include the work which women did – preparation and packing, cleaning and

12 An alternative to the 'natural' family: girls and young women working away from home often lived in lodging houses such as the YWCA hostel depicted on this postcard. (Photo: Roger Taylor)

cooking, record-keeping and marketing – as well as the main, core function in which they often stood in for partners or worked in their own right. The industries where women worked – such as food and drink, clothing, services – may be considered as well as those of the Industrial Revolution. The boundaries of home and work might be expanded to emphasize their interdependence, for example, the effects of shift work at home. The vignette of the reconstruction room occupied by the 'natural' family might be shifted to reflect different households, with diverse patterns of paid and unpaid work among family members. Dramatic and powerful interpretative methods might be used to inform and illustrate where, in less object-rich displays, the objects and milieux do not 'speak for themselves'.

The museum's relationship to its public is also pertinent. Visitors have been kept at arm's length from the museum process, as consumers of a finished product, the display, which claims a single, unambiguous meaning, 'this is how it was'. There is little room for questioning or doubt. Museums of social and local history strive to show 'typical', generalized domestic settings, which do not admit the partiality of records or collections, nor the difficulty of 'reconstructing' past histories. Incomplete records from individual households, defined by local and personal circumstances, are almost the only surviving information to work on. A more honest statement might thus be: 'we think this is how it might have been, for these people, at this time in their lives'. A few museums, such as the People's Palace, explain to the visitor how material is selected and grouped in different ways within the museum, and thus demystify and qualify the historical statements which they offer.

Museums have also responded slowly to shifts in public interest, appearing to be indifferent both to the materials offered by 'new' areas of history, such as women's history and Black history, and to the more general issues which they raise. The organization of WHAM has provided a focus and contact for people outside the profession with an interest in women and in history. The group has begun to explore the issues for women in relation to museums, with practical projects, such as a joint exhibition, and with discussion of the effects of, and alternatives to, aspects of current practice.[26]

One of many ways of opening up the museum process is to involve people outside museums with relevant insight and experience in both analytical discussion and practical, positive programmes within the museum. It is precisely through looking at one detailed area, gender, that the limitations of underlying assumptions in

13 The touring exhibition 'Fit Work for Women', compiled and designed by the north-west group of Women, Heritage, and Museums in 1986, looks at the experiences and common issues of women's work in the key industries of the region. (Photo: Women, Heritage, and Museums)

museum practice can be understood, and that alternative approaches to classification, collecting, and display can be explored.

Notes and references

1 Using the analogy of the museum display with the written text, and the visitor with the reader, I have drawn on Belsey, C. (1980) *Critical Practice*, London: Methuen, particularly ch. 1, 'Criticism and common sense', pp. 1–36.

2 Equal Opportunities section in the Museum Association annual questionnaire, 1983, analysed by Val Bott and Jane Legget. Summarized in Legget, J. (1984) 'Women in museums – past, present and future', *Women, Heritage, and Museums Conference Proceedings*, pp. 14–15.

3 Mattingly, J. (1984) *Volunteers in Museums and Galleries*, Berkhamstead: Volunteer Centre.

4 WHAM! conference introduction, (1984) *Women, Heritage, and Museums Conference Proceedings*, pp. 1–2.

5 Porter, G. (1987) 'Gender bias: representations of work in history museums', Museums Professionals Group Transactions 22: 11–15.

6 Davidoff, L. (1976) 'The rationalisation of housework', in D. L. Barker and S. Allen (eds) *Dependence and Exploitation in Work and Marriage*, London: Longman, pp. 121–51.

7 Davidoff, L. (1976) *The Best Circles: 'Society', Etiquette and the Season*, London: Croom Helm.

8 Higgs, E. (1986) 'Domestic service and household production', in A. V. John (ed.) *Unequal Opportunities: Women's Employment in England 1800–1918*, Oxford: Basil Blackwell, p. 125.

9 ibid.; see also Porter, G. (1973) 'Domestic servants 1870–1914', unpublished MA dissertation, University of Edinburgh.

10 Both the diaries of Hannah and of Arthur Munby, to whom she was secretly married, carry many references to dress. Hudson, D. (1972) *Munby: Man of Two Worlds*, London: Sphere; Stanley, E. (ed.) (1984) *The Diaries of Hannah Cullwick, Victorian Maidservant*, London: Virago.

11 Hiley, M. (1979) *Victorian Working Women: Portraits from Life*, London: Gordon Fraser.

12 Best uses Charles Booth's census reconstruction to show the growth of middle-class occupations from 10.4 per cent of the occupied population of England and Wales in 1851 to 13.8 per cent by 1881. Best, G. (1971) *Mid-Victorian Britain 1851–1875*, London: Weidenfeld & Nicholson, p. 85. In Thompson's class structure for the Edwardian period, based on men's occupations, 3 per cent occupied men are upper class, 22 per cent middle class, and 78 per cent working class. Thompson, P. (1975) *The Edwardians: The Remaking of British Society*, London: Weidenfeld & Nicholson, p. 17.

13 E.g. Thompson, P. (1975) *The Edwardians: The Remaking of British Society*, London: Weidenfeld & Nicholson; Roberts, E. (1984) *A Woman's Place: An Oral History of Working Class Women, 1890–1940*, Oxford: Basil Blackwell; national interview study of family, work, and community life, Department of Sociology, University of Essex. Many local groups are also publishing their own histories and autobiographies from this period.

14 *Museum Procedure: Classification*, Reading, Museum of English Rural Life; SHIC Working Party (1983) *Social History and Industrial Classification (SHIC): A Subject Classification for Museum Collections*, Sheffield, Centre for English Cultural Tradition and Language, 1983.

15 SHIC, p. vi.

16 Murdock, C. P. *et al.*, *Outline of Cultural Materials*, New Haven, Conn: Human Relations Area Files Inc., several editions.

17 Kavanagh, G. (1983) 'SAMDOK in Sweden: some observations and impressions', *Museums Journal*, 83 (1); Stavenow-Hidemark, E. (1985) *Home Thoughts from Abroad: An Evaluation of the SAMDOK Homes Pool*, Stockholm: Nordiska Museet.

18 Leaflet 'Every home should have one', York, Castle Museum, 1985.

19 Introductory panel to exhibition, 'Every home should have one', York, Castle Museum, 1985.

20 The image is based on an advertising poster by John Hassall for the British Vacuum Cleaner Company, 1906, which hangs in the Science Museum's domestic appliances gallery: a maid with a handbrush runs away from a vacuum nozzle thrust through the rooflight by a male hand (Science Museum inventory 1973–155).

21 Gershuny, J. (1982) 'Household tasks and the use of time', in S. Wallman and associates, *Living in South London: Perspectives on Battersea 1871–1981*, Aldershot: Gower, pp. 149–79; Oakley, A. (1985) *The Sociology of Housework*, Oxford: Basil Blackwell; Bereano, P., Bose, C. and Arnold, E., 'Kitchen technology and the liberation of women from housework', in E. Arnold and W. Faulkner (eds) (1985) *Smothered by Invention: Technology in Women's Lives*, London: Pluto, pp. 162–81.

22 The impact of public and private transport has been closely studied in the USA. Schwartz Cohan, R. (1985) 'More work for mother: technology and housework in the USA', in L. Levidow and B. Young (eds) *Science, Technology and the Labour Process*, London: Free Association Books, pp. 88–128.

23 E.g. Coyle, A. (1982) 'Sex and skill in the organisation of the clothing industry', in J. West (ed.) *Work, Women and the Labour Market*, London: Routledge & Kegan Paul, pp. 10–26.

24 Westwood, S. (1984) *All Day Every Day: Factory and Family in the Making of Women's Lives*, London: Pluto; Cockburn, C. (1985) *Machinery of Dominance: Women, Men and Technical Know-How*, London: Pluto.

25 Winship, J. (1978) 'A woman's world: "Woman" – an ideology of femininity', Women's Studies Group, Centre for Contemporary Cultural Studies, *Women Take Issue*, London: Hutchinson, p. 137.

26 In the past three years a number of meetings and projects have taken

place at local, regional, and national level. In particular, the North West WHAM group has organized an exhibition, 'Fit Work for Women', touring throughout 1986–7. At the time of writing, events are planned on racism, flexible working practices, and access to museums.

6

Tomorrow's yesterdays: science museums and the future

ALAN MORTON

This essay is intended to contribute to a discussion about the future of museums of science and technology. The views given here are my own and not to be taken as representing the opinions of either the staff or the trustees of the Science Museum.

It is difficult to predict what will become of museums of science and technology because there is little agreement at present on their function and there are many possible developments. Bearing in mind that my task might be as useful as reading the horoscopes for last year, I set out in this essay to examine some of the issues facing the staff and visitors of these museums. Some of these issues, for example to do with the funding of museums, have recently become acute, but others, such as the effect of the museum as a medium of communication, have been with us for much longer. Since similar factors are likely to constrain future developments, I hope to glean a few clues about what the future might hold by looking at the effects of these constraints in the past.

Messages and the museum medium

Today there are several patterns for what might be done in the future. Some museums display objects in 'traditional' ways and other institutions, the science centres, such as the Exploratorium in San Francisco or the Ontario Science Center in Toronto, offer 'hands-on' experiences. Both approaches have their followers and a high-tech attempt to integrate them has been made recently at the new and expensive enterprise at La Villette on the outskirts of Paris.

However, all these institutions devoted to science and technology enshrine the relentless march of industrial society, a progression which has led to a bewildering array of products, from television to shopping malls but also including the consumers that go with them. Apart from providing the objects for exhibition, these developments have affected museums in many ways. Sometimes new inventions, like moving pictures or television, have appeared which compete with museums for their audience and one consequence has been that museums have become outmoded and almost the victims of the very progress they collectively applaud.[1]

In recent history, outmoded technologies have often come to rest in museums, perhaps a fate that awaits museums themselves. A selection could be preserved under the wing of English Heritage in a 'Museum of museums', as examples of late-nineteenth- and early-twentieth-century follies marking the triumph of consumer society. The marketing of this museum could develop the concept of it as the 'nation's scrapyard', a sanitized version of an essential feature of any industrial society. (Until recently the Victoria and Albert Museum was advertised as 'the nation's treasure-house', an ambiguous term which can be taken to imply that the collections inside the building are there only because they are valuable and have to kept locked away.) Visitors to this 'Museum of museums' would gape at the quaint surroundings of warders and curators in the way they do today when visiting monasteries or stare at musty exhibitions, with the same feelings they have when going round a grand dining-room full of grotesque knick-knacks.

If that is not to be the fate of museums, can they be given a new identity and their staffs find novel ways of appealing to the public who would find it more worthwhile and interesting to visit them? A partial answer to this question comes from some of the factors which have affected the growth of museums in the past since many of these are still operating today.

As private and public institutions museums have a long history but those which specialize in science and technology are essentially late-nineteenth- and twentieth-century institutions.[2] In Britain the origins of the Science Museum in London can be traced to the Great Exhibition of 1851. This exhibition led to the setting up of the South Kensington Museum which later split into the Victoria and Albert Museum, dealing with decorative arts, and the Science Museum. During the construction of the Science Museum in the early years of this century, the government was implementing a number of policies to promote science and technology, largely to counter the growing military and industrial might of Germany. (Interestingly the largest museum of science and technology in Germany, the Deutsches Museum in Munich, was founded in 1903.) These policies included the founding of Imperial College of Science and Technology in 1905 and the setting up of the Department of Scientific and Industrial Research during the First World War. This department had responsibility for funding research in universities and for helping to set up research associations for industries, jointly funded by government and the firms involved.

But building a museum of science and industry is quite a different project from attempting to support science and technology directly. The aims, methods, and the results are quite different.

The construction of a museum is a signal that the government and others want to influence public attitudes to science and technology, to increase the standing of these subjects (and that of their practitioners in particular). However, it is not only the medium of the museum that can be used to achieve these ends. Here it must be very significant that at the time this type of museum was first set up (and I am thinking of the Deutsches Museum, Science Museum, Chicago Museum of Science and Industry, and Palais de la Découverte as examples), for most people, the other sources of information about science and technology were printed, encyclopedias, newspapers and books, all of which are two-dimensional.[3] The museum medium had the advantage of another dimension and with it came the romance of seeing the 'real' thing on display. Sometimes these devices could be made to move by a visitor, creating fleeting allusions to both the role of the operator and questions about the control of the production process. The conception of reality on offer in the museum was very plausible.

Some eighteenth-century writers suggested that sculpture, painting, and the written word were each suited to conveying different ideas. Perhaps in a similar way, the use of a museum format permits only certain ideas to be presented and places constraints on the information available to the visitor. The museum is a medium which conveys messages explicitly and implicitly (in a McLuhanesque Medium-is-the Message sense); a medium which lends itself to imparting certain views of science and technology and to being part of the process of socially constructing these in a particular way.

An example of a deliberate message in the format of a museum display was the arrangement in the early nineteenth century of the 'natural objects' from the collections of the Ashmolean Museum in Oxford. These were laid out according to a framework drawn from Paley's 'Natural Theology' so as 'to induce a mental habit of associating the view of natural phenomena with the conviction that they are the media of Divine manifestation and by such association to give proper dignity to every branch of natural science'.[4]

However it is not just the intentional message supplied by one or several curators or sponsors which is important in a museum display. Many other issues can be raised about the way people interpret and understand museum exhibits and the implicit messages they receive from them. The most obvious and in many ways also the most complex problems arise because museum exhibits use 'objects'. Like a fossil in a natural history museum, it is very easy to accept that such an 'object' exists but very difficult to understand why it does. Let me pursue this analogy for a moment. If the machines in a museum of science and technology are fossils left by the changes in industrial society, then this record, like any fossil record, is difficult to interpret because the living elements have disappeared. But curators and indeed visitors have also the further problems of 'inventing' a Darwin and deciding how his or her theory of machine evolution explains what they see in an exhibition.

Several consequences result from this object-centred approach to history. One is simply that if there are no objects available, it becomes very difficult to mount a museum display. The development of many early technologies used in agriculture or in the preparation of food literally become invisible as far as museums of science and technology are concerned because the implements have not survived. Often these implements would have been used to destruction, unlike many machines today which become obsolete before they are used up. The net result is for these museums to concentrate on the recent past and to present a foreshortened view of history.

This object-centred approach provides too a version of the past that is inhuman because it has become separated from human beings. While any historical enterprise is inhuman in this way, there is a particular problem in a museum because the 'objects' constrain the story in important respects. For example what machines in an exhibition do not show (except in very exceptional circumstances) are the actions and reactions of human beings to existing techniques or new developments in the production process. Any references to these have to be supplied by the curator. By contrast, in, say, an agricultural community in Britain in the nineteenth century, many technologies would be familiar, baking, flourmilling, blacksmithing, and so on, and these technologies would be understood in a context where the baker or blacksmith would be known individuals, a very human context in which the characters, skills, and life histories of these people would all be relevant.

The idea of progress

Deriving from this foreshortened view of history is an idea of progress which may be conveyed by an exhibition (though of course this message may be intended). Any exhibition where earlier and later devices are juxtaposed, such as one on hand- and power-looms, and social context is completely ignored, will have this effect. As well as inculcating the view that progress is a straightforward and uncomplicated technical matter, this idea of progress expands to become 'history'; that recent history is simply an assembly of sequences such as the one illustrated. Bound in too with this version of progress is a view of modern technology as being the best of all possible technologies.

In a museum this view of technology is cast in a mould formed by a nationalist ideology. National economic factors, a government's desire to promote industry, or an industry's desire to fend off nationalization, help to form a patriotic view of technology in a museum. When language is taken into account as well as the point that it is easier for a curator (and perhaps more relevant to the public) to publicize local technology, such a view of technology is very difficult to avoid. For example the Science Museum in London has an exhibition on nuclear power which emphasizes the Advanced Gas-cooled Reactor, a reactor designed and used only in Britain. The equivalent display at the Palais de la Découverte in Paris shows the French design of Pressurized Water Reactor but the National Museum of American History in Washington ignores this controversial topic altogether (though it does have a display of Atomsmashers, a field the USA dominated until recently).

Other problems arise for museums from this view of technology because in many industries today production is arranged globally. The latest technology may be developed in Japan, making it difficult to arrange a museum display about that technology in Britain or the USA since factors such as a desire to boost local industry may not operate if, for example, the foreign firm doing the research is in competition with a local one.

For museums, another question coming out of the global nature of industry comes in the matter of sponsorship. A multinational company is likely to support activities dealing with its technology in its home country but will be more sensitive about doing so in a foreign country. There it is more likely to prefer to sponsor arts events which have high cultural status and show respect for that nation's culture, perhaps that part of culture they want to be seen to be heir to, unlike the national science and technology. Such a policy may reflect a desire to be seen to contribute to the common good but without raising questions about their industrial role in any country. (One exception to this pattern seems to be IBM who sponsor exhibitions, often their own, on science and technology. Perhaps in their case this attitude reflects the dominant part they play in the world computer industry.)

There is a further point to make. In a country like Britain there is historical material from an industry like watchmaking, but little that is modern because the watches sold today in Britain are made instead in Switzerland, Japan, and now Hong Kong. A historical exhibition on watchmaking would then be a story of decline from a glorious past, a parable for Britain's industry, and a case of the message of progress being read backwards, with the result that museums here can often be seen as mute monuments to the 'glorious past' of British industry.

Another problem with museum exhibitions using this particular view of progress arises because this view often conflicts with perceptions about science and technology which people have formed from other sources, like television, newspapers, or their own work-place. The result may be a cynicism about museum displays. For example such displays may be seen as ambiguous, the ostensible message being supplied by the creators and then another, conflicting message being supplied by the viewer. The long-term result of this credibility gap may be that visitors are less interested to visit museums.

Having dealt with some of the consequences of using 'objects' in a museum, I would like to examine the way these same objects are used in wider society to see what implications there are for museums.

Objects as commodities, art versus science and technology

An important attribute of 'objects' in our society is that they are commodities to be bought and sold. Different commodities have their different uses and this apparently banal point has had some profound repercussions for museums. At one end of a spectrum, some objects are valued for their artistic qualities. Often these were made for decorative purposes and are usually unique. Such objects are housed, when in an institution to which the public have access, in art galleries or museums for the decorative arts where they can be viewed by a suitably respectful (and respectable) audience. Though the historical context of these objects may have changed drastically, a function of the object as something to be appreciated by a viewer, is still recognizably the same (or at least has been so for a considerable portion of the history of the object).

At the other end of that spectrum of objects are machines which have a use, that is they occur as a part of a production process, and these become the objects displayed in a museum of science and technology. Curiously, though such machines may be shown moving in a museum display, they are rarely shown working and virtually never shown operating as part of a production line. A beam engine, for example, often can be a 'working' exhibit in museums but it leaves the impression that the engine exists to rock the beam when in fact it would have powered a pump or a factory. Thus in the case of a machine, and unlike the art object, the context of the museum display is quite different from the one for which it was originally made, both historically and functionally.

Clearly this distinction between types of objects is not clear cut since some objects can be both utilitarian and decorative, for example scientific instruments or the chalices used in religious services. Cutlery can be on display in a museum of design or a kitchen. (Since many of these distinctions are made by housing such objects in different buildings, like museums, churches, department stores, houses, or auction houses, perhaps we can learn a lot about our society by comparing museums with these other institutions.)

These distinctions between 'art' and 'utilitarian' objects are also observed outside museums through the prices of these items and the ways in which these are determined. Because 'art' objects are unique (or occur in limited editions) and there are finite numbers of works by those who are both acknowledged as masters and dead, the prices for these objects reflect the demand for them which is very high at the moment. By contrast, one result of industrial innovation may be that some equipment is virtually worthless even though it was made in limited quantities and has great significance for the history of contemporary technology, for example a production line for 4K RAM chips now that 256K RAM chips are standard.

In such cases the scrap-dealer rather than a collector in an auction house is the one who sets the price.

Ironically it is the objects produced in the past using now obsolete technologies which have supplied the wealth to create the art market. The objects used in the production wealth are not valued whereas other commodities, with other properties, are used to signify wealth. These valuations impinge on museums because the cultural status of different types of museums are reflections of these valuations with art galleries at the top and science museums lower down the scale.

So different types of museums, as well as providing settings which have different implications for the various categories of objects on display, also reflect and reinforce different categories of contemporary culture (decorative arts, natural history, industry, or whatever).

Of course there are many other ways which are used to define the categories of contemporary culture and some of the media which have this role have themselves had an effect on museums.

Television

If museums provide cultural niches for certain objects, the coming of television, and even more modern variants like the video cassette recorder, has provided competition for the museum medium. Television provided a new medium of popular instruction and entertainment. With television, viewers have access to images of distant people and places in a way that a museum can never match. Even more than that, television has the potential to show what is in a museum.

Television can also be used to record complex and lengthy processes at the place where the process is normally carried out. By going to the original a more 'realistic' and detailed account is possible than would be the case in a museum display. In the past museums provided access to parts of a differentiated society and were modest microcosms of industry, a role which television now plays today. (Braudel mentions 90 crafts listed in 1568, two centuries later 250 were given in the Encyclopedie, and over 800 mentioned in 1826, figures which may go some way to explain the need for museums as places where people can learn about parts of the world they might not otherwise encounter.)[5] In these respects the medium of television has great advantages over that of a museum and may even be able to supplant the role of museums.

But science and technology museums are in a particularly ironic position because they are expected to cover new subject areas, such as television, which have tended to make the museum medium obsolescent. This point can be illustrated by an example, a display of a television set with an explanation of how it works. The television set is an important and complex piece of technology but such an exhibition would miss all the important attributes of television as a mass cultural medium. This hypothetical example throws into sharp relief some of the limitations of the museum medium to date. But all may not yet be lost since the newer media are now being feted in museums devoted to photography and the moving image.

The coming of television has had other effects. Because the television picture is so dominant a cultural medium, the techniques of television have become norms in many areas. The way a scene in a television soap-opera or a shot in a documentary are constructed is having an effect on museums. There the use of room-settings and story-lines is being influenced by the practices of television with the result that exhibitions become a series of views in which a small number of points are put across and the visitor is expected to be a passive viewer of the exhibition. (In Washington DC television has had a dramatic impact. JR's hat is one of the 'Treasures of the Smithsonian', judging from its appearance in the exhibition of that name in Edinburgh in 1984.)

The result of the competition from television and the other pressures I have described has been that, like other institutions in society, museums have had to change to adapt to new historical circumstances. The original aims of their founders may have been lost or even enhanced over time and new purposes may have been grafted on to the existing structures of staff and buildings. But during the evolution of science and technology museums there has been an important shift. This shift had its starting-point in institutions which represented useful objects, those illustrating the novelty and progress of an industrializing society. These objects were displayed simply as the commodities produced in that society in exhibitions which took place in buildings designed within a tradition of museum architecture and public displays. These buildings were public spaces used for educational and improving purposes and while these facilities had to be paid for, they were not run as commercial organizations and often they were free to visitors at the time of use.

Today in contrast, in a society of consumers, some functions of commodities are well understood (and endlessly reiterated by advertising). New techniques like colour printing and television have appeared to provide competition for the museum medium and in doing so have pushed museums into the market-place. Government policy too has reinforced these trends and endeavoured to make museums cost-effective and market-oriented. The introduction of charges to visit several museums in Britain has been one result. Consequently museums have become more like other commercial leisure institutions and distanced from an idea of education as something which is valuable but none the less should be 'free' at the time of consumption. The result of this spread of 'market values', in other words the bottom line, is that the museum visit has itself become a commodity. The transformation which began in part with the museum representing objects as commodities has come full circle.

Similar changes have affected many other aspects of life. In the same period educational organizations like schools and universities have suffered from some of the same pressures. Other recent examples are whether blood should be donated or bought to supply blood products or whether surrogate parenthood should become a commercial service. Each of these marks a step in a process of alienation.

Competing in the market-place

If there is no intention that public museums should compete directly with commercial organizations (and there are certainly not the resources to do that effectively) then an important problem for museum staff is to fashion and maintain a clear identity for museums as different kinds of institutions from those in the commercial arena.

Some of the contemporary pressures operating on museums come from the growth of tourism and the industries devoted to leisure. For instance 'theme parks' compete directly with museums as alternative places for visitors to go. A shopping mall sets out to attract consumers and to occupy their free time with the pleasures of consumption in a public space whose architectural features are reminiscent of those found in museum buildings. Such 'gallerias' function as museums dedicated to consumption but where you can buy and possess the exhibits with all the gratifications that are entailed. (A new shopping mall in Edmonton, Alberta, is the largest in the world. It has 817 shops, a palm-lined beach with waves, an amusement park with 47 rides, and a zoo. The Fantasyland Hotel offers Arabian harems or 'truck stop' rooms with a model policeman at the jacuzzi and a bed on the back of a real Ford pick-up truck.)[6]

Some aspects of this 'competition' may very well be beneficial in raising the quality of the facilities for visitors, for example, but there are problems too. The greater the success of these malls and theme parks, the greater the pressure on museums to emulate these in various ways; to mount spectacular and expensive displays (to compete with, say, the Disney organization's EPCOT in Florida) or even to place a museum 'shop' in a prominent site.

Interestingly in the heartland of the philosophy of the free-market today, the USA, it is accepted that there are certain things which are worth doing – and doing well – but which cannot be done by the private sector. Some of these tasks are carried out for the government by an agency, the Smithsonian Institution, and the Smithsonian is a graphic example of the interplay of the forces working on museums today. (There are many museums in the private sector such as the Getty Museum or the Metropolitan but in these cases the government has affected their development through a framework of tax law.)

In Washington DC, along the sides of the Mall fronting the Capitol building, some of the museums of the Smithsonian Institution and other galleries are arranged like a cultural Stonehenge. In many of the museums the mixing in of politics with the displays is more overt, partly because the museums have a greater role in portraying the history of the USA and partly because these institutions reflect the major business of the city as the seat of government. There you have an exhibition of good taste, that of the presidents' wives, the First Ladies, in a display of their dresses. It also seems quite natural that the National Air and Space Museum should be in front of NASA, a clear reminder of the role of space in the nation's psyche post-Sputnik. (After the Space Shuttle disaster, an earlier film about the Shuttle *The Dream is Alive*, has now a different meaning in Washington.) Taken as a whole, the Smithsonian functions as a national shrine for American visitors fulfilling needs analagous to those met by the nearby Vietnam Memorial.

But the role of national shrine is not the only possible identity or use for museums in the future. An earlier theme was that the role for museums of science and technology has been circumscribed by the very technologies they display. If that is the case, are other opportunities opened up which might compensate? Because a tangle of issues is involved, it is very difficult to come up with a glib prescription for what might be done to forge a new identity for museums of science and technology.

Making changes

Unless oil is struck in South Kensington or some equally far-fetched endeavour provides large amounts of money, and the commissioners for the 1851 Exhibition decide to rebuild all the museums in Britain, any discussion about the future has to start with the existing museums, their staffs, and collections of objects.

As the collections are an obvious feature of these institutions it is very tempting to build an argument on this foundation. But there are both strengths and weaknesses in this approach. The strength lies in that the collections are unique, something to distinguish one museum from another and also from any other type of institution. But a weakness appears if the argument is left at that point. While that argument may demonstrate that a museum has a unique identity, that argument by itself does not justify the existence of a museum. The same argument would apply to a collection of used milkbottle tops. That collection too would be unique but the fact that it exists is not a strong enough reason for providing a museum to house it. Other arguments have to be advanced.

If this argument about uniqueness of museum collections is not to be seen just as special pleading by curators looking after their self-interest, curators have to explain how objects might be used more constructively as part of museum displays that would engage the attention of their publics. But object-based displays, as I have tried to point out above, often have great weaknesses and the difficulty is to see how the worst of these can be avoided.

One of the points I made about object-based displays in most industrial museums was that they are basically inhuman, a few mannequins and some throwaway remarks about social history notwithstanding. What is missing from this approach are aspects of the human condition, such as arguments about technology, the negotiations and trade disputes that centre on it, and how these are resolved.[7]

One technique which can be used to inject more of a human element into exhibitions would be to tame video and have it perform in museums. With video it would be possible to capture the motion of machines together with the skills and reminiscences of the human operator. His or her conditions of life could be preserved in an oral and visual account of what they did.

Similarly questions about skill are often ignored (along with the consequences of such issues for domestic life). Perhaps these topics could figure in museum displays. For example some aspects of skill can be brought out because today mass production methods are used to manufacture many household goods but similar items are also produced by 'craft' methods. Furniture, ceramics, and food all fall into this category. Mass and craft production processes could be contrasted by exhibiting the products and the processes side by side. The difference in the qualities of the finished products and their uses could be illustrated and the history of mass production methods and the technologies developed to achieve them could be shown. The differing roles of human beings in craft and mass production could be brought out and craft skills could be demonstrated, by for example a potter (making the point that these methods are not necessarily low tech). Incidentally such exhibitions might help too to break down the art/science divide which has bedevilled museums.

Earlier I made the point that one distinction between art museums and museums of science and technology is that the former contain emblems of wealth, the latter the means for producing wealth. If this distinction is now well understood in our society, perhaps it is no longer quite so necessary to continue to reinforce these distinctions by housing these objects in different institutions. Today 'art' and 'technology' could be housed together. The advantages in doing this are that in many cases it would become possible to link up the finished product, the fabric, the furniture, or the metalwork with the technology used in their manufacture. The usefulness of the manufacturing process would be illustrated by the end product and aspects of the design of the product could be explained in terms of the production process.

In some respects museums are in the pre-Henry Ford era since very little attention is paid to that emblem of modern industry, the assembly line. This is surprising because a large amount of research and development work, often involving advanced technologies, is done to speed up production carried on by these methods. If this research is going to be illustrated in a museum, it would seem obvious to show it as something with a bearing on the production process, yet this does not seem to happen. Ironically, in a way the production line is ideally suited to being shown in a museum because there is a product at almost every stage, though the size of the line is sometimes a factor which may work against this.

Such an approach could be expanded. Rather than illustrate just the processes carried out on a production line, the line could be used as the thread of a more ambitious exhibition on modern industrial society, the additional material illustrating the ramifications of the production line. These could range from the production of the raw materials to the cities populated by the workers on the line; from the systems developed to control the flow of work and parts on the line to the skills needed by the people and machines arranged along it; and even from ancilliary services like coffee-vending machines to the banking machines used by the workers.

Though the current state of an industry is an important topic for a museum, the evolution of industry is also something else that can be featured. Here techniques could be adapted from archaeology and industrial archaeology. Rather than depict an industry at a particular time, an attempt could be made to illustrate the economy and the changing industry of a small area. The different 'levels' of Trafford Park in Manchester or the East End of London could be shown and the changes which occurred both locally and inter-nationally to produce these levels could be explained.

A novel approach that might be taken in museums would be to copy techniques used in newspaper articles. Many problems with technology, and the issues about employment that are connected with them, surface in debates carried on in the newspapers. A typical format is an article written by a journalist who quotes selectively from people whose views he or she has solicited. It would be quite possible to copy elements of this approach in a museum exhibit. A snapshot view of a particular issue could be provided by a curator selectively quoting from a number of sources. If the issue was limited in scope (though it could still be important), small and relatively inexpensive exhibitions could be mounted and museums could respond more quickly to issues as they arose.

In the longer term it is quite possible to think of more radical solutions. Museums using the advantages of new computer-based technologies could truly become centres for providing the public with information about technological and social issues of all kinds. The museum building itself (compare La Villette) could itself become an exhibit of high technology. But in any discussions it is important to remember that a museum has many in-built advan-tages. It can offer the real thing, which in some cases may have a romantic aura of its own (like steam engines). A museum provides an opportunity for a visitor to browse, to have the potential of choosing what to see, and then to reflect on what is being shown (unlike the case of television). They and their children can have the unalloyed pleasure of pressing a button. The excitement and wonder induced in a visitor to a museum should never be underestimated. A museum visit provides an uncommon opportunity to experience a unique public space, unlike the shops with 'designer'-produced styles which make every High Street identical.

A museum is an institution for informal education. Part of that remit is to illustrate aspects of what has happened in the past to help people understand the present and make informed choices about the future. History is too important to leave it to be ruthlessly plundered for images by the advertising industry.

Notes and references

1 See the excellent and stimulating article, Shaw, J. (1985) 'Museums an obsolete medium', *Museum Professionals Group Newsletter* 21, winter.

2 See Finn, B. F. (forthcoming) 'The museum of science and technology: historic outline', in M. Shapiro (ed.) *The Museum: A Reference Guide*, Westport, Conn: Greenwood Press, ch. 6.

3 An intriguing coincidence is the near-simultaneous appearance of the Theory of Special Relativity (1905) and the development of motion pictures around 1900. In a museum, for example, a visitor walks forwards (or backwards) in time, from an earlier to a later object. The 'time' in the exhibit is experienced as something laid out in space. However, in a moving picture, as the film goes past on the screen, you travel forwards in the time of the action (or backwards through flashbacks). Both 'time travel' (backwards and forwards in the time of the action) and travel in the space of the action each happen in the time of someone watching the film. Do reactions to the first appearance of films that treat time and space in this novel way explain aspects of the reception of Einstein's work on Special Relativity which deals with the relationship between events separated in time and space?

4 Catalogue of the Ashmolean Museum published in 1836 and quoted in Murray, D. (1904) *Museums: Their History and Use*, Glasgow, p. 229. A more recent example comes from the facade of the British Museum (Natural History) in South Kensington. A figure of Adam graced the front entrance until his fall during the Second World War. Perhaps in this case the fact that he has not been raised up again is as significant as his being there in the first place.

5 See Braudel, F. (1981) *The Structures of Everyday Life*, London: Collins, p. 432.

6 See the *Financial Times*, 19 March 1987, p. 14.
7 These issues affect the very conception of objects. See for example Noble, D. F. (1984) *Forces of Production: A Social History of Industrial Automation*, New York: Knopf.

7

The future of the other: changing cultures on display in ethnographic museums

BRIAN DURRANS

Since the end of the colonial era, museums displaying artefacts from the developing world have been coming to terms with new conditions affecting the way they exhibit other cultures and document them with new collections. Changes in museum practice have usually been made *ad hoc* rather than thought through strategically. There has been a marked, if unsurprising, reluctance to anticipate further shifts of context so that museums might plan appropriate responses. As a result, ethnographic museums face the twenty-first century ill-equipped to deal with reality, and risk substituting antiquarian interests for the concern with contemporary cultures that has guaranteed their vitality in the past. In this chapter I shall review some of the challenges confronting ethnographic museums, and argue for new approaches to research and public work as the best and perhaps the only way to realize their potential in changed conditions.

The stigma of evolution

Ethnographic museums are influenced by the time-machines we conventionally use to represent other people's societies. At the Jorvik Centre, in a series of scenes like film-sets, familiar layers of history are stripped back one after the other – Victorian, Georgian, and so on – until the visitor reaches the reconstructed bustle of Viking York. Most archaeological museums and textbooks work in the same way, except that instead of moving from the present to the past, the progression of exhibits and chapters tends to be from past to present, like time itself. Museums and books dealing with contemporary or recent cultures often borrow this chronological device, suggesting (even if claiming otherwise) that people alive today can be graded on a scale of social evolution. Modern hunters and gatherers, whose type of economy emerged early in the archaeological record, then seem more 'primitive' than cultivators or city-dwellers, whose economies developed more recently.

It should be clear, however, that every contemporary community, whatever its way of life, and whether dominant or dominated, inherits a stake in the whole of human evolution. Whether fractured or continuous, exclusive or interwoven with that of other groups, the past development of all surviving societies has the same time-depth. Within that time, their responses to different cultural and environmental opportunities are as interesting for their unique qualities as for what they share in common. This does not mean they meet the needs of their members equally well or are equally prepared to cope with current or future pressures; but it does mean they cannot be evaluated according to the idea of intrinsic 'primitiveness'. This is an important challenge to which many ethnographic museums have responded as well as they can by stressing the complexity and sophistication of traditional ways of life. In a world where the 'primitive' other has long been the victim of imperial domination, this is one way of attacking the ideology that supports it. But representing other cultures also raises problems about the adequacy of existing evidence and about the attitudes of curators, visitors, and those being represented.

What we know of the past depends partly on what survives into the present, and partly on how we interpret it. What we know of our contemporaries, whoever they are, depends on how far we can share their experiences, either directly through a common way of life, or vicariously through anthropological participant-observer fieldwork, trying to grasp how they see the world. This is never easy to do, but gets harder as the target of analysis shifts outwards from oneself, through family, friends, colleagues, neighbours, and co-citizens, to people of different societies. On this gradient, the shared cultural basis for mutual understanding declines. Differentiating between self and other, and within the category of 'the other', is necessary for any kind of grasp of the world, and is therefore also a potential source of error. How we project ourselves is subject to bias: what people would like others to know about them usually differs from how they actually live. Collectable evidence provides some measure of the material conditions of social life, and, interpreted sensitively, can also give insight into the way people misrepresent those conditions ideologically.

Other peoples' artefacts are among the most 'objective' data we can expect from them, and provide an intelligible baseline from which to begin the more difficult task of interpreting cultural meanings, even though cultural symbolism is never confined to material objects, and the same objects in different cultures may be used, practically and symbolically, in different ways. These caveats remind us that collecting needs to be based on field research if these variables are to be exposed and the objects themselves better understood; but even with scant documentation, an object can still shed some light on its parent culture. Details of where and when it was originally collected may give an accurate if incomplete idea of a culture's provenance in time and space, and thus alert interpretation to the possible influence of historical and geographical circumstances. An object made of iron, for example, implies a minimum set of technological prerequisites for iron-working, or an exchange system for bringing in such objects from outside; a textile similarly implies weaving apparatus, and so on. On the other hand, the cultural meanings attached to objects are enormously variable, and cannot usually be predicted from objects alone. Involvement with ongoing fieldwork, analysis of collections, comparison between collections, and bringing together artefacts and written records can, however, considerably advance our knowledge of different societies through their material cultures, and it is this potential that puts ethnographic museums among the most valuable archives of social knowledge.[1]

When people make and use artefacts or alter their environment, they do so in distinctive ways that amount to unconscious 'statements' about themselves. Sometimes they are aware of this potential communication and transform materials deliberately to inform, as when artists sign their work or committees bury time capsules. Alternatively such 'statements' can be deliberately misleading, as when signatures are forged or rich people conceal their wealth to avoid theft or taxation. Shifting needs, techniques, and influences amend these conscious or unconscious messages but important habits and relations of social life get expressed in the observable or collectable evidence of what people do or leave behind them. This is obviously a basic principle for an anthropology that interprets past and present, and familiar and exotic ways of life, and tries to pass on its findings in lectures, books, journals, or exhibitions.

But the same principle also applies to what curators do with the material they collect. On what basis are objects classified? A distincitive subdiscipline of anthropology, ethnosystematics, is devoted to exploring this subject in many societies around the world. How we categorize other people's artefacts is a similar, equally interesting, but still relatively neglected problem. More than this, it is a particularly interesting and urgent problem because of its great influence on those exposed to the representations that are based upon it.

Cultural property relations

Museums may be valued in the abstract as sociological data banks, and whatever their present shortcomings may be, their collections will probably be even more appreciated in the future than they are today. But their current usefulness is largely determined by what they do and who controls them. This provides a baseline for any future developments we might anticipate or prefer. In their modern form, ethnographic museums, like academic anthropology, emerged as adjuncts of European expansion and colonialism. This by no means reduces anthropology to an ideological device; simply because imperial relations facilitated and made some practical use of the work of specialists from metropolitan societies in other peoples' cultures does not mean that the results of that work are of value only to imperialists. Often, the work was of little interest to nineteenth- and twentieth-century empire-builders; often again, it could be used to modify imperial policies against the wishes of their authors. Moreover, not all empire-building societies cared to collect examples of their subjects' material cultures, or, when they did collect such things, to display them in a certain way. In 1775 the Admiralty was pressing the British Museum to display objects from the Pacific 'in a particular manner and in a distinguished place as a monument of . . . national exertions of British munificence and industry'.[2] On the other hand, the desire for appropriate 'monuments' to British exertions around the world (as if the country, and London in particular, did not already have enough of them), was not always satisfied. In 1930 a Royal Commission recommended that a national ethnographical museum be established, observing that the absence of such a museum 'in the capital city of the British Empire is a glaring defect'.[3] Evidently this was a tolerable defect, since no such separate museum was ever established. The ways ethnographic collections and anthropology in general served and were influenced by colonial policies are complex and contradictory. Nevertheless, the largest and most important ethnographic collections derive from the heyday of colonialism in the nineteenth and early twentieth centuries and have ended up in the major museums of some of the main western powers of that period.[4]

As anthropology developed in Europe, North America, the Antipodes, and most recently in the former colonies, its horizons have broadened. What might once, in the colonial era, have been dismissed as empty rhetoric about universal cultural understanding while real domination was being reinforced, can now be taken seriously for two interrelated reasons. On the one hand, with the imperial system running into unprecedented problems, there is now a prospect of ending that domination for good. On the other hand, the balance of influence in world anthropology is shifting away from its old heartlands, and this trend seems likely to continue.

At the same time, while the imperial system remains, based nowadays on neo-colonial relations between countries, any way of representing other cultures in the museums of metropolitan powers has implications for political links with the developing countries concerned. This is reflected by the interest that diplomats often take in ethnographic displays. Prominent western ethnographic museums increasingly operate in a diplomatic mode, in order to establish or maintain possibilities for further collecting and research, as well to assist the foreign policy objectives of their funding authorities. Except for some private museums, most now refuse to acquire material known to have been smuggled out of its country of origin.

Museums have been less consistent, however, in their attitude to claims for repatriation of artefacts acquired during the colonial period: some have returned things, while others have refused. The relatively small number of cases and the special circumstances of each make it hard to generalize about the approach to restitution claims of museums in possessing nations. Soviet and East European experience suggests that close control over museums by state organizations in countries otherwise sympathetic to the predicament of Third World nations by no means guarantees that claimed objects are returned as requested, while elsewhere a degree of independence from the state gives museums the option of meeting or – more often – refusing requests.

The period in which restitution has been seriously debated is not yet long enough to reveal clear trends, but it seems likely that nations already well entrenched as neo-colonial powers will probably have little to gain by agreeing to return cultural property, while the more *arriviste* nations, anxious for their economies to compensate for earlier missed opportunities, may be tempted to encourage trade-offs in the museum field. Examples here might be Sweden, which never had an empire in the first place, and countries like Belgium, the Netherlands, and (West) Germany, all of which lost major overseas territories without arranging an orderly transfer of political power to facilitate strong economic ties after independence. Another factor influencing the outcome of restitution claims in the coming decades is how ethnographic material, and the Third World in general, feature in the cultural life of the metropolitan country concerned. Paradoxically, where these are imaginatively presented and enjoy a high prestige – as they are beginning to through forms of multicultural education, for example – pressure for the return of objects might be resisted on the grounds that they are playing an important part in the contemporary culture of the possessing nation, thus transcending arguments based only on the historical conditions in which they were originally acquired. Conversely a narrow evaluation of national culture may so marginalize the products of other societies as to make them seem, from the perspective of the possessing country, expendable and returnable.

The important point is that on both sides of the argument, deeper implications tend to be neglected, whether for the future control of museum work, for wider co-operation between the countries concerned, for the prospects of new replication technology or alternative ideas for the 'ownership' of universally valued cultural property subject to multiple and legally irreconcilable claims.[5] As far as most countries are concerned, even including active claimant states, the restitution issue is only one factor influencing the prospects of additional or alternative forms of co-operation that are being sought for the preservation of cultural heritage and the continued growth of collections and international scholarship based upon them.

It is possible, however, that neo-colonial pressure may prise some items out of established collections if direct appeals from claimant states fail. Neo-colonialism and transnational corporations are major factors in the world of ethnographic museums. If exhibitions and catalogues can hardly avoid mentioning imperial dominance, this is discreetly done so as to close its history at the end of the colonial era itself, at political independence. As a result, transnational companies, which today perpetuate the imperial system in its neo-colonial form, feature only in the list of exhibition sponsors. For investment and to boost their corporate images, some of them even collect ethnographic art.

If there are definite limits to the kinds of representations that can be expected from this international setting, there may also be partially compensating opportunities. First, exhibitions with a 'diplomatic' component may be the only practical way for museums to acquire scientifically valuable collections of interest to future generations. Second, the balance of advantage in any diplomatically initiated exchange may go beyond the calculations of either side. Whether or not multinationals profit from the experience, there may be advantage for developing countries in associated trade deals, especially when these involve competition between rival capitalist countries or with socialist ones. Better cultural exposure for a Third World nation beyond its own borders is not facilitated by corporate sponsors or other states as a way to get to heaven; it is, rather, a means to advance their own worldly interests. But such means may incidentally help develop wider public knowledge of and sympathy for the predicament of the developing country concerned and for the developing world in general.

The prevalent images of most Third World countries among the public of former colonial powers are nevertheless racist or patronizing, reflecting historical experience of dominance rather than sympathy or solidarity. Provided it is done thoughtfully, re-presenting the cultures of such countries more on their own terms therefore does something to redress the historical balance, but good intentions or a commitment to 'realism' cannot guarantee that stereotypes will not be reinforced in other, unforeseen ways. Conditions of life in many developing countries cannot be reproduced directly in a museum setting: to attempt to do so may simply confirm prejudices. Different visitors respond to different messages, so this must be taken into account in planning any exhibition designed to bring people closer to an understanding of how another culture operates. Provided it is based on detailed knowledge, there is no reason why a critical attitude cannot also be encouraged towards some aspects of other peoples' way of life – the dowry system in India, for example, or female circumcision in parts of Africa. Simply acknowledging the extraordinary cultural achievements of other peoples is, however, a stage that many in Britain (and elsewhere) have yet to reach. Accepting these achievements is not, of course, particularly radical, and remains compatible with a neo-colonial ideology, leaving the basis of continuing exploitation intact, but that is no reason to dismiss it. If this limited but important degree of understanding were attained on a large scale in Britain, it would indicate substantial progress in shaking off the ideological legacy of colonialism. Better appreciation of other peoples' cultures makes their demand for full independence that much more persuasive.

Beyond this, any progressive programme for museums in the immediate future must confront the problem of reduced funding and other attacks on access and scholarship. Piecemeal objections to particular restrictive policies are patently insufficient when such policies are rooted in a deep economic and political crisis. But in the present 'postmodernist' anomie there is also a related need to reassert a suitable theory or philosophy in which museums have a role in a preferred future. Since the increasingly dominant, postmodernist cultural style of our own society involves an effacement of history, even an awareness of subjective bias in representing other cultures can end up legitimizing how things are.[6] This it does by collapsing the critical distance between ourselves and the real world – the basis for comparison – that alone can guide interpretation and social action. Existing problems, open to practical solutions either directly or through deeper structural changes, are then denied by definition (becoming 'opportunities') or made to seem inevitable. At the theoretical level, therefore, it is essential to retain a strong sense of critical distance and of historical time. In this effort, ethnographic descriptions and collections are immediately useful in achieving a distance from which to criticize our own society. But this is only a form of resistance, a first step in formulating an appropriate response to postmodernist ideology. The second step is to expose the systematic constraints on museum work that keep published or exhibited comparisons safe or obscure. These steps can be taken not as an unrealistically new departure, but in parallel with existing modes of representation, enlarging the scope for serious interrogation of collections, displays, methods, and cultures, including our own.

Museums and images for the Third World

International cultural links can belatedly help establish or assist museums outside the western world. Museums in developing countries are fewer and generally less well funded and staffed than their counterparts in the west, but the contrast between the best and the worst is not very different from what can be found elsewhere. In most developing states, local, regional, and national museums operate not just as repositories for things of the past, but as instruments for building new national identities, whether the effort involved is genuinely mass-based and democratic or sectional and élitist. Some are wide-ranging cultural centres with a strong community focus. Others are sadly neglected, doing little more than keeping the curator in a job.

We know that museums emerged from classical antecedents as a peculiarly western phenomenon in the eighteenth and nineteenth centuries. During their development they have acquired many culture-specific features, like grandiose and sometimes intimidating architecture, the tendency to put more material on display than anyone can hope to see in a single visit, and either too much information on labels and panels or else too little. The basic functions of museums as they have evolved are to collect, preserve, research, and exhibit – implying two relevant 'audiences': the present-day public, and posterity. How far is this basic model relevant to Third World countries, and how far can museums carrying out these basic activities in the developing world take on additional characteristics that are innovative or appropriate to local traditions?

How far they succeed in the objectives required of them is usually determined, in the last analysis, by the wider problems that most developing nations have to deal with – such as economic dependency, inter-ethnic conflict, and neo-colonial intrigue – rather than, as is sometimes suggested, an abstract 'unsuitability' of museums and academic work derived from a dominant colonial culture. The idea that such institutions, as they are usually understood, are appropriate for some parts of the world but not for underdeveloped countries – where 'distortions' of their established functions are more or less inevitable – is effectively Eurocentric and racist even when it takes the apparently progressive form of recognizing the right of other cultures to resist the encroachment of western values.

Rights are meaningful only when there is a context in which they can be exercised. While prevailing inequality in world economics, politics, and communications denies such a context, past and present influences from the west have created demands that distort traditional culture within developing countries and yet cannot be satisfied from outside. Give people schools and they will demand

152

universities; give them a reason for taking cultural heritage seriously, or for using it to accumulate 'cultural capital', and they will attempt something along the lines of what museums do in the west. To argue that museums are not an authentic part of many cultures, and that people have the right not to 'museumize' their societies, is fine but beside the point. Coca Cola, blue jeans, electric guitars, and higher vocational education are not promoted, desired, or consumed simply as accessible objects; they also symptomize a whole repertoire of goods, services, institutions, and values from which eclectic choices can be made. For those marketing a western way of life, and also those wary of it, the aim is for only some of these things to be accepted while others are refused; but the stock-lists and shopping-lists rarely coincide. Thus the concept of the museum may come from the west, but its appeal cannot be explained only in terms of any prestige that western values may possess: on the contrary, it is attractive to many Third World countries precisely because it offers a means of recapturing, elaborating, or inventing their own distinctive cultural traditions as a countermeasure to past or present domination.

The view that such institutions – like high technology – are 'inappropriate' to developing countries also implies that museological and academic work cannot be improved by exposure to new experience, or that any new challenge to how they have operated in the past threatens their basic functions. But there are many ways that museums can carry out their traditional tasks more effectively by attracting visitors and playing an active social role. Even if they sometimes put different kinds of collections and displays under the same roof because of lack of alternatives, or uncritically apply the social and museological policy conventions of imperial powers, Third World museums need not develop the same culture-specific features as those in Europe and North America.

Because of their different history, Third World ethnographic museums occupy a different place among their countries' cultural institutions than western museums do in theirs. The peasants of continental Europe and their emigrant offshoots in North America merit museums of their own, a legacy of nineteenth-century bourgeois nationalism that sought the allegiance of the *Volk* as it drew inspiration from their real or supposed traditions. In the larger cities of these countries, if you want to see artefacts from the Third World and its ancestral cultures, you don't seek them primarily among fine art or archaeological collections; you go to – of all places – natural history museums. This is because, in the late eighteenth and nineteenth centuries, evolutionary theory was applied to society as well as to the natural world, and was the basis for arranging museum displays. In accordance with imperial ideology, colonized societies were not thought complex or important enough to deserve museums of their own, as were provided for ancient Mediterranean civilizations or the high arts and sciences of modern capitalist states.

In a recent television interview the exiled South African-born pianist, Abdullah Ibrahim, recalled a Black figure in traditional dress, displayed like a game animal in a glass case, that disturbed his childhood visits to the Cape Town Museum. At the Smithsonian Institution's National Museum of Natural History in Washington DC, contemporary visitors, young Black and native Americans among them, find plaster mannequins posed in ways of life that have now almost completely disappeared. Outside the display cases are several Black figures – larger than lifesize bronzes – including one that embodies the romantic idea of the noble savage: an improbably naked West African carving a wooden object. As a figure, it is rendered accurately rather than in any kind of caricature, unless the 'naked savage' is a relevant stereotype (most carvers, in Africa or elsewhere, work with clothes on). The convention of a giant bronze nude would fit perfectly well into an environment like an art gallery or sculpture garden. But this one is in an ethnographic exhibition, alongside real artefacts and realistic images. You would not expect to find an outsize sculpture of a nude Caucasian, whether whittling an artefact or just looking decorous, in an exhibition of European or Euro-American folk culture.

What classification of reality do such images express? What does the classification itself imply about the kind of society in which it is generated? The idea that scholars and curators should just get on with a disinterested pursuit of knowledge is harder to support the clearer the interaction between that knowledge and the 'outside' world becomes. Museums, after all, are nothing if not public institutions; even private ones depend on visitors. Moreover, it was the colonial domination of most of the world that furnished the ethnographic museums and galleries of Europe and North America with their collections. Museums not only benefited from this experience by inheriting collections, but also helped legitimize it through their displays. Museums could play a legitimizing role, however, only because of their relative autonomy as cultural institutions from the economic and political business of running an empire. In order to work effectively as legitimizers of imperial exploitation, they had to retain an image of detached objectivity, and the simplest way to retain that image was by working as they had done before, with a positivist orientation and commitment to science. The same orientation also allowed museums to acquire things from other parts of the world where Britain had no particular imperial designs, and to show objects that not only legitimized colonial domination in a general way but also simultaneously undermined its logic, at least to some extent, by revealing evidence of the technical and aesthetic sophistication of peoples who were otherwise denigrated as needing the benefit of British civilization. A degree of detachment from colonialism was therefore essential to the role of ethnographic museums in supporting it, and a degree of support for it was equally a condition of their independence. The positivist orientation of museums and anthropology was in any case appropriate to a stage of rapid capitalist development.

But does this entanglement with past and present politics mean that nothing can be salvaged from the traditional project of museum anthropology? That project, as generally understood, was to help those interested to understand the human condition more deeply through exposure to less familiar aspects of it. Is this just a Eurocentric affectation? A strongly relativist view suggests that it is. Museums are increasingly criticized not only for the way they represent certain themes in exhibitions, but also for their choice of theme in the first place. Sometimes this criticism is legitimate: too little thought is given to the likely effects of displays on visitors. But often the criticism is naive precisely because so little is known about how museums influence their public relative to people's prior assumptions and the impact of other media. Critics might therefore claim that a given exhibition 'represents' something unintended by the curator; but while this is probably true, it is hard to specify and substantiate and would remain a risk in any kind of exhibition. If there can be a kind of knowledge that is not just propaganda, how can it be developed in a way that takes account of the lives of real people who are not merely anthroplogists' informants? How, in other words, can ethnographic museums be sensitive to contemporary social issues (that is to say, politics) without abandoning their legitimate objectives?

It might be argued that ethnographic museums provide collections, displays, and specialized research techniques that complement the work of anthropologists in colleges and elsewhere. This is true up to a point, although by historical accident rather than design. While academic and 'applied' anthropologists are now

engaged in an enormous variety of research programmes in societies of different kinds, their museum counterparts are still largely
preoccupied with relatively small-scale 'tribal' and exotic cultures.
For practical reasons, the material dimension of life in complex
industrial settings is almost completely ignored by museum
anthropologists, although the scope of anthropology is supposed to
be universal. Even in social history museums the challenge of
comprehensively documenting the present-day culture of industrial society is more often discussed than taken up. This not only
perpetuates the impression that such museums are exclusively
outward-focused, but also discourages comparisons with more
familiar cultures and therefore discourages comparison in general.
It is no accident that the contemporary bias in ethnographic
museums is towards monographic presentations of particular
cultures or limited comparison within regions. While detailed,
localized studies are essential if there is to be anything to compare
in the first place, these are usually carried out most productively
when they are geared to some larger theoretical motive that gives
point to comparison. In contrast with the academic disciplines from
which they claim inspiration, the bias of ethnographic and social
history museums is, with few exceptions, particularistic and empi-
rical.

The everyday life of ethnographic objects

Pressure toward more mundane, representative, and 'democratic'
collections and exhibitions may help overcome this defect. Ironically one sign of hope is the problem museums have in collecting
objects now highly valued in the art market. Things that would
once have been received as donations increasingly go through
dealers, and the price usually puts them beyond the reach of most
museums. As the market seeks more and more lowly categories of
objects to satisfy its appetite, so those with such artefacts in their
attics have become more aware of the prices they can fetch, and
more in need of the money. For economic reasons, if a museum has
an acquisitions policy at all, it is now more likely to obtain contemporary or recent things brought back by travellers than to buy older
and more expensive ones. But there are also dangers in the same
process. Much of the earlier material from societies that were later
drastically changed by colonial contact has survived into the
present only through the care of ethnographic museum curators,

and its documentary importance is now unique. For private collectors and dealers to retain artefacts on an increasing scale, when these could be used in museums for the scientific documentation of relict societies, is a form of privatization of history that posterity will not easily forgive, however unreasonable it might be, given the present character of British capitalism, to expect exemption for ethnographic objects when so much else is commoditized.

Ethnographic objects have in any case invaded the key arbiters of established good taste and fashionability in our society: the art galleries, glossy magazines, and television. In almost any city, it is now possible to see works of art from tribal cultures of Africa, North and South America, the Pacific, and elsewhere, in museums, art galleries, or the showrooms of private dealers. Some of this material was once hardly even noticed outside a narrow circle of anthropologists, museum curators, eccentric collectors, and avant-garde artists. Today, ethnic sculptures are admired outside their original cultures for qualities that usually derive more from aesthetic conventions of the west than from those of their makers.

It is standard practice to present such objects as self-evidently artistic. At the same time, western connoisseurship may be able to acquire, at least for some categories of object, a grasp of aesthetic criteria capable of differentiating standards of artistic achievement that would also make sense in the original context. If it is possible to understand another culture even to some extent from its material output, then there is clearly a point in studying and collecting it, and beginning this task by investigating how material objects are created and deployed in their original setting.

What is curious, however, is that while 'ethnic art objects' have been cut loose from their social moorings by the western art world, to be displayed in flattering solitude, most ethnographic museums have been obsessed with doing just the opposite. For them, a prerequisite for understanding the art object is an appreciation of its original meaning(s) for those who made and used it. Some museums of western art have also been moving in this direction; no longer content simply to hang a painting in a gallery, they sometimes provide a package of background information that allows it to be assessed in something approaching its original context.

These communicative techniques have much to commend them, for it is certainly true that the world of Vermeer or Caravaggio is as remote and unintelligible to most contemporary gallery-visitors as are the Amazon rain-forests or the highlands of New Guinea. But there are two major problems with the idea that only the lack of sufficient 'background' information prevents anyone appreciating an object aesthetically as it would have been appreciated in its original setting. These are worth considering because of their implications for how museums might exhibit ethnographic material.

First, appreciating the social and cultural setting of an object does not exhaust and is not a substitute for an appreciation of the object itself. The object might be experienced through a combination of sense-impressions, each responding to a different quality or configuration of qualities. These qualities may depend not simply on the material or form of the object, or on how it is confronted, but on a complex interplay between these variables. If an object is made to be seen in a particular position, against a specific background, from a certain angle, with a range of other objects implicitly in mind, then its creator will take this into account when deciding its form. If the object is then viewed in another position, against another background, from another angle, or by an observer familiar with a different range of other objects, it will be impossible to reproduce the aesthetic effect intended or anticipated by the artist. Since sensory aptitudes are culturally varied, it might in any case be impossible to reproduce this aesthetic experience even if all the circumstances were faithfully repeated. But despite these strictures, it seems likely that certain formal qualities – such as scale, proportion, texture, 'balance', or 'harmony' in the distribution of detail in available space, or combinations of these – given to objects in one culture are nevertheless capable of being appreciated in others. Even if the original and subsequent aesthetic experiences are very different, there may still be a degree of shared sensitivity to rather generalized formal qualities and this may be a measure of overlap in basic cultural orientation. That there must always be some overlap of this kind is a corollary of being human. In other words, context counts for a very great deal, and is always worth knowing about, but it does not cancel certain abstract qualities that artefacts can relay between cultures, irrespective of context, such as in a museum. These qualities may play an important role in the aesthetic appreciation of objects.

The second objection to the argument that an aesthetic experience can only be reproduced in another culture given sufficient information is based on knowing how a museum display works. Reconstructing a version of the original context of a displayed object apparently conceals, as effectively as putting it on a pedestal, the real new context in which the object is being offered up to

14 Artefacts shown 'as found' – or as plausible – in part of one society. Context of cultural function alone; classification hidden behind artful naturalism. From the Museum of Mankind's temporary exhibition, 'Vasna: inside an Indian village', 1982. (Courtesy of the Trustees of the British Museum)

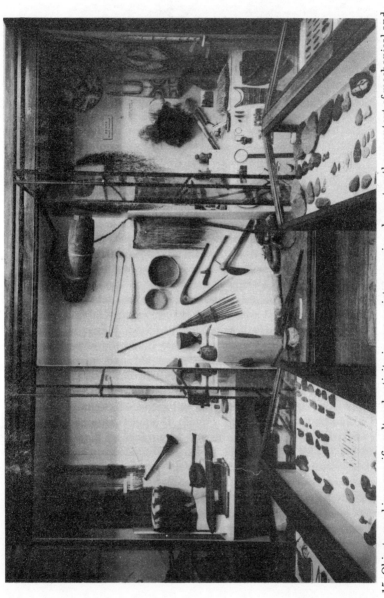

15 Objects used in a specific cultural activity in one society or region shown together: context of mechanical and cultural function. Classification imposed but looks more 'natural'. From the British Museum Ethnography Gallery, permanent exhibition, 1968. (Courtesy of the Trustees of the British Museum)

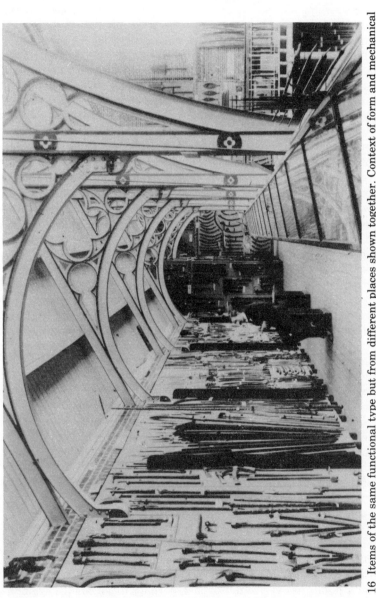

16 Items of the same functional type but from different places shown together. Context of form and mechanical function; classification obviously imposed. Henry Balfour, the first curator at the Pitt Rivers Museum, University of Oxford, photographed working in the top gallery, c. 1896 (Photo: Pitt Rivers Museum, Oxford)

experience. This is true whether the original context is conveyed verbally in information panels or non-verbally in an 'authentic' reconstruction. The wider setting in which the object is now experienced has to be taken into account if a museum object is to be appreciated in all its significance. The museum display is a context in its own right, and not just more or less of the original context it may seek to reproduce. In fact, the greater the effort to 'naturalize' the artefact in a display, the more it may also look alienated from its original context. The more stridently a reconstruction proclaims its 'authenticity', the more obvious its artificiality will become. The standard experience for a museum visitor contains a tension between these two sides of the museum object's predicament. Museums tend to be informative about the 'naturalized', original context of the object, yet silent about its alienation. To redress the balance, they might draw visitors' attention to the circumstances in which objects were not only made in their original setting but also acquired by the museum in which they are now displayed. How have they been exhibited in the past, and why are they now being shown differently? This need not be done routinely for every exhibition, but could well provoke intelligent questioning if combined with other types of display. Just as some kinds of objects tend to be shown in display cases while others make more sense in a 'reconstructed' setting, so visitors' experience of almost everything shown in museums would be enhanced by highlighting the 'transactional history' that brought a particular object or collection into its current, museum context. This narrow history could be linked not only with wider historical experiences such as explorations or colonial relations but also with earlier uses and presentations of the material by previous generations of anthro-pologists and curators, emphasizing the value of reinterpreting collections. The growth of a museum's collections could also be indicated, giving an interesting angle on its history, with charts showing which major categories of material came from which part of the world at different periods through different kinds of people (missionaries, colonial servants, travellers, dealers, and so on); and some attempt could be made to interpret this information.

Providing a variety of display styles, of types of artefacts, and of angles on original and subsequent contexts would in this way enlarge visitors' perceptions of museums themselves, and alert them to the idea that since the relationship between museums and their public has varied in the past, perhaps it can change again in the future. Yet presenting exhibitions, even in an apparently satisfying variety, does not mean that visitors necessarily experience what curators would like them to. We can say that visitors may be encouraged to think deeply about certain specialized themes if these are featured in exhibitions, but experiencing an exhibition is a more complex phenomenon than is usually allowed for. Whatever the past permutations of display techniques, the chances are that many of the most enduring and important responses of visitors were unintended and unpredicted by designers and curators; people seem to experience idiosyncratic and mysteriously enriching reactions to displays that professional critics and the curators themselves might not share.[7] The appropriate curatorial reaction to this is not despair but a determination to cater sensitively to the public's imagination by means of a variety of display styles and themes that between them will help prevent visitors becoming complacent about what they expect to find in an ethnographic museum. It also argues for trying different methods of conveying thought-provoking information, and for investigating visitors' attitudes more thoroughly.

The 'contextualizing' effort of many ethnographic museums, especially over the last thirty years, has not just omitted what is special and interesting about the museum context itself; it has also abandoned a still-significant aspect of the traditional view of ethnographic artefacts: how they represent alternative solutions to technical problems experienced in most societies. The 'context' with which such museums have been preoccupied is a very partial and atomistic one. Instead of explicitly classifying the world's cultures in evolutionary terms between primitive and advanced, apparently progressive museums have treated them relativistically – each a uniquely 'valid' configuration. Exhibitions have tended to stress the complexity and integration, and (at most) the regional affiliations of cultures, rather than their susceptibility to change or how they compare with others in different times, locations, or degrees of complexity. This conforms to the dominant paradigm of academic anthropology of at least a generation before, and thereby confirms how marginal museum ethnography has been to mainstream anthropological thinking.

A new role for the museum?

Besides this time-lag in their dominant background assumptions, academic and museum anthropology have different relationships with the public. Although in some respects this has put museum anthropology at a relative disadvantage, the public role of museums, imaginatively interpreted, might now provide an opportunity for revitalizing anthropology itself. Museum ethnographers do not carry out one set of functions as if they were academic anthropologists, and a second set specifically appropriate to their museum. Exhibitions are not a completely separate activity within museum anthropology: most aspects of museum work relate to a public function. Neither are exhibitions the only way in which anthropology, even within museums, reaches a wider public. Nevertheless, alongside television, ethnographic museums provide perhaps the main public face for anthropology. More than television, they can legitimize certain ideas and attitudes, since the prestige of the museum is generally greater than that of modern mass media. Far more than academic anthropology, museum anthropology is exposed to public scrutiny and criticism. Because of their subjects, ethnographic displays are often widely reported on, and increasingly in the countries from which the displayed material derives. This exposure to criticism is enhanced by the reliance of many more important or prominent exhibitions on some kind of diplomatic co-operation, as referred to earlier.

In Britain, most ethnographic collections, from the small to substantial, are housed in more general museums typically funded by local authorities; only the largest is in a national museum (the Museum of Mankind, the Ethnography Department of the British Museum), while the two next largest (in the Pitt Rivers Museum at Oxford, and the Cambridge University Museum of Archaeology and Anthropology) and a handful of others are in universities. The fourth largest, in the Horniman Museum in south London, has up to now been local authority based. Public interest and display activity tends to be greater in national and local authority museums than in most university ones, so it is not surprising that the public image of the ethnographic museum that was also influential among academics themselves tended to be that of an unsettling and relatively unprestigious interface between an apparently freewheeling academic discipline and the more restrictive world of public controversy or triviality. For a long time, this helped make the prospect of working in such a place less attractive than a college department for most anthropologists in Britain.

This contrast between academic and museum-based anthropology has remained essentially unchanged for half a century, but what has definitely changed in recent years is the way it is interpreted. Partly because of the coincidence of economic crisis with an overproduction of graduate anthropologists (relative to the existing job market), ethnographic museums have been able to appoint more highly qualified and field-experienced anthropologists to their staff than ever before. If these people became more enthusiastic about the idea of working in museums than their predecessors did, it was probably because they already anticipated their future job prospects before graduating or completing their postgraduate research; but in any case, the prestige of a formerly undervalued job is bound to rise if alternatives are scarce. Although a degree of frustration with established expectations is probably inevitable in these conditions, these newer curators tend to find ways to apply their anthropological ideas in their museum work, and to some extent they may help shake up existing procedures. But the traditional disciplines of the job have not been abandoned. For anyone to apply academic interpretations in a public context requires an ability not only to think and write clearly but also to assess priorities and objectives. As museums themselves become more cost-conscious, their staff are encouraged to acquire appropriate organizational skills. People with a specialized academic background therefore find themselves pressured from different sides to perform more effectively in a public role. It would be shortsighted simply to resent the erosion of specialized curatorial research time that this pressure undoubtedly involves. As museums take their enduring public responsibilities more seriously, new prospects are likely to emerge for anthropological research. Much depends on who is exerting the pressure. If it comes only from administrators, the advantage is likely to be limited to efficiency. But if curators themselves recognize that engaging with the public can enhance their work, the advantages might be shifts in scholarly objectives and in the whole orientation of ethnographic museums.

Restricted funds and growing demands on staff lead to the idea that museums must 'adapt or die'.[8] Many existing procedures certainly need rethinking, whatever the incentive to do so. However, the 'streamlining' of museums currently proposed ought to raise the neglected question of what museums are being adapted to. This requires a wider interpretation of the social role of ethnographic and other museums than most specialized curators have been ready to attempt. Once the idea of adaptation or 'new realism' is questioned in this way, several alternative scenarios can be considered. The main thing is not to accept as inevitable the existing, historically conditioned relationship between museums on the one hand and the public on the other. Harsh new realities

might set in motion changes not just in museums or their administrative structures, but in whole sets of assumptions and relationships undreamt of by the apostles of cost-effectiveness.

There is no reason why insightful academic research in or about
ethnographic collections or the cultures from which they derive
need be limited to the labouring of self-sacrificing individuals in
libraries or storerooms. The general level of education in our
society, even despite the current falling-off resulting from restricted funding for schools and colleges, is still quite high. The
proportion of television and printed media coverage of other cultures and anthropological insights is probably greater than in the
past. If museums begin to interact with their public rather than
just expect visitors to come to exhibitions or attend lectures or
film-shows, the impact could be enormous. Some signs of the
potential can be seen in the way school students' imagination is
captured by creative and 'hands-on' experiences of different kinds.

But these are still 'services' provided by museums for their
audiences. Much more exciting is the idea of harnessing the
imagination, insight, and experience of visitors in the interest of
the main objectives of the museum. Some museums have
discovered that visitors like to see exhibitions being constructed,
and occasionally provide a route or vantage-point from which work
in progress can be observed. Given the increasing reliance of
museums on voluntary assistance or on sponsorship money to
mount exhibitions, it seems only a small step to have at least some
displays put on by members of the public themselves. With curatorial supervision, students or others might plan a display from the
beginning, devising new ways for representing objects that might
not have occurred to professionals, and complementing their own
exhibitions. 'Draft' previews of exhibitions might be tested on
interested members of the public before the final version is decided;
critical comments and practical help might then be obtained to
improve the end result.[9]

This need be only one aspect of greater public participation. It
might be more productive to have people help with basic research
and identification tasks. Most museums have significant numbers
of objects in their collections of unknown purpose, provenance, or
even material. Few curators, however extensive their knowledge of
the ethnographic material culture of particular regions, can be
expected to identify all these things. On the other hand, it is
possible to contact members of the public – whether they would
normally visit the museum or not – who have special knowledge,

either of particular parts of the world, or of certain technologies, and who might be able to suggest likely identifications. One way of contacting people would be to arrange identification sessions to which they are also encouraged to bring things in their own possession. An extra spin-off might be new acquisitions for the museum, although this would not be the main objective.

People from many different countries can be found in Britain, either as permanent or temporary immigrants, or else as short-stay residents or tourists. For at least some cultures represented in ethnographic museums, their views might be a valuable addition to what is already known about the collections, as well as a source of potential future acquisitions to fill gaps and create ensembles suitable for display. Where local authority museums are encouraged to use their resources in anti-racist and multicultural education, some of these opportunities are already being used; but the potential also exists where this kind of pressure has not yet been or is unlikely to be applied. If social change encourages changes in museum practice, it can also bring about a shift in the social role of museums and other cultural institutions. A less élitist image could greatly extend the influence of ethnographic museums. New perceptions of the public as an audience and collaborator could enhance the appreciation of anthropology and encourage the systematic cross-cultural comparison of ethnographic material, especially if contemporary mass culture also becomes a legitimate focus for collecting and exhibitions. Greater social accountability should also mean democratizing the governing bodies of museums so they represent wider community interests. At present, it is not merely that women, young people, consumers, staff, Black and working-class citizens are under-represented on such bodies, or absent altogether, but that this is not even recognized as a problem. In any country, culture of whatever level is too important to be permanently entrusted to cultural élites.

One of the reasons why museums have been reluctant to involve members of the public in these ways in the past is that curators have been scared to reveal that they are not, after all, the omniscient experts of popular imagination. There is also the institutional affectation that a museum should be able to mount all its exhibitions and conduct all its legitimate research activities using its own resources. That may be a justifiable view, and argues for renewed pressure to improve public funding, but provided existing staff complements are not put at risk there is no reason why freely given public enthusiasm, that demands nothing, or nothing unreasonable in return, should be less acceptable than private sponsorship money. Besides, the key criterion is whether exhibitions and other ways of reaching a wider public, and the collections and associated documentation that will be handed on to future generations, will be enhanced or not. The ideas suggested seem likely to help in these respects. Whether or not such ideas will be able to secure a useful future for museums that some myopic critics have already written off as relics of colonialism depends only in part on what the museums themselves do. But if the main task of relevant specialists is to protect ethnographic collections and the enlightening study of cultural variability from the crises that lie ahead, this might at least be done with optimism and panache.

Acknowledgement

I am grateful to Malcolm McLeod for helpful criticism of an earlier draft of this paper. Any remaining errors, bias, and unjustified assumptions are, of course, my own.

Notes and references

1 For examples of documentary and research uses of ethnographic artefact collections, see Cantwell, A.-M. E., Griffin, J. B., and Roth-schild, N. A. (eds) (1981) *The Research Potential of Anthropological Museum Collections*, Annals of the New York Academy of Sciences, vol. 376.

2 Miller, E. (1973) *That Noble Cabinet*, London: André Deutsch, p. 75.

3 ibid., p. 327.

4 On the colonial background of anthropology, see Asad, T. (ed.) (1973) *Anthropology and the Colonial Encounter*, London; divergent views are given in Berreman, G. D., Gjessing, G., and Gough, K. (1968) 'Social responsibilities symposium', *Current Anthropology* 9 (5): 391–435. On the role of museums in the same context, see Avé, J. B. (1980) 'Ethnographical museums in a changing world', in W. R. van Gulik, H. S. van der Straaten, and G. D. van Wengen (eds) *From Field-case to Show-case*, Amsterdam, pp. 11–28.

5 The term 'custodianship' might be preferable to 'ownership' since 'it allows for the concept of universal culture': Mulvaney, J. (1985) 'A question of values: museums and cultural property', in I. McBryde (ed.), *Who Owns the Past?*, Melbourne, pp. 86–98.

6 Jameson, F. (1984) 'Postmodernism or the cultural logic of late capital-ism', *New Left Review* 145: 53–92 (see especially the section on 'The abolition of critical distance', 85–8).

7 On this aspect of experiencing ethnographic exhibitions, see Clifford, J. (1985) 'Objects and selves – an afterword', in G. W. Stocking, jun. (ed.)

Objects and Others: Essays on Museums and Material Culture, History of Anthropology, vol. 3, Madison, pp. 236–46.

8 For this abrasive approach, see Cossons, N. (1987) 'Adapt or die – dangers of a dinosaur mentality', *The Listener* 117 (3007) 16 April: 18–21. For a stimulating perspective on anthropological museums in particular that raises many useful points yet fails to recognize that there might be a case for changing the context rather than just adapting museums to it, see Ames, M. M. (1986) *Museums, the Public and Anthropology: A Study in the Anthropology of Anthropology*, Ranchi Anthropology Series, vol. 9, Vancouver and New Delhi.

9 I owe the idea of draft exhibitions to Len Pole, curator of the Saffron Walden Museum, who mentioned it in a paper presented to the Association of Social Anthropologists' and Museum Ethnographers' Group's conference on cultural representations held at the British Museum in February 1986.

8

'Astonished and somewhat terrified': the preservation and development of aural culture

JEREMY SILVER

Sound and society

Sound is one of the basic senses through which we experience the world. In a recent essay called 'Le Bruit c'est l'autre', Marion Segaud wrote:

> Sound makes space comprehensible; it introduces time, rhythm, action, all of which are the active ingredients of daily life.[1]

Such is the definitive power of sound in our everyday life, it locates and renders comprehensible much of our experience of our fellow human beings, of animal life, of geo-climatic changes, and of machines – everything which is 'other' than ourselves.

For those of us fortunate enough to be in possession of most of our sensory faculties, our lives are filled with movement and with sound. Yet there are powerful factors which, until very recently, had induced us to create the still, silent worlds of books and museums whenever we have sought to set forth some detailed exposition of a part of our own or of other cultures. On one level it is the case that, almost since its invention, recorded sound seems to have been the exclusive domain of commercial and 'media' professionals. This is, perhaps, an inevitable result of the close commercial involvement in the research and development of sound recording and playback technology. It is also the result of legislation; the Copyright Act, 1956, makes the familiar provision for brief quotation of extracts of written texts without the need to pay royalties. Such provision is clearly essential for the pursuit of academic research, for criticism, and for journalism. Yet the Act makes no similar provision for sound recordings nor is any likely to be made in the new legislation. For society as a whole an ignorance of the principles and potential of audio technology has led directly to its construction as a specialized field; sound is not participatory but something either to be consumed (a number one single) or to be just plain ignored (muzak).

The field of recorded sound is so vast that it is almost impossible to talk about it as a whole without focusing on particular areas such as broadcasting or recorded music or oral history, but all of these are linked by the medium that carries them and to some extent all suffer from the same restrictive cultural views of who can make recordings, who or what can be their subject, and who can merely consume the results.

This sense of alienation from the technology also effectively obscures some more profound difficulties which derive from the highly literal nature of liberal humanist culture. It is surely as a result of this traditional influence that in educational contexts, in exhibitions, and in scholarly research, problems are so frequently experienced in making use of recorded sound. Similarly it is as a result of this orthodoxy that researches into sound recordings themselves are rarely met with the kind of recognition which would give them broader cultural validity. Even some of the most widely listened to forms of speech recording – the BBC's frequently excellent radio drama productions – suffer from inadequate critical attention. Esslin recently commented:

> It is one of the tragedies of a mass medium like radio that a play that may have one hundred thousand listeners – a thousand times more than say, the audience in an experimental theatre – will get far less critical attention than any Soho lunchtime production.[2]

This kind of negative response typifies a failure to recognize the validity of recorded audio materials as cultural documents which has been widespread in many of our academic, educational, and cultural institutions.

Ironically, even as these difficulties have been encountered, western culture has become increasingly oral in character. As Ong observes:

> Many are aware of the marked orality of our culture today when compared with the culture of thirty years ago, before the

electronic potential first mobilized in the 1840s with the tele-graph had matured and become interiorized in life styles and world views.[3]

More recently non-professionals have grown more confident in the use of the technologies of sound recording and production. The last twenty years have seen a tremendous increase of activity in the field of oral history, paralleled by more locally oriented, participa-tory forms of radio (BBC local radio began experimentally in 1967 and grew rapidly throughout the early 1970s) and by a strong growth of independent record labels. More recently still, the growth of CB, pirate, and community radio stations, and cable transmis-sions, have contributed to a much wider dissemination of all kinds of audio communication. The centrality of sound has indeed 'become interiorised in life styles and world views', but the rapid increase and diversification of the contexts in which sound record-ings are made and used has hardly been reflected or built upon in the culture's activities of self-documentation, interpretation, and exposition. The potential to tune in to all kinds of sounds on the radio, to have a constant source of recordings on disc and cassette, and to be in oral contact with others on the telephone are all aspects of a widely shared 'life-style'. Yet little has been explored of the significance of these changes or of their effects on social relations and cultural development.

While many cultural institutions currently retain collections of audio materials, there is an absence of consciously developed strategies which archivists, curators, teachers, and researchers might adopt to improve the exploitation of ever-increasing quanti-tites of recorded materials and to render them more accessible to users. In order to move towards the development of such strategies, it is necessary to examine in some detail the function and status of sound in a wider social and historical context.

The history of sound recording is little over a century old. Edison first recorded his own voice, reciting 'Mary had a little lamb', in 1877. Asked to record his response to the new invention directly on to a cylinder in 1888, Sir Arthur Sullivan commented:

> I can only say that I am astonished and somewhat terrified at the result of this evening's experiments. Astonished at the wonderful power you have developed and terrified at the thought that so much hideous and bad music will be put on record for ever.[4]

This amusing but telling ambivalence encapsulates many of the suspicious attitudes to recordings which exist in more sophisticated guises today. I shall attempt to reveal here a few of the reasons for this kind of prejudice by exploring some of our cultural attitudes to sound (both 'natural' and recorded), by examining the ways in which these attitudes are embodied in institutional structures, and by drawing out some of the relations between these institutions and their users. I shall explore a few of the ways in which attitudes are beginning to change in a number of distinct but related fields.

One of the characteristics of contemporary urban society is the massive proliferation of intrusive transient sound, much of which is derived from recorded sources. City-dwellers frequently express a desire to retreat to the country for 'peace and quiet'; the city has become synonymous with vast amounts of artificially produced noise, while the country is still idealized, within a Romantic discourse, as a place of organic aural integrity. Similarly the qualities of stillness and quiet are still largely associated with most kinds of 'serious' learning processes. Commerce and trade are regarded as noisy while study and instruction are seen as requiring silence.

This sort of somewhat archaic attitude is often to be seen reflected in the role given to sound in museums and in exhibitions. Many museums are now involved in gathering recorded documentation in the form of oral history projects to complement their collections of artefacts. Yet the invasive quality of the medium which might disrupt the hushed holy atmosphere of the gallery is often cited as a reason not to use sound. Another reason for preserving the silence is that sound would prevent visitors using their own imagination to interpret the artefacts for themselves. Judging from the use of background or ambient sound at the Boilerhouse Project exhibitions at the Victoria and Albert Museum, or at the Natural History Museum, visitors do not appear to have any difficulty in choosing to read printed panels, listen to music or ambient sound, or ignore both as they choose. Sound has the potential to attract attention to a particular display but it can also hold and stimulate the imagination of the visitor.

Recorded sound and critical discourse

It is frequently pointed out that recordings convey far more of an event than can any written account; yet little or no vocabulary has been developed to articulate the full signifying functions of particular sounds, above and beyond what is conveyed through discourse. The many aspects of nuance and intonation, implied reference, or allusion through affectation of pronounciation or accent, or unexpected intrusions of ambient sound, all embody a complexity of meaning which, as skilled listeners, we all understand without necessarily being aware of how we do so. There is little or no vocabulary available with which to discuss the very qualities of sound which make it so effective a medium. These are the aspects of sound which are integral to our understanding what we hear and yet which are incapable of being acknowledged by current forms of literal, critical discourse. Shepherd has recently observed the nature of the problem in relation to music:

> The insusceptibility of timbre (timbre is the quality which distinguishes a note performed on one instrument from the same note as performed on other instruments or voices) in particular to analytic notation is symptomatic of the problem addressed here. For timbre, more than any other musical parameter, appears to be the nature of sound itself. While it is possible to conceive of sound with infinite duration, sound without fixed pitch and sound without gradations of amplitude, it is not possible to conceive of sound without timbre. It is the texture or grain without which sound cannot reach us, touch us or move us. It is the very vibratory essence that puts the world of sound in motion and reminds us, as individuals, that we are alive, sentient, experiencing.[5]

This is a crucial point because it indicates the extent of the linguistic problem raised by efforts to use recordings in educational and critical contexts. The development of the technology has not been accompanied by a development of discourse or methodology with which to articulate the intricacy and the immediacy we experience on hearing a sound recording. In the context of spoken word recordings (such as the oral history interview), the vocabularies and methodologies of phonetics and applied linguistics may undoubtedly contribute significantly but, as Shepherd suggests elsewhere, the difficulty lies in the subtlety of the sounds and also, frequently, in their intrinsic lack of referentiality.[6]

This lack of suitable critical discourse may not seem to present an immediate problem to the curator designing a display, nor indeed is the historian seeking oral testimony likely to be worried by a lack of critical vocabulary. Inevitably, however, a stage is reached where the 'timbre' of a voice may effect decisively the significance of what is uttered and this stage is not as far removed from the general usage of recordings as might be supposed.

Recorded speech, like music, poses a problem to a culture which is still primarily literal in its evaluative processes. While the medium of the written word is more direct, in terms of the limited technology required in order to be able to read a printed page, the processes of production from the linguistic and rhetorical formulation of phrases, editing, typesetting, through to printing and publication, are much more complex (and much more the province of a privileged, educated social group) than need be the case with sound recording. As Thompson says of the 'oral approach':

> It is about individual lives – any life is of interest. And it depends upon speech, not upon the much more demanding and restricted skill of writing. Moreover, the tape recorder not only allows history to be taken down in spoken words but also to be presented through them.[7]

An audio record offers much less distance betwen subject and audience, the subject is much more accessible or more vulnerable; a word spoken lightly, a wrong note played, may be made available, for ever, for serious scrutiny. This non-discriminatory function represents the supreme value of a sound recording and at the same time is the main source of anxiety elicited by its being made. In essence a sound recording lacks precisely the kind of 'authority', derived literally from authorship, upon which a literal culture has, until relatively recently, appeared to depend in order to evaluate and interpret a document. The influence of semiotics and post-Saussurean critical theories has begun to displace simple Romantic notions of a singular 'author' and this departure may eventually assist in developing the interpretation and analysis of sound recordings where the relationship between the recordist and the recorded is by no means straightforward. In the mean time, the pragmatic use of sound recordings in audio-visual displays may influence popular thinking, not only about the theme of a particular display, but also about the medium being used. So there are important questions to be asked about the use of, for example, actors as opposed to 'real people' in making recordings for displays, the functions of middle-class white male voices in commentaries in order to convey information with 'authority', or the use of pop-music to glamorize a theme.

The most commonly held experience of sound recordings is either in listening to radio or playing commercially issued discs. Perhaps the most complex aspect of the creation of a sound recording is its potential to turn a *natural* process of events into a product (for example an LP or a single) or into a programme, and the more 'mixed' or 'edited' the result the further it departs from the primacy of the original. It has been forcefully argued, for example by the Musicians' Union, that even in making an unedited 'straight' archival recording, the mediation of the event has been initiated and a potentially threatening or exploitative process has been conceived. Clearly the nature of the threat in this case directly relates to who is making the recording and for what purpose it is used.

The recording forces the subject immediately to relinquish control over his or her performance and it renders the subject directly and vulnerably accessible to all members of the culture – although the 'author' of the recording (for example the recordist, dubbing engineer, or producer) may remain utterly obscure. A recording may thus seem at once highly *natural* (people seem to *come across* as close to how they actually *are*). At the same time recordings may appear most *unnatural* because the uniqueness of a passing speech or musical performance is isolated from the context and process of its production. Just as quite a number of different cultures equate having their photograph taken with the physical theft of their living spirit, so the recording of the voice, whether in speech or song, may connote a similar kind of theft and the thief in this case may indeed be the 'author' – recordist or the producer. There is, of course, a significant difference between the recording of 'a passing speech', spoken extempore, and the musical performance which is itself an isolated framed phenomenon, but in both kinds of situation a similar feeling may arise. The most successful oral history projects are, for these reasons, frequently those where the collective involvement of the community is emphasized and the element of theft by an outsider is minimized.

Such is the literal nature of our culture that the forms of distancing and control which are exerted by the author over the written word are understood and widely accepted as a norm. A sound recording is more obviously *unnatural* than writing because of the technology required both to make it and to replay it. Audio recording technology is less culturally familiar, less immediately transparent in its role. While it may appear that these distinctions are rapidly falling away, the cultural status of the oral, whether recorded or directly spoken, still stands in direct opposition to what Ong has described as

the massive and deep-set subconscious defenses which writing sets up in the psyche to sustain the restructuring of personality which it brings about. Or, to put it another way, it shows how the acquisition of writing brings those who acquire this skill to structure their entire world view around a feel for the written word to the positive (but not often conscious) exclusion of the oral as such.[8]

The exclusion of the oral by the written has often accurately been perceived as reflecting the cultural and historical exclusion from documentation of those people least likely to contribute to printed publications (that is women, the working class, and cultural minorities). Oral history has therefore often seen its goal as being to document the lives and experience of those who would otherwise disappear from 'history'. This communal approach not only occurs in opposition to the literal, as Ong has pointed out, but also confronts professional media operations and commercial 'product'. Sound archives and museums are frequently faced with the confrontation of these different forms of recording where the conflict for resources ultimately centres on the question of the cultural validity of the recordings. Cultural institutions do not always recognize the influence which they exert in how they choose to treat materials in this context, particularly if the decision is not central to their own collecting policies.

The commercial product and the cultural document

The shifting distinctions at play which construct the perception of recordings as cultural documents or as commercial products are highly complex. Nowhere are the complexities of these relations seen more clearly than in the field of pop music. No other cultural art form has developed so closely with an evolving technology and for this reason commercial pop music may be described as the hyper-space of sound recording. The explosion into western culture of rock and roll in the 1950s coincided exactly with the development of magnetic tape and the tape-recorder. As a result the whole sophisticated notion of a studio sound, and of production techniques, played their parts almost from the outset in the developing self-identity of the music. This is quite different from the demands of classical music or of drama where the technology had to mould itself to the existing audio patterns. The questions of authenticity which arise in talking about recordings of our voices are exacerbated in the pop field where, some have argued, everything is almost equally 'artificial' and where contradictions abound.

On the one hand, there is a recurrent desire in pop music to present a 'natural' unprocessed sound. Much of the aggression of Punk, for example, was devoted to breaking down high production values and the creation of a more 'natural' sound. On the other hand, a band like Frankie Goes to Hollywood devoted considerable energy to the mixing and production of a specific 'studio' sound. They subsequently had to work very hard in order to recreate their own recorded sound in their live act. It is interesting to note that the musical trend of hip-hop subculture in the mid-1980s is towards cutting up and reassembling all kinds of other recordings, as heard in scratch and in some rapping. As Frith has recently pointed out, this represents a significant subversion of notions of 'original' musical talent and 'authenticity', The newly created music may bear the commercial traces of its origins, but the corporate shackles of control have, at least provisionally, been subverted and the music effectively challenges any simple notions of 'authorship', reasserting its own identity as a creative art form and not as a commercial product.[9]

All forms of music, but particularly pop, are frequently used and abused to set a mood in a film, to create an atmosphere in an exhibition, or to sell a car or a breakfast cereal. Cultural institutions ought to be at least as alert as the more sophisticated practitioners of this art. The use of music in this way is a cultural phenomenon in its own right, but perhaps before turning their attention to that, institutions ought to become involved in exploring just what the music communicates about the society and cultural conditions from which it emerges.

Technology and the question of access

The content of a disc or a tape is, by its very nature, invisible and access is acquired only by its being played. Similarly recordings cannot be held in the equivalent of a freeze-frame for analysis; nor can they be easily scanned at speed to establish basic information content. The effect of these simple facts is to make users very dependent upon a high standard of documentation and detailed cataloguing to facilitate research. It is an extremely lengthy, time-consuming business effectively to create a catalogue of recordings. Whereas a book may be identified with more or less adequate accuracy by its author, title, date and place of publication, a recording, if it is for example a commercial disc, will consist of several tracks, each of which may contain different speakers or musicians, performing works by different composers in different locations with different orchestras. Each track needs to be itemized and entered separately for a catalogue to be effective and of service. The result of this is that most of the world's major sound archives have extremely low levels of holdings catalogued (on average around 10–15 per cent of total holdings according to the International Association of Sound Archives). Equally one of the recurrent flaws in locally initiated oral history projects is the lack of documentation assembled concerning the provenance of any particular tape. It seems likely that industry-fed computer data bases will, in the next few years, alleviate some of these difficulties in the commercial domain. The partnership of the British Library National Sound Archive and the Mechanical Copyright Protection Society in setting up a national discography is a significant development. Yet it only goes to emphasize the weakness of the position at the local level and outside the commercial domain.

It seems quite likely that sufficiently motivated technical research might be able to overcome some aspects of these problems, but technology tends to be developed along strictly commercial lines. Recent efforts in this area, for example, have been devoted to making track selection on cassette decks more flexible in order to increase the resemblance of tape-use to disc-use. Similarly the ease of programming track-selection as facilitated on compact discs has been emulated on both cassette-decks and disc-turntables. As Griffin has recently pointed out:

> With state-of-the-art digital technology an extensive concert performance and all the discographical data needed to identify the performance can be digitally recorded on the same optical disc ... However, the implementation of new technological systems ... requires extensive financial and political commitment.[10]

While there are few signs at present that record companies would be persuaded to provide this kind of information on compact discs, the production is already beginning of machines which could read and play back both high-quality audio signals and a visual one in the compact format.

The advent of new audio and visual carriers, such as the compact disc, create constant problems for the technician. It is a basic requirement of any active sound-collecting organization to be able to replay all the variety of carriers in its care (from wax cylinders to optical discs). As technological developments increase in speed and sophistication, the problems of obsolescence become very real and call for detailed technical knowledge. This is the sort of area where collections are increasingly dependent upon the willingness of large corporations to provide long-term maintenance and training.

Similarly the preservation of audio materials is a major issue which must be addressed by any serious collecting organization. Recent developments in digital technology have improved significantly the possibilities for the long-term preservation of sound recordings by allowing copies to be made from digital recordings without deterioration of the audio signal. Archival considerations of this kind, however, are rarely at the forefront of commercial corporate thinking, nor, alas, is there much awareness of preservation needs in institutions where recordings are only incidental to their core activities. As a result the technical requirements which are basic to the establishment of sound archives as essential cultural institutions are very often subject to the whims of the general market. In a few, more peripheral fields of audio research, for example voice identification, where motivation behind the research is very strong (police forces make increasing use of voice-identification technology), advances have been more marked and so, by a coincidence of interests, the development of digital sound spectrography offers all kinds of new possibilities for research into the composition of audio signals, but this remains an exception rather than the rule. There is now a growing need to lobby commercial manufacturers of discs and audio equipment, in order that they are made more aware of the wider uses of audio materials, and of their cultural significance.

Collections of recorded sound

In most of the world's 'developed' countries, sound recordings are preserved as cultural resources in a number of different kinds of organizations. The most obvious are the archives of large broadcasting organizations, but recordings are also preserved in separate national sound archives, in the archive collections of most record companies (major and independent), as well as at local radio stations, county record offices, museums, public libraries, community recording groups (such as oral history groups or wildlife sound recording groups), in the hands of specialist private collectors, and, of course, in the relatively small personal collections of large sections of the population.

The extent of this disparate set of insititutions, organizations, and individuals has only recently begun to be charted in by the

National Sound Archive. The archive began collecting data for a National Register of Collections of Recorded Sound in 1984 and, to date, some 600 entries (excluding public lending libraries) have been collated covering all forms of recording including commercial discs, broadcast materials, private recordings, and field recordings. There are several distinct categories of collections distinguishable in the UK currently as shown in Table 8.1.[11]

The relationship between these different collections is complex, but may perhaps be best understood in terms of the purposes for which the recordings are made and the uses to which they are put. Almost inevitably a kind of tacit hierarchy of collections emerges, constructed not only by the scale of budgets of the different collecting groups, but also by the social and cultural status attributed to the recording work being carried out. Technical factors, such as equipment used and expertise of recordists, may also affect the status of the recording. Thus recordings held in the BBC Sound Archives may acquire a greater perceived value than those held by an extremely competent local heritage recording unit. This value is not necessarily simply related to the actual content of a recording, but may also be linked to the systems of production and dissemination of which it is a part or to which it has access.

The national infrastructure of collections contains many different functions and may appear to move in several different directions. The needs of the local community group may often be directly at odds with those of broadcasters. This may be reflected in the methodology of making the recording, where the interviewee or musician, for example, may be treated either as a subject or as a participant, with very different results.

As the details in Table 8.1 reveal, the collections of the BBC and the National Sound Archives are by far the largest in the UK. It is quite difficult to reconcile the situation at a local level, where collecting policies vary enormously from one part of the country to another, with these large, institutionally formulated collections. There is probably as much material held in these two large national collections as in the rest of the country put together. For most researchers and members of the general public, access to the national radio archive collections is obtained through the National Sound Archives for reference and study purposes only. At the local level different institutions offer access under differing sets of locally devised conditions; the amounts of radio materials held in local archives is small although growing and tends to be selected

Table 8.1 *Examples of collections of recorded sound*

Type of audio collection and examples	No of discs	Hours of tape	Access	Comments
Collections of national importance				
Imperial War Museum	7,800	8,000	Researcher by appointment	
National Sound Archives	1,000,000	45,000	General public by appointment	NSA is a department of the British Library
Network radio archives				
BBC Sound Archive	Over 130,000 items on about 50,000 tapes and discs		BBC staff and limited researchers	
BBC Gramophone Library	1.5 million		BBC staff and limited researchers	
Regional centres				
North-West Sound Archive	12,000 hours		General public by appointment	
Welsh Folk Life Museum, St Fagan's	700 hours	4,300	General public by appointment	
Ulster Folk Life Museum	350	1,500	General public by appointment	
School of Scottish Studies			Academic researchers	A department of the University of Edinburgh
Local oral history projects				
Bradford Community Heritage Research Unit				
West Midlands Oral History Group				

Local radio archives			
BBC Bristol	3,500	Educational and researchers	
ILR-Viking Radio (Hull)			Receives sample output from ILR
Local passive repositories			
Berkshire County Record Office			
Birmingham City Library			Provides public access to Birmingham museum, originated oral history tapes
Specialist and academic collections			
Pitt Rivers Museum, Oxford	900 cylinders	No public access	Valuable materials with no allocated resources for preservation
Leeds School of Folk Life Studies			
Cardiff, Christmas Archives			
Collections for and by disabled people			
RNIB Talking Book Service	6,000 master 10.5 hour tapes	Access for registered visually handicapped only	RNIB Talking Books are produced by volunteer actors reading on to special tapes
Commercial archives			
Major record companies (e.g. Polygram)	60,000	Internal company use only	

on the basis of either random representative selections or under *ad hoc* 'interesting and historical' criteria.

The responsibility for selection and retention of network broadcast materials rests mainly with the BBC and in the past this has resulted in some unfortunate omissions; the junking of the first series of 'Goon Shows' in its entirety, for example, is a great loss to the modern history of popular comedy. More recently a policy to retain a far higher proportion of broadcast output has been introduced (around 50 hours of radio broadcasts per week). But it is probably because of the earlier, relatively low level of retention, in proportion to transmission, that producers currently make such little use of archive recordings as well as the effects of the constant urge for the 'new'.

This neglect may also occur because of the very clearly defined ways in which programmes made around archive materials have been given their own kind of stigma. Most people tend to think of sound archives as the dusty vaults of broadcasting organizations which are drawn upon for a particular kind of programme which has become characterized by the successfully lighthearted whimsy of Glyn Worsnip exploring the BBC Sound Archives at 8.45 in the morning on Radio 4. The internal use to which programme-makers put archive materials is rarely recognized and indeed producers themselves are often less than imaginative in their use of the wealth of archive materials at their disposal. There is consequently a vicious circle typified by the early BBC archive selection policy, where unimaginative use of archive recordings led to a low estimation of the status of the archives which in turn led to the limited allocation of resources to provide access to recordings which led to unimaginative usages. It is also ironic to find a distrust of the medium itself on the part of administrators in the BBC which led to the retention of all written scripts while the programmes themselves were lost; this attitude was not, on the whole, shared by producers.

It is ironic that those who have access to the BBC Sound Archives for broadcast use seem less likely effectively to use the materials in innovative ways, while those with imaginative ideas have so far been excluded from access for any purposes other than study and research, except where the high copyright charges have been met. This should not, however, merely be interpreted as an imperative to improve access to sound archives alone. There are more organizations producing and collecting sound recordings, at all levels of professionalism and community involvement, now than at any time since its invention.

Oral history and cultural utterance

Much of this activity takes place in the field of oral history. Since the mid-1960s oral history has grown in popularity to an enormous extent, both in this country and as an international movement. It developed out of growing popular interest in folk history and a widespread concern to explore and preserve memories and reminiscences of the local roots of rapidly declining communities particularly in rural areas. Early pioneers in the field, like George Ewart Evans and A. L. Lloyd, concentrated almost entirely on rural communities, carrying out interviews and recording the music of elderly men and women in efforts to document all aspects of their lives from their working experience to their folk-music and songs. More recently, with the increased interest and the availability of MSC funds, many groups have broadened their scope to include topics of highly contemporary relevance, such as life in the inner cities and the experiences of different immigrant communities.

Unfortunately, however, oral history has not really succeeded in gaining the broader recognition of its own validity which it so clearly requires. One reason for this is the variability of the results of many interviewing projects and an accompanying reluctance on the part of oral historians to make too many 'value-judgements' about the validity of recorded material as a historical document. Results may be variable because both technical skills and available equipment may not be of very high standards, but disciplined interviewing techniques and thorough subject-research are also qualities which make or break a good oral history project.

The reluctance to attribute academic values to oral history recordings is, perhaps, partly explicable in terms of some of the problems which I raised earlier. The lack of critical vocabulary with which to discuss a sound recording clearly makes it difficult to evaluate a piece in purely audio terms. At the same time, frequent insistence on the transcription into textual form of recordings represents, on the one hand, an erosion of the notion of the value of sound, and on the other hand, a somewhat compromised attempt to translate the oral into the literal. The result of such a compromise, certainly in purist terms, is to lose many of the subtleties and complexities of the oral and to produce a poorly written (since not 'written') piece of text into the bargain.

Another of the pioneers who helped to broaden understanding of the oral history method was Charles Parker, who died in 1980. Parker, a committed Marxist, was Senior Features Producer for BBC Radio Midland Region between 1954 and 1972. The example of his particular experience in attempting to use oral history as a powerful and legitimate form of modern social history reveals quite strikingly some of the ideological problems which surround the cultural uses of the medium. It had always been the practice in the BBC when making features about 'real' people to use actors and provide them with carefully scripted parts. When, in the early 1950s, the BBC began to make regular use of the new technological possibilities of the portable tape-recorder, their main value was seen as a research tool. If 'actual' people in the 'real' world were to be interviewed, it was in order to make the scripts more 'authentic' and certainly not because their 'real' voices were to be heard on the air.

In the course of researching one particular story, however, Parker was struck by the power and intensity of emotion expressed by the people telling their stories. In response to this he created the first of a series of dramatic documentaries, the 'Radio Ballads', which were acclaimed internationally as a new departure in radio programme-making. Parker was very much influenced by three people with whom he worked quite closely at this time: folk-musicologists, Ewan MacColl and Peggy Seeger, and Alan Lomax, a Texas folklorist and broadcaster who was in Britain as a refugee from MacCarthyism. Another colleague of Parker's, Trevor Fisher, encapsulates what was innovative about the 'Ballad of John Axon', the first documentary to take the new form:

> What made John Axon distinct was firstly the use of the speech of the actual participants through tape-recording; secondly, the absence of narration and actors, letting the actuality tell the story; thirdly, the use of folk song and jazz; and fourthly, the attempt by MacColl to use the form and techniques of the folk ballad as the model for the programme.[12]

Parker went on to make a series of 'Radio Ballads', covering such subjects as the lives of trawler-men, miners, polio victims, and teenagers, each of which further developed and extended the technique over a further eight programmes, the last of which was made in 1964. During this period Parker became more committed to radical left-wing politics and produced further programmes after the Ballads which developed the possibilities for radio of directly transmitting the voices of the people in ways which still challenge orthodox broadcasting techniques today. In a talk transmitted on Radio 3 in 1971, Parker demonstrated that he was not just a great producer, but that he was also thinking carefully about the role and the challenge of oral history, particularly in relation to teaching oral English:

> I think there is the intellectual's difficulty in exercising humility . . ., in that what it means is that brilliant minds, men who have had an experience of life, are well educated, who have had great achievements, if they're honest in this they've got to go back to school, they've got to go back and sit at the feet of . . . a Connemara construction worker, or an East Anglian herring fisherman . . ., and learn what language is like on the lips. And this, of course, is an exercise in humility that very few of us are prepared to make, involving, as it does, all the difficult questions of identity . . . if you begin to question a person's language, or his ways of speech, he's terribly vulnerable to this. We are so sensitive in these areas. So it's a very difficult question, but I don't think there's any alternative . . .

He continued:

> The point is that this is not simply a matter of English, of language, or preoccupation with speech, which indeed I have, but it's much deeper than this. I think it is the survival of the race. I think that inbuilt into our language is our memory, is our past. If we lose this we lose ourselves: this, I think, is where we die. I came across an extraordinary quotation from Adorno and the phrase which sticks in my mind is where he stated: 'The spectre of mankind without memory . . . in a galloping technology of mass production where men are expected to have four completely different jobs in their lifetime, the inherited skills and all the cultural utterance that surrounds them are discredited.' Therefore there is economically a danger that all the cultural heritage, the history, of this people that goes with this will also be put on the scrap heap, and this, I think, is precisely our danger.[13]

Parker's recognition of the fundamental function of spoken language, of 'cultural utterance', to reflect the political, social, and economic history and present circumstances of a society is of great importance. It encapsulates all that motivates serious oral history, and it is challenging in its crucial assertion that it is not simply the construction, syntax, and reference of spoken language which must be understood, but also the oral complexities of utterance. Parker's declared Marxism, his 'difficult' personality, and his insistence on the frequent use in his programmes of actuality recordings, of 'cultural utterance' which was both very expensive to produce and threatening to orthodox forms of broadcasting, no doubt all contributed to his being dismissed from the BBC in December 1972, yet his contribution to radio and to the understanding of the cultural role of sound remains to be fully appreciated.

The theme park model: Wheels and Jorvik

One aspect of the clash between Parker and the BBC stemmed from Parker's insistence on the use of non-professional, untrained voices. This conflict between the professional and the community is also to be seen in the presentation of audio-visual displays in museums. Discussions on the use of pure sound are often distracted into talking about the audio-visual in such a way as to neglect the audio, however the function of sound is crucial in such presentations (whether tape-slide or video). All of the difficulties relating to using sound in other contexts also occur in the creation of audio-visual displays; the frequent tendency is towards studio-produced sound-tracks and actorly (white male voice) commentaries.

While many public museums sponsor oral history projects and have found the results useful aids to interpretation, very few have sought to make any extensive use of sound derived from these sources in their displays, despite the fact that audio-visual presentations are now quite commonplace. In the private sector, ironically, the popularity and lucrative commercial potential of such presentations has led to more adventurous uses of sound. The Disney World, theme park model has been successfully followed in several locations such as the Wheels display at the National Motor Museum, which sets out to illustrate the history of the motor car, and Jorvik, which is 'a journey back in time' to explore the Viking settlement which predates the modern city of York as revealed by recent archaeological excavations. Both displays take the form of 'dark rides' in which the visitor sits in a moving car or 'pod' and is transported around a series of animated audio-visual displays. The audio content of the display combines a spoken commentary, relayed directly to each moving car, with a changing sound-track played externally which complements, by spot effects, the various sets through which the visitor is taken.

This is the basic model which is followed in different ways by both Jorvik and Wheels. Jorvik is the larger set-up involving static near-life-size reconstructions of cottages, a village street, and the archaeological dig itself. All of the sound used at Jorvik was especially recorded in the field with the emphasis on being as 'authentic' as possible. This included bringing in a linguist specially to devise the 'reproduction' Viking-language which is heard at various points and sending a recordist to Iceland to tape the sound of Faroese Ring Doves which most closely resemble the kinds of birds found to have been present on the original site in Viking times.

Wheels, on the other hand, incorporates a changing music-track which, almost subliminally, evokes the various periods covered in the history of the motor car. Most of the sets at Wheels are small self-contained animated cameos; the sound-effects are nearly all studio produced along with the music to create a sophisticated but utterly artificial sound-track. The displays operate simultaneously on several different levels, feeding the audience with a rapid succession of relatively small points of information. Wheels is technically sophisticated and incorporates a number of new features of audio-technology, notably the solid-state digital sound-stores which are used to provide a very flexible synchronized commentary to the individual cars while being almost maintenance free.[14]

Jorvik also displays a high level of technical competence. Its strength perhaps lies in its open transport system which moves along tracks hidden beneath the floor, as distinct from the track-guided cars at Wheels which revolve the visitor from left to right to be shown each new cameo. At Jorvik visitors have more time to look around the display as they move through it; one of the more disturbing qualities of the Wheels version of the 'dark ride' is the way in which it manipulates the attention of its captive audience; at its best this happens subtly without seeming to force the point.

The educational value is a little higher than might be expected; Jorvik in particular succeeds in conveying a good deal about its subject although the efforts to be 'authentic' are wasted by the lack of anything to draw attention to the nature of the work which has been put in. The recorded sound is successfully used both to communicate basic narrative information through the spoken commentary and to create the series of changing atmospheres necessary to simulate a 'total experience'. It never becomes more than a simulation and the sense of the artificial is foremost; the synthetic 'smells' which are released at various points in Jorvik are easily mistaken for the odour of the operating machinery. Considering that the total running time is very short, between 10 and 15 minutes, the displays do manage to convey a surprising amount of informative detail and to offer an enjoyable show.

David Willrich, the technical manager at Beaulieu, explained that the motivation for Wheels began with a desire to tell the story of the motor vehicle. This was something which it was felt could not easily be done in the mainly silent, static display of cars which is the museum's principal attraction. Several full-scale installations in the main display also use sound to evoke the social context in which the motor vehicle operates but the general effect here is closer to being an amusing gimmick. For example, if you listen carefully you can hear the rattle of crates, doorstep conversation, and a cat miaowing to suggest, faintly, the street in which the milk van on display might have made its rounds. Elsewhere in the main display commercial-style audio-visual presentations offer other 'live' attractions.

Beaulieu's motoring theme has enabled the museum to attract significant sponsorship from industry and this is reflected in the audio-visual presentations in the main display from Champion, Lucas, BP, and others. It is also seen in grants to help fund Wheels received from the Kenning Motor Group, the Ford Motor Company, and the British Tourist Board. Thus from the management point of view, if the display attracts visitors and entertains, it has succeeded; if it also educates them, this is a bonus.

The National Motor Museum, and its Wheels display, is of course only one of Beaulieu's several attractions and to that extent it fits in better with the Disney World model of the theme park than with the more orthodox museum. Yet, arguably, the half million or so visitors a year are more stimulated and informed by this kind of dynamic audio-visual display than by more traditional museums.

The professional 'media' approach to audio-visual presentations adopted in the theme park model is probably only an exaggerated extension of the current practice in many public museums and libraries. The sponsored buying-in of complete services from a professional audio-visual production house is not simply a pragmatic step, but also represents a political decision to present a subject in a commercial way. The model of Wheels and Jorvik is felt by orthodox museums, however, to represent an insidious threat to their continued funding. The superficial attractiveness of the theme park model both as an 'experience' and as a money-spinner will certainly find favour in the eyes of local councillors and politicians who might wish to appear trendy and to bring prestige 'culture' to their areas. There are plans to open similar 'environments' in other historic cities which, like York, already have a well-established tourist infrastructure, for example Oxford, Canterbury, and Edinburgh.

Yet, although these 'environments' are based on accurate scholarship, they lack the basic collecting and cataloguing functions which represent the core activity of traditional museums. It would be a seriously damaging move if public funds were redirected away from museums, with their innately preservative functions, to new centres of this kind. Jorvik makes a gesture towards recognizing some responsibilities in this respect; while the centre continues to make money, its profits are constructively fed back into the York Archaeological Trust. If, however, profits began to decline, Heritage Projects, the commercial production company and managing agents, would doubtless have little hesitation in closing the centre down. Yet the fact remains that the use of sound in these new-style centres is considerably more inventive and exciting to a broad cross-section of the general public than most of what is currently on offer in the majority of the country's local or national museums.

The theme park model therefore raises several questions for public museums or even for libraries. Is it possible to combine the widespread and desirable involvement of a local community in producing recorded documents of its own history with a 'professional' presention? Is the 'professional' style of presentation itself a factor in distancing the visitor from the subject or can it be used to encourage further a real form of participation and involvement? And does the Wheels/Jorvik approach have to mean that the sound recording becomes a mere adjunct to the overall 'entertainment' or could its intrinsic value also be demonstrated in such a way as to encourage further study and awareness? These are among a number of questions which public museums ought to address and which are clearly linked to the larger issues of how exhibitions can be brought to life and made more attractive to more people.

The oral history interview can be used very effectively to this end. If members of a particular community are recorded explaining aspects of their culture, as for example at the Manchester Jewish Museum, the directness of the voices puts the visitor in much closer contact with the subject of the exhibition. Instead of a detached, possibly authoritarian label explaining a particular display, the mediation of audio technology is much less obtrusive and much more likely to offer a sense of immediacy and contact. As Davies has argued, 'oral information may help to bring "dead" objects to life by giving a poignant backcloth to material remains'.[15] Whether or not this revived form of 'life' bears a direct relationship to the original is a more complex question and relates to the many different ways in which sound is manipulated and perceived. As has been shown, a variety of roles are socially constructed for sound materials and the ways in which recordings are used in cultural institutions can either reinforce these set roles or seek to alter and to develop them.

One very important but largely unconscious distinction is often made between the transient domain in which sound occurs 'naturally' and the recorded domain in which sounds are stored for replay at a required moment in any context. When sound is experienced as transient it seems to retain its natural 'authenticity'. Once a recording has been made accessible, however, there is an altogether different relationship established between the subject and the listener; it becomes more resonant because of its repeatability and therefore more open to critique. These different relationships to sound can be usefully exploited in exhibition and display design. Ambient sound can be used to create a particular atmosphere, which may not need to be carefully attended to, while recordings of voices which require more concentrated attention can be made available if the visitor so desires. Very few institutions are even beginning to exploit this potential. Despite its popular appeal, sound remains very low down on the agenda.

Conclusions

Perhaps more than any other medium, the sound we make – whether in speech or song or in our music – gives us our identities. To hear that sound confirms our very existence and to hear the sounds of others brings about a greater understanding of the world. Sound possesses the immense power to transform our experience on a level which exceeds most literal forms of explication and all cultures, whether modern or 'primitive', demonstrate a remarkable underlying desire to listen in a wide variety of contexts.

The work of oral historians, in some respects, only reflects the natural impulse of earlier societies to retain the memory of its history in the oral poetry and song of its artists. The development of modern recording technology has enabled us to document, with less likelihood of distortion, the audio content of our lives and yet the contemporary drive towards professionalism and institutionalism has confined such activities to the margins of our culture. Equally the primitive desire to hear our experiences and our different histories confirmed through the accounts of others has been transmuted into a restless consumption of the marketable products of both record companies and broadcasting channels.

There has always also been an undercurrent of opposition to this inexorable drive towards the obliteration of cultural memory and cultural utterance. The work of Charles Parker remains as a testimony to this, as does the ever-growing number of oral history groups. The fact of Parker's dismissal from the BBC emphasizes the fact that, in contemporary society, freedom of expression must also encompass the freedom to record and to broadcast. Equally, although they romanticized the attempt and were perhaps hopelessly monotonous in their output, the struggles of the pirate radio stations in the late 1960s and early 1970s to transmit programmes which, at least, sought to identify more strongly with a known body of listeners, indicate the consistent will of the community to speak to itself without restrictions.

The recent decision by the Home Office to cancel its planned two-year 'experiment' in setting up community radio stations is only the latest expression of official anxiety at permitting free access to the airwaves.[16] There has been some suggestion that the reversal of policy on the community station proposals was, at least in part, due to cabinet fears that the stations would be used by subversive groups to transmit messages fermenting social unrest and civil disobedience. The fear that the full, exuberant multicultural nature of our society might find itself more powerfully reflected in such transmissions was not even privately expressed, and yet it is the continuing lack of this reflection in the mainstream media which perhaps more accurately reveals current institutional prejudices.

It seems likely, therefore, that similar anxieties and prejudices have led to the lack of attention devoted to diversifying the usage of sound-recordings in exhibitions, scholarly research, and in education. One of the functions of a modern museum, library, or sound archive should be to seek to extend and to develop an awareness of the cultural roles of sound in challenging new ways; drawing extensively on local archives and on the work carried out by local groups at the community level. Despite the restrictive nature of copyright legislation, there is much more which could yet be achieved. The task might simply be stated as the need to offer to all sections of society, on an individual level as well as on a mass scale, the opportunity to hear, to enjoy, and to study our own and other peoples' experiences – past and present.

Ultimately the functions of sound recordings, and indeed of all audio-visual media, in cultural institutions centre on questions of power. The power behind technical and production knowledge; the power to obtain access to materials; and the power to be able to disseminate them. There is a whole world of sound, beyond processed pop however palatable, which we could be listening to at home, in cars, in galleries, or – on personal stereos – almost anywhere, and there is a huge gap in our museums' exhibitions where there should be the voices, songs, and other sounds of what is on display. The notion that we could use ambient sound, for example the natural, wildlife sounds of the Amazonian rain-forests, to provide a relaxing environment or an exotic atmosphere has hardly been explored at all. A truly radical innovation in broadcasting might include the transmission, without commentary or narrative, of the natural sounds of waterfalls, rivers, forests, or thunderstorms for extended periods at little cost and tremendous effect; why insult the art of musicians by playing their work as 'background' when the technology exists to bring us the endless variety of the world's own sounds? The situation is changing, but the directions which recorded sound will take depend upon the imagination and the political motivation of those who wish to hear for themselves. We will, no doubt, continue to be astonished by what we hear, but it is surely time to stop being terrified by the immense possibilities of recorded sound.

Notes and references

1 Segaud, M. (1982) *L'Oreille oubliée*, Paris: Centre de Création Industrielle, Centre Georges Pompidou, p. 54 (my translation).
2 Esslin, M. (1983) *Meditations: Essays on Brecht, Beckett and the Media*, London: Abacus, p. 186. See also Lewis, P. (1978) *Conference Papers from the Radio Literature Conference 1977*, Durham.
3 Ong, W. J. (1971) *Rhetoric, Romance and Technology: Studies in the Interaction of Expression and Culture*, Ithaca and London: Cornell University Press, p. 284.
4 Edison Cylinder (1888) recording, reissued (1970) on 'The Wonder of the Age: Mr Edison's New Talking Phonograph', Argo, ZPR 122–3.

5 Shepherd, R. (1986) 'Music consumption and cultural self-identities: some theoretical and methodological reflections', *Media, Culture and Society* 8: 305–30.

6 ibid., p. 314. Using some of the methodology of linguistics, the American anthropologist and sociologist, Irving Goffman, began some valuable work in the context of 'radio talk'; see his (1981) *Forms of Talk*, Oxford: Blackwells, ch. 5, pp. 197–330. For a useful summary of other possible sources of theoretical approaches, see Ong, W. J. (1982) *Orality and Literacy: The Technologizing of The Word*, London and New York: Methuen, ch. 7, pp. 156–79.

7 Thompson, P. (1978) *The Voice of the Past: Oral History*, Oxford, London, and New York: Oxford University Press, p. 15.

8 Ong, W. J. (1971) *Rhetoric, Romance and Technology: Studies in the Interaction of Expression and Culture*, Ithaca and London: Cornell University Press, p. 293.

9 Frith, S. (1986) 'Art versus technology: the strange case of popular music', *Media, Culture and Society* 8: 263–79.

10 Griffin, M. (1986) 'Access to performance from Bach to Wynton Marsalis', *Phonographic Bulletin* 45, June: 25–32.

11 This is the first time that such a comprehensive survey seems to have been carried out, certainly in this country and possibly anywhere in the world.

12 Fisher, T. and Parker, C. (1986) *Aspects of a Pioneer*, Birmingham: The Charles Parker Archive, p. 4. For a detailed study of the Radio Ballads, see MacColl, E. and Seeger, P. (1968) *I'm a Freeborn Man*, New York: Oak Publications.

13 Charles Parker, 'The tape recorder and the oral tradition' transmitted BBC Radio 3, 11 September 1971.

14 For a useful and detailed technical analysis of the Wheels audio set-up, see Simpson, R. and Smith, P. (1985) 'Dark rides', *Studio Sound*, September: 82–6. Also useful for technical information is the article on Walt Disney World's sound system in Florida: Nelson, T. (1985) 'Theme park sound at Disney', *Studio Sound*, June: 64–70.

15 Davies, S. (1984) 'Museums and oral history', *Museums Journal* 84(1): 25–7.

16 It is worth pointing out that this anxiety is a peculiarly British disease; in many other 'developed' countries such as France and the USA, community radio stations have for several years operated in abundance offering, more or less, successful alternatives to the public service networks and the commercial channels.

PART 3

Sociology of the museum public

9

The Pompidou Centre
and its public:
the limits of a utopian site

NATHALIE HEINICH
Translated by Chris Turner

The Georges Pompidou National Centre of Art and Culture ('Pompidou Centre' or, more simply, for many Parisians, 'Beaubourg') is a complex object. It is complex in a literal sense in that the building contains several distinct departments, such as the Public Information Library (BPI), the National Museum of Modern Art (MNAM), and the Centre for Industrial Creation (CCI), as well as being the home of a number of other activities (children's studio, *cinémathèque*, meetings/forums, audio-visual unit, publications and periodicals) and having the Institute for Acoustic and Musical Research and Creation (IRCAM) close at hand in a basement in the *Place* Stravinsky.

It is also complex from the point of view of administrative organization. The range of its activities and the cultural quality of its objectives mean that it might best be thought of as a kind of large-scale and typically Parisian descendant of those Maisons de la Culture, created in a handful of provincial towns by André Malraux in the days when he was Charles de Gaulle's Minister of Culture. It does, however, have a special status within the 'integrated cultural establishments' of which it is a part, as 'a national public establishment of a cultural character', attached to the Ministry of Culture.[1]

It is complex also from the point of view of what is at stake in the project. It was created by a 'right-wing' minister (from whom it takes its name) who was, paradoxically, a fervent admirer of contemporary art with a desire (at least in this case) to 'democratize' culture – an objective which distances him from the traditional image of his political bedfellows. The project of building such an institution could in fact easily have been conceived ten years later by the Socialist government and its Minister of Culture, Jack Lang. We have seen that government pursuing a policy which reconciled – or aimed to reconcile – the imperatives of mass consumption (what in the 1970s was called the 'socio-cultural') with 'higher' cultural production. Sadly this is only too often a contradictory project, both in general and at Beaubourg in particular, for although that establishment has been unassailable from the point of view of its (massive) success with the public, it is often attacked by cultural professionals for giving over too little space to the avant-garde artistic creation which it was originally supposed to spearhead.

This reservation, however, is lightweight indeed beside the principal criticism which has been and continues to be levelled against it (though less forcefully): this concerns its architecture, which is, to say the least, original (no one disputes the fact) but which is accused by some of disfiguring the area or of bringing a dignified cultural establishment down to the level of a vulgar factory (on account of its pipes and chimneys). Yet even these polemics are tending to die down now, partly because people are becoming used to it and partly because it has proved so undeniably popular, both in specifically tourist terms (the building is an attraction on account of its architecture and the view of Paris it affords) and for more cultural ends (such as the major exhibitions on the fifth floor – 'Paris–Moscow', 'Paris–Berlin', 'Vienna', and so on – which have played a large part in establishing its reputation) or quasi-professional uses (such as the many visitors – students and others – to the library).

It is also, then, at the level of use that Beaubourg shows itself to be a more complex and many-faceted object than one might suppose from its square and transparent external structure. It will therefore come as no surprise that we find a similar complexity when we come to look at the Centre's visitors. Ten years after its creation and beyond all the polemics and issues it has stirred up, we now have sufficient data and we have had enough time, to be able to attempt a first assessment of the Centre's users. What then is Beaubourg's public, or better what are its publics? And what is Beaubourg for its public or publics?

The statistics

Whatever one thinks of it, it cannot be denied that Beaubourg's success with the public has surpassed all forecasts. Forecasts based

17 The Georges Pompidou Centre, Paris.

on studies carried out in the early 1970s suggested there would be between 8,500 and 15,000 visits per day, making an annual total of between 2.5 and 4.5 million. In reality, the figure has been much higher, the daily average being some 25,000 visitors, giving an annual total of 7.3 million visits.[2] There have therefore been almost double the expected number of visitors and this has happened in the very first years of operation.

Such success can, of course, be ascribed in part to the quality of the service offered; it is also an effect of the general increase in cultural consumption that has taken place since the end of the 1960s, an increase that can be seen merely by looking at the growing success of exhibitions in Paris.[3] Its causes are to be found in the general raising of levels of education in the post-war ('baby-boom') generation, whose consumption has tended to become increasingly oriented towards 'cultural' goods in the broad sense (television, music, theatre, art gallery visits, and so on), by contrast

201

with the previous generation which was more eager to equip itself with cars and domestic appliances.[4] Consequently, as Pierre Bourdieu remarked at the very opening of the Beaubourg Centre,

> Though it would be naive to attribute to the 'supply effect' exerted by Beaubourg what is, rather, the effect of an increased demand linked to the effects of education, it would be equally inaccurate entirely to deny the existence of a specific 'supply effect'.[5]

We cannot, however, simply be content with such general data, on the one hand because, in spite of the architectural unity of the building, it is put to a multiplicity of very different uses, and on the other because, as the logic of a cultural establishment is not that of a business, the mere fact of having attracted a large number of users does not of itself mean that the particular policy followed has been successful. That policy can never in fact simply be about the number of users; it must also aim at quality of use as well, as at a diversity of types of audiences, since we are talking about a public service, where the taxes of each must go to serve the needs of all. As a result, the by no means necessarily convergent demands of culture and democracy have to be taken into account in what is consequently a more complex process of evaluation – a process which a purely commercial logic would simply have carried out in terms of financial balances.

The selection of the public

In general terms, then, who are the types of people using Beaubourg? They are predominantly male: 61 per cent are men and only 39 per cent women. They are also relatively young: the average age is 30 and the 18–25 and 26–35 age groups predominate (42 per cent and 32 per cent respectively). In other words, more than three-quarters of Beaubourg's visitors are under 35, whereas those of retirement age (65 and over) form less than 2 per cent.

The visitors are primarily Parisian (40 per cent) or from the Paris area (18 per cent) and, paradoxically, there are fewer French provincials among them (approximately 13 per cent) than foreigners, who form at least a third of the public – or more at certain times of year. As regards social origins, we are generally dealing with a highly educated public. More than half of Beaubourg's visitors have spent at least three years in higher education. Almost a third have passed their baccalaureate and/or have two years of advanced general or technical education. Only 15 per cent do not have their baccalaureate.

It will come as no surprise that a large number of Beaubourg's visitors (around 40 per cent) are students. Nor will it be surprising that they do not represent a broad spectrum of the general public; only 3 per cent are manual workers (who formed 18 per cent of the adult French population in 1982) and another 3 per cent are self-employed workers such as farmers, craftworkers, and tradespeople (7.7 per cent of the general population). By contrast, almost 30 per cent are executives and professionals (4.4 per cent of the population), 11 per cent are from the intermediate strata (technicians, middle management, schoolteachers, nurses: 9.2 per cent of the population) and approximately the same number are white-collar workers (13 per cent).

Overall, then, Beaubourg's audience is completely atypical in structure. It is atypical above all with respect to the French population as a whole, of which it is entirely unrepresentative, given that a high degree of selection has taken place here, not in terms of 'economic capital', but as a function of 'cultural capital'. The typical Beaubourg user belongs to what Pierre Bourdieu terms the dominated fractions of the dominant class, by which he means those categories enjoying relatively high to moderate incomes, who are highly qualified or who engage extensively in cultural activities. [6] This structure is equally atypical of findings obtained by the various surveys that have been conducted to determine the nature of the traditional gallery-going public. [7] Beaubourg in fact possesses all the characteristics of the great tourist attractions which are visited by foreign tourists in their thousands (Louvre, Versailles), as well as displaying – though to a lesser extent – features common to 'high-brow' cultural institutions (Grand Palais, national galleries and museums, Musée d'Art Moderne de la Ville de Paris). In addition, it boasts a large number of characteristics that are specific to a library, the Beaubourg library being unique in France in that it is open to the general public, non-specialist, free, and more flexible in its opening hours than any equivalent establishment. This explains the large number of student or para-student visitors, which give the centre its young, or as some see it, 'marginal' image. However, the truly marginal characters are to be found among the tramps and hippies who have taken advantage of the free access to lay siege not only to the outside of the building (the 'piazza' is currently the high spot of Parisian popular culture with its buskers, pavement artists, and fire-eaters) but also the ground floor and even the toilets. Although these people are relatively few in number, their presence is strong enough to confirm the doubts of those elderly or, perhaps, upper-class individuals who might think that Beaubourg is definitely not the place for them.

Contrary then to the objectives proposed at the time of its launch, Beaubourg is in no way a popular centre, if we mean by that it has attracted large numbers of visitors from the 'popular classes' – thus abolishing, as if by magic, age-old social barriers. This only goes to confirm that the (relative) absence of an entry-charge,[8] which may at one time have been seen as a key weapon in the battle to demo-cratize culture, has little actual impact on visitor numbers, since the barriers to culture are themselves cultural and not economic.[9] Nevertheless, when we compare Beaubourg's visitors to the tradi-tional art-gallery public (and, whether legitimately or not, the spontaneous tendency is to think of it as a gallery), it is undeniably the case that an overall democratization is taking place. It is simply the fact, however, that this democratization benefits not the workers, but the middle classes, whose strong presence has edged out the upper classes, for whom Beaubourg consequently repre-sents some loss of their prerogatives in cultural matters. The age factor plays a role here, the youthfulness of Beaubourg's visitors meaning that in large part they have not yet risen as far in the hierarchy of their professions as they ultimately might.

As we shall see, however, this 'democratization' is merely an artificial construct, resulting from the presence of diverse activities in the building, a factor which invalidates any direct comparison with the world of art galleries in general.

The diversity of publics

The 'typical Beaubourg visitor' with the statistically most repre-sentative characteristics would be a man of 30, living in Paris, working in education, research, or journalism, having a university qualification, and using the library regularly. However behind the falsely unambiguous image of a single model visitor constructed by this statistical operation, the sociological diversity of Beaubourg's audience, which is itself activity-related, is as great as the cultural diversity of activities which go on behind the apparent architectural unity of the building. These activities range from study to merely browsing around, from artistic education to language learning, from having a drink in the café to learning about contemporary artistic creation, from tourism to research, from cinema-going to computing.

Naturally, these different activities attract differing quantities of visitors: the latest surveys show that around 47 per cent of visitors went to Beaubourg to use the library, some 17 per cent for the art gallery, and about 10 per cent to see the major exhibitions on the fifth floor (though this figure varied by between 3 and 20 per cent).[10] As for the rest, they went to visit the other galleries (contemporary art, CCI, forum, BPI, and so on) or the *cinémathèque* (3 per cent) or were among the 10 per cent or thereabouts of 'wandering' visitors unable to give any precise reason for their visit.

Now there is inequality not merely in the numbers of people pursuing the various different activities, but also in the type of audience for each activity, each of the various sites having a quite distinct 'profile'. Thus, for example, the library has the highest number of student and working-class visitors, mostly people from Paris and its suburbs, and the greatest number of 18–35-year-olds. The gallery itself has a large proportion of foreign visitors and of highly qualified people; it also has more visitors from a higher age range (46–55) and with upper-class or educated middle-class backgrounds. The profile for the large exhibitions on the fifth floor is somewhat similar, though a little younger (36–45) and includes more women.

Of course, such diversity represents a quite normal state of affairs; it is part of the Centre's programme and fits in with the declared aim of making it a multipurpose establishment. It also perhaps corresponds to the unconscious programme of its designers, if one accepts the observation that there is an homology between the architectural structuring of activities and the social structure of their respective audiences: 'The higher you go in the building', notes Pierre Bourdieu, 'the higher the social status of the visitors'. The problem remains, however, of discovering to what extent this diversity represents increased possibilities of access for the various categories of visitor, or to what extent rather it merely reflects a compartmentalization of activities which are as strictly partitioned sociologically as they are topographically. In other words, in statistical terms, to what degree are the different social categories of audience mutually exclusive? Do they actually mix or do they merely rub shoulders in the same building?

Wandering and compartmentalization

It is possible to provide statistical answers to these questions. For example 45 per cent of visitors questioned are making 'single-purpose' visits or, in other words, using only a single part of the Centre to the exclusion of all its other attractions (most often they are going to the library where the level of single-purpose visits is as high as 60 per cent and where the figures show that 24 per cent of the users have come only to use the library and only ever come to the Centre for that purpose); 'dual-purpose' visits make up 23 per cent of the total, the remaining 32 per cent being divided up between the other possible options (triple, quadruple, and so on).

Similarly a substantial proportion of visitors questioned had never been – either on the day of the survey or at any time before – to any other part of the Centre than that to which they were going. We are therefore obliged to conclude that there is a considerable separation of audiences in relation to the different activities. This hyperpolarization, though it runs against the Centre's declared aim of multipurpose use, transparency, and internal fluidity, very frequently has a symmetrical opposite. This is the phenomenon of 'wandering' which applies to at least a tenth of visitors, who, though they have just been through various parts of the Centre, are unable to name any particular one. This 'wandering' which is particularly common among older visitors, as well as among visitors who are not very – or not at all – familiar with the building (provincials, foreigners), reflects a lack of points of reference or an inability to use the reference points offered, a problem we find elsewhere in many aspects of the Centre's operation. It is the case, first of all, with the topography of the Centre. A complementary study on the basis of interviews revealed how difficult it was for most of the visitors to say how many floors the building had.[11] Answers ranged from two (the library on the first floor and all the rest above it) to six; and this is to leave out of account the problem of actually applying the notion of 'floor' with all the mezzanines, basements, and 'sunken areas' that there are.

Such topographical vagueness produces problems when it comes to naming and signposting the parts of the building. It has, in fact been necessary to give names to some fifty different points and to do so in such a way that the elegance or the suitability of the name does not obscure the actual nature of the place (which the outsider needs to be able to identify). Early in the Centre's life some name-changes of this kind were made, the 'forum pit' being transformed into the 'forum' or the 'fifth floor temporary exhibition area' into the Great Gallery. Since, as a general rule, a name designates but does not describe, the ambiguities of the topography are compounded for the visitor by the obscurities of the 'house' names. These are in turn complicated by the use of strange initials (BPI, CCI, MNAM, and so on), which are of course familiar only to the administrative personnel. This kind of guerrilla warfare between the 'house' names which are official but purely internal, and unofficial names, which are unsanctioned but widely used, extends even to the name of the establishment itself: it is the 'Centre' to those who work there, the 'Gallery' to the inhabitants of the area, 'Beaubourg' to Parisians, and the 'Pompidou Centre' for others.

Among the various sources of the 'wandering' that results from more or less heterogeneous activities being lumped together in the building, there are then topographical ambiguities (risk of getting lost) and semantic ambiguities (lack of reference points). To these we must also add ambiguities relating to the functional identification of activities, particularly as regards their temporary or permanent character. In fact, by contrast with an art gallery, which is almost exclusively permanent, or an exhibition, which is temporary by definition, Beaubourg brings together very stable elements (the library), others which are less stable (the Gallery collections, where the hangings change periodically) and others which are very ephemeral (small exhibitions). How are unfamiliar or inattentive visitors to distinguish between these different types, and if they can, will they also be able to develop points of reference that will serve them again on a subsequent visit? For example, a person from the provinces on her first visit, who had spent a long time visiting the Beaubourg, said she had greatly enjoyed the 'Exhibition of Impressionists', though she had not heard of the National Museum of Modern Art (MNAM).[12] On the other hand, was an installation by Nam June Paik in the forum perceived by many visitors as 'televisions awaiting repair'?

All these (metaphorically and literally) misleading factors produce perceptions of Beaubourg that are as different as the forms of activity or the different categories of audience. One person will see it as a large library on two floors with a cafe on top. For another, it will be a huge art gallery filled with exhibitions of all kinds – books, pictures, posters, and so on. For yet another, who has never ventured on to the escalator leading to the upper levels, it will be seen as a large, warm, busy hall, where you can pass the time without anyone bothering you (an immigrant worker on sick leave who spent all his afternoons there told me, 'I'm like anyone else, I just like to be among people'). Someone else, who has taken up residence in the square among the street entertainers and the hippies, will simply see it as a sort of large mysterious factory in the heart of Paris, where they never seem to finish the building work. All he or she will know of it will be the groundfloor or basement toilets which are not only free, but also cleaner and more accessible than those in the stations.

The distribution of these different types of perception and use is, again, no random matter. For we do find actual examples of the 'ideal visitor' (generally young, Parisian, and highly qualified) though they are far from being the norm. They are likely to feel at ease in this labyrinth, to be able to find their way about or, in the absence of any clear bearings, they can accept with equanimity a principle of 'drifting' which will take them, on their regular visits, from one exhibition to another, from the library to the gallery, from the fifth-floor *cinémathèque* to the theatres in the basement and from the restaurant to the library. It seems, however, that many visitors have great difficulty in coping with this abundance of possibilities, to which they possess no prior key – either because they are not used to the building or, more importantly, because they feel less than assured there. In this case, they have the choice of admitting defeat at the outset, by asking for assistance at the reception desk (such cases are rare and consist either in admissions of total failure or, by contrast, in individual enquiries from those who are secure in the feeling of being 'at home' in the building and do not experience such a step as an admission of failure) or of turning back on themselves the humiliation of not being able to find their way around, in which case they will blame their own incompetence and will find solace in the idea that the place really is not for them after all. There is a further solution which consists in avoiding any risk of becoming lost by keeping entirely to a carefully planned route from which one allows oneself no deviation.

This latter course of action, which as we have seen is particularly frequent, implies a renunciation, from the very outset, of the possibilities of free circulation offered by the Centre, as if in the absence of reference points afforded by regular contact with cultural sites, its objective openness and transparency engendered an individual closure and an increased segmentation, destined to compensate for the objective instability of possibilities by the fixity of subjective habits. Such an attitude is indicative of a kind of mental rigidity, a difficulty to adapt which is also found in this type of visitor's attitude to other people: these are in fact the visitors among whom one finds the greatest sensitivity to the seething mass, distaste at the presence of other people, fear of the 'crowd' or 'people' and suspicion of bystanders, tourists, tramps, and thieves. In other words, it is exactly as if the aggression experienced in this need to orientate oneself without any proper markers – external and internal, objective and subjective – became transformed not on this occasion into humility as with those who blamed their own distractedness (leaving aside for the moment all those who do not even go there for want of being able to imagine themselves in such a place), but into aggression towards the Centre, its architects, and officials, or even against the government – in short against 'them'. As a result the under-use of Beaubourg's capacities is accompanied in many cases (typically among the regular users of the library who belong to the upwardly mobile fractions of the middle classes) by general bad feeling towards it and a low opinion of it.

It is not insignificant in these circumstances that the image of the labyrinth is frequently used to characterize Beaubourg (the images of a ship or a refinery being more frequently used to describe its outward appearance): it is a closed space in which you are both forced to circulate and yet deprived of orientation, a Kafkaesque place *par excellence*, as the replies to a survey carried out among season-ticket holders showed on the occasion of an exhibition on Kafka. In that survey Beaubourg itself was often referred to as typically Kafkaesque.[13] The public space – which is divided up into individual units and which you are free to wander through without really being able to master its organization since there are no markers to enable you to orientate yourself – is in fact a good illustration of the figure of the labyrinth, where the freedom of individual circulation supposedly guaranteed by the neutralization of references only serves to highlight a dependence on subjectively internalized criteria, which visitors possess in varying degrees. Indeed, that distribution is all the more unequal since these criteria relate to a field which is subjective above all, namely the field of culture. It appears therefore that the cases in which visitors' confidence in the organizational project (which is often, in fact, nothing but their confidence in their own resourcefulness) allows them to stroll happily through the building, experiencing each step as the realization of a preconceived plan, are rare indeed. More often, rather, the outward appearance of freedom (which in reality implies an increased dependence upon the architecture, since no way of gaining mastery over the building's space is available) is likely to give rise to aimless wandering which itself becomes transformed into anxiety; the capacity to 'drift' is not so easy to acquire as one might think.

The ambiguities of a success story

Beaubourg remains, however, undeniably an overall success. This can be measured by the entry figures, by the wear and tear on the carpets or by the length of the queues outside. To what extent, however, does this success, which indicates the satisfaction of a need, also satisfy the objectives initially aimed at? The question is certainly worth asking. As regards the desire to democratize access to culture, we have seen that this remains a marginal effect, if not a mere perspectival illusion, given the fact that the specific audiences for the principal activities have approximately the same characteristics as the audiences for these activities elsewhere: the art gallery audience is similar to art gallery audiences everywhere and the library users are like other library users. Similarly, the desacralization of art, which was initially at the heart of what Bourdieu called the 'Beaubourg effect', could be brought about only if the intended mingling of heterogeneous activities was actually practised and experienced by the visitors.[14] We have, seen, however, that this is merely an ideal, against which we may quote numerous cases of over-compartmenta-lization and of increased rigidity of itineraries, postures, and behaviour. Simply putting activities together in the same place (as the Maisons de la Culture attempted to do) cannot of itself conjure up a space which would allow people to consume 'culture' in general, with all hierarchies abolished. By the same token, the mere act of bringing together socially heterogeneous groups of people who would normally be separated does not produce a unified audience that is somehow magically homogenized in a common celebration of the cult of culture. On the contrary, as we have seen, such an operation is very likely to engender defensive reactions, though one may of course choose to view such reactions as the inevitable consequence of an experiment whose results can be seen as generally positive, by virtue of the blow they would have struck against the habits and unspoken assumptions of our current forms of social life.

In a certain sense then, what might have been a fear even before the Centre's opening (that 'risk of compartmentalization behind a facade of interchangeability', as Bernard Pingaud put it)[15] has been partially confirmed: the degree of compartmentalization appears indeed to be in direct proportion to that desire for interchangeability and transparency, for which the glass building, with all its structures open to view, in a sense provided the architectural guarantee.[16] And all that remains intact of the 'dream of a utopian site, which would suspend the established sociological laws of cultural consumption' (Bourdieu) is, the specific – and perhaps necessary – virtue of utopian dreaming.

However, in spite of what may seem a pessimistic conclusion, we must not forget that Beaubourg has enabled some quite new forms of behaviour in relation to cultural installations to develop, including practices without any preordained plan, in which the visitor does not determine in advance the objectives of his/her visit, but is carried along by the 'supply' proposed to him/her on site. More generally, it has introduced a diversification of cultural practices within the same building – for the effects of over-compartmentalization should make us forget that there are none the less some doubly 'felicitous' uses of the Centre, in the sense that they exploit to the full the possibilities the Centre offers and these themselves meet the more or less explicit dispositions of the visitors concerned.[17] And lastly nothing prevents us, once we have abandoned idealist and probably unrealistic ambitions, from seeing the Pompidou Centre as a daily sum of (more or less well-adapted) answers to, or (more or less well-used) proposals for meeting all sorts of quite real needs: needs for documentation, information, contemplation, and contact. In spite of everything, Beaubourg can pride itself as much on having in part created these needs, as on the degree to which it has managed to satisfy them.

Notes and references

1 Decree of 27 January 1974. Cf. Mollard, C. (1976) *L'Enjeu du Centre Pompidou*, Paris: Union Générale des Editions – 10/18.
2 It should be noted that it is important, in statistics of this nature, to distinguish between the number of *visitors* as we may compute them per day and the number of *visits* or entries. Looked at over a twelve-month period, this latter figure is inevitably higher than the number of visitors, since one person may make several visits in a year. The calculations that have been made for Beaubourg enable us to estimate that the ratio is roughly one visitor to every nine visits: in other words, we may estimate that 7.3 million visits means approximately 800,000 distinct visitors.
3 See *Des chiffres pour la culture* (1984) Paris: Service des Etudes des Recherches du Ministère de la Culture.

4 See *Pratique culturelle des Français* (1973, 1981) Paris: Service des Etudes des Recherches du Ministère de la Culture.

5 Bourdieu, P. (1977) *Enquête sur le public du Centre Pompidou*, Centre Pompidou.

6 This social overselection becomes even more evident if the figures are based not on the interviewee's profession, but (to take into account the social background of the many students) on that of the head of the family (which may be the interviewee, their father in the case of students, or a housewife's husband). The proportion of executives and professionals then rises from 30 to almost 50 per cent.

7 Cf. Bourdieu, P. and Darbel, A. (1969) *L'Amour de l'art*, Paris: Minuit, as well as the various studies summarized in Heinich, N. (1986) 'La Sociologie et les publics de l'art', in papers of the conference, Sociologie des Arts, Marseille, June 1985, Paris: Documentation française.

8 Though access to the building itself is free, there is an entry charge for the gallery, the fifth-floor exhibitions, the contemporary collections, the *cinémathèque*, and for the various events.

9 See Bourdieu, P. and Passeron, J.-C. (1964) *Les Héritiers*, Paris: Minuit.

10 See Heinich, N. (1986) 'Enquête aux portes du Centre' (Centre Pompidou) (the visitors to IRCAM are not included in these results). Surveys have been carried out regularly since the Centre opened, first by a team led by Bourdieu (J.-L. Fabiani, P.-M. Menger) in 1977, then by H. Berestycki (1979) and N. Heinich (1981) and, later, by N. Heinich (1983, 1986).

11 Cf. Heinich, N. (1983) *Pré-enquête*, Centre Pompidou.

12 Since then, the directors of the MNAM, having become aware of these identification problems, have had the interior of the space remodelled by the architect, Gae Aulenti. The same has been done to the gallery entrance, which is now more clearly signposted.

13 See Heinich, N. (1984) 'Kafka vu par vous', Paris: Centre Pompidou. See also on this subject Heinich, N. (1986) 'Les Immatériaux – un événement culturel', Paris: Expo-Media, 108 Rue Saint-Maur, 75011.

14 'The specific effect of a relatively de-sacralized and desacralizing building, which brings together cultural objects of very different "supply levels" (from modern paintings to postage stamps) and very different cultural functions (from the Gallery of Modern Art to the Library)', Bourdieu, P. (1977) *Enquête sur le public du Centre Pompidou*, Centre Pompidou.

15 Pingaud, B. (1975) 'Un Choix culturel', *Beaubourg et le musée de demain, L'Arc* 63: 25.

16 And it is difficult not to draw a parallel between what goes on in the administrative offices – where the level of internal tension rises as more offices themselves become open-plan and visible to everyone – and the process of re-compartmentalization carried out by a large proportion of the public.

17 Cf. Barbier-Bouvet, J. F. and Poulain, M. (1986) *Publics à l'ouvre – pratiques culturelles à la Bibliothèque publique d'information du Centre Pompidou*, Paris: La Documentation française.

10

Counting visitors
or visitors who count?

EILEAN HOOPER-GREENHILL

Too many visitors are bad for the fabric of our buildings, and our displays, and push up maintenance bills, too few visitors and we scent failure and we rush off to commission visitor surveys.[1]

To many museum workers, visitors are faceless ciphers, feet to be counted across a mat, but none the less a necessary evil as a museum is, by definition at least, a public institution. It is rare that museums know who visits them and why, although any curator will be able to quote endless 'visitor figures'. Quantity not quality seems to be the name of the game, and evaluation of the work of the museum is measured by weight of bodies rather than by depth of experience.

Visitors are generally understood as those people who come to the museum to view the displays, and a more subtle notion of different user groups is not often developed. All museums are used in different ways by different groups, which might include those people who come to identify an object, researchers, and volunteers. Volunteers might be not only people working in a voluntary capacity in their spare time because of some accumulation of experience that is of value to the museum, but also young people trying to get some experience to enter the profession. Other user groups include teachers, children, scouts, WEA, and so on. The museum is also used by groups that are visited by museum workers. This outreach work might involve handling sessions for elderly people in a nursing home, follow-up work after a school visit, the development of networks in a particular section of the local community, or a museum bus or train visiting a site. Loan services

213

from museums have been valued by many educational institutions since the beginning of the century.

In many museums a vast amount of this kind of work is being carried out, but typically, in an uncoordinated, fragmented way. It is extremely unlikely that there will be a co-ordinated communications policy that is related to a researched knowledge of the total clientele of the museum. It is probable that the museum will not have stated policies of any sort, and that specific objectives in relation to provision for visitors, potential visitors, and the public at large will not have been defined.

Most museums, in spite of apparent evidence to the contrary, work at a frenetic pace. In addition, resources are scarce and becoming scarcer. The response is often to try to work even faster. But with a lack of aims, a lack of knowledge of what the museum is doing, and a lack of knowledge of why and for whom this work is being done, this increase in pace is absolutely meaningless. Most museums in Britain actually need to stop work for a while, for curators to talk to each other, for educationalists and curators to meet, for all the staff of the museum to identify and discuss common aims and methods. The Rayner Report pointed out that the two large national museums that it examined, the Victoria and Albert Museum and the Science Museum, were operating without aims or objectives.

> Neither . . . had aims: nor were there even *obita dicta* or tablets from the past from which valid aims for the present could be clearly deduced. Equally the Department of Education and Science, though it gave them our money, could not say, other than extemporaneously, what the museums were there to do.[2]

Many museums that have been in existence for a long time are continuing under their own momentum and are only just beginning to question their relevance to the late twentieth century. Large questions of what a museum has been, is now, and should be in the future, need to be asked and answered. Much of the answer will depend on the interaction of the museum staff with those to whom the museum can be of use, of delight, and of educational value. Here we should consider not only those who can be identified as current users but also, most importantly, those who are potential users.

It is however true that now museums are becoming aware that they have disregarded their publics and the perceptions of their visitors for too long. It is becoming clear that museum curators have worked from within their own world views and have assumed that visitors share the values, the assumptions and the intellectual preoccupations that have guided not only the choice and presentation of exhibitions, but also, more fundamentally, the selection and acquisition of objects.

It is perhaps rare that professions are self-conscious about what they do, and the museum profession is no exception to this. The grounding assumptions that guide museum work have been operating at a common-sense level for a very long time, but museum workers are now beginning to feel the need for the conceptual apparatus that will enable a more critical examination of these taken-for-granted notions that underpin daily practices.

One of the most essential aspects of this will be the beginnings of an understanding of the experience of the visitor to the museum. Decisions about the work of the museum have rarely taken into account the needs, wishes, or feelings of the audience. Statements such as the following are unusual and are generally to be found in the newer museums, most of which are operating as independent charities:

> The independent museums first of all *depend* on visitors; they are consumer oriented; they are user-friendly, so they have an instinct to reach out and serve their public. They have a dialogue with their clients; we cannot possibly forget that we are there to serve. . . . And we must continue to be of service as we grow . . . we harness the work of disparate groups of people and we have to be good at communicating with all of them and making them feel cherished, whether they are volunteers, unemployed, the elderly, scholarly, or MSC: they are all needed by us. What they can give us is of value to us; we must make them feel we value them.[3]

The idea that museums might value, or even cherish, their visitors and their user groups is a new one, although increasingly curators will be adopting this point of view. The quality of the experience is beginning to matter. The Henley Centre for Leisure Forecasting indicates that people now no longer define themselves by their occupations, but use their interests as a way of identifying and describing themselves.[4] A major American report on the future of museums, *Museums for a New Century*, confirms that the museum that is succeeding best in a time of recession in the USA is the one with a well-established and qualitative relationship with the community it serves. This report further points out quite unequivocally that the educational role of the museum, understood in its broadest sense, is going to become of greater and greater importance.[5]

Museum visitor surveys and their limitations

During the last twenty years there have been many small-scale visitor surveys carried out in individual museums across the country.[6] In general these have been executed with lack of staff, money, time, and often, without professional guidance. The surveys represent sincere attempts by museum workers to find out who their visitors are, and in some cases valuable insights at the local level have been gained. However, all too often this work, crucial to both the determining and evaluating of museum policy, has not been accorded the importance that it deserves. The design and execution of the surveys has often been left to inexperienced, untrained, temporary staff, and vital questions as to the objectives of the work have not been asked.

The results of these surveys are not always made generally available. For many reasons, most of them are regarded as internal documents and are therefore not written up in the professional journals, or discussed except within the museum itself. Compilation and comparison of data are therefore difficult, both for the museum worker and the museum researcher.

During the last five or six years a few larger-scale surveys of national museums have been produced either by government departments or commissioned professional researchers.[7] Although weightier and more thorough than some of the earlier surveys, these projects are limited to the study of the museum visitor, the in-museum situation, and do not set out to relate this to either the local area or the population in general. The reports are produced for management as information relating to policy decisions, which has therefore limited the approach to the collection of quantitative data concerning those people who have visited the museum. Few sociologists or cultural theorists have directed their attention to the museum as a site to study. There has been no large-scale, detailed survey of the general public and its uses of museums, such as the one that was conducted twelve years ago by the Canadian government when a national museums policy was put into effect.[8] This survey dealt with demographics at a national level and also looked into fundamental attitudes of Canadians to museums as a leisure pursuit. These were considered in comparison with other ways of using leisure time. It remains the most comprehensive, accessible, and professional account of the interaction of museums to people that exists and as such provides a model for future research in Britain.

Government statistics include some vital although limited information about the nature of the museum public. The *General Household Surveys* include some figures on museum visiting in analyses of how people spend their leisure time.[9] *Social Trends* will also yield some information of this nature.[10] From these sources we can see that in relation to the British population as a whole that section that visits museums is of a higher social class, better educated, younger, and more mobile. The patterns of museum visiting are closely related to those for theatre, opera, dance, and classical concerts. The *General Household Survey* from 1977 breaks down the figures by gross weekly household income, and demonstrates that as the weekly income rises, so does the number of museum visits. In other words, the more highly paid you are, the more likely you are to visit a museum. Although there are indications that this is the case for other related activities, it is particularly marked for museums.

The English Tourist Board (ETB) carried out a survey of museum visiting in 1982.[11] This report identified the same demographic characteristics in museum visitors and also showed how this is likely to vary between types of museums. Dividing museums by governing body, a more democratic audience was identified in the local authority museums than in national museums, although the visitors were still more privileged in all aspects in relation to the population in general. The ETB survey additionally pointed out that 24 per cent of all British adults visited a museum at least once during the year (1981) that it was investigating. This survey was carried out expressly to justify charges and confined its conclusions to this issue. On discovering a relatively small, highly select audience for museums, the report proposed that charges would be justified on the grounds that visitors could afford to pay them, and the report further suggested that the majority of visitors would welcome them. This report has since been quoted to demonstrate that 'the British public' voted in favour of charges.[12]

It has been argued that the sample of museums used by the ETB was not well chosen (the sample was grossly skewed in favour of national museums), but more worrying was their assertion that the proportion of British adults visiting museums is only 24 per cent. From research in other countries, it would seem that the proportion of the population that visits a museum is regularly about 50 per cent. Is Britain so out of line?

Further figures that relate to this point can be found in the reports of the Henley Centre for Leisure Forecasting, who have produced percentages of 45–48 on a quarterly basis for some years.[13] The regularity of these findings, carried out over a period of time and in the context of a broad-ranging survey of trends, would seem to lend weight to the conclusions, but more specific research is required before we can be certain whether nearly half or only a quarter of the British population visit a museum at least once a year.

Further research is also needed to clarify how far the general rather depressing picture of the nature of the museum visitor relates to specific types of museums. Art galleries seem to attract the most highly privileged people, while infrequent museum visitors are more likely to visit general or site museums. There is some evidence that more women than men visit art galleries and that in science museums the converse is true.

Research carried out in Sweden, Canada, the USA, France, Germany, and Britain over the last fifteen to twenty years confirms that education and wealth are important variables in determining who will become a museum visitor. Both the Canadian and the Swedish reports say that the dominant variable is education.[14] The more you have been exposed to higher levels of education, the more likely you are to become a museum visitor. Is this the case in Britain? Recent research carried out at the British Museum[15] and the Victoria and Albert Museum[16] show that visitors have a very high terminal education age: in both museums the average seems to be about 21.[17] The percentage of people in Britain that have had the benefit of education up to this level is 8 per cent. Even bearing in mind that both museums attract large numbers of people from countries where the percentage of highly educated people is higher, it would seem that on this dimension museums are attracting a non-representational cross-section of the public.

However these quantitative data can present a misleading picture of an unchanging monolithic institution. More qualitative data are required to reveal the efforts made by some of the museum staff to break down this stereotyped image. Merely looking at 'visitor figures' obscures the fact that in the British Museum, for example, the Education Department works to make the museum more accessible to groups who are not necessarily highly visible. In so doing new ways of working are explored that affect the traditional practices of the museum.

Over the last three years the Education Department of the British Museum has produced two exhibitions of sculpture that could be handled. The first of these, 'Please Touch', was evaluated on a professional basis and the findings related to the second, 'Human Touch', which made for quite radical changes in the design of the second exhibition.[18] Bright colours were used behind the objects and on the hand-rail; the objects were arranged in the space in a linear way with the hand-rail acting as a guide to position, texts were large and simple without being simplistic, and seats and audio-cassettes were provided. Most radical of all, perhaps, was the reproduction of a repeat image next to the object. This was drawn in a firm black outline, with black shading, and was on a smaller scale than the sculptures. Those with some vision could get an idea of the totality of the object that complimented the touch experience that of necessity is limited to only one part at a time. This image was repeated in the catalogue, as were the label texts. The catalogue could act as an aid during the exhibition, perhaps while sitting down having a rest, but also worked as a reminder after the exhibition.

Listening to a group of blind people discussing their experiences of many special exhibitions of 'Sculpture for the Blind', it was clear that they enjoyed going back to the experience in a quiet time at home, and for those with some residual vision, the catalogue reminded them of the feelings they had had at the time, and enabled them to explore this further. Those with no vision would have liked access to the tapes that they had used in the exhibition, but had had to leave behind. It was also clear that all the group, while appreciating the opportunity to 'see' those things that sighted people have access to whenever they want it, bitterly resented the fact that they were dependent on special provision as and when the museum chose to produce it. 'Why can't the local museum have a small permanent table of things to handle available all the time? Then we could go when we wanted, and could manage ourselves without a special trip.'

Counting visitor numbers, or measuring the social class of visitors, will not reveal this kind of qualitative data, that means the museum researcher 'getting her hands dirty' and actually listening to people and their own opinions of their needs. A more flexible model of research that moves beyond demographics into interpretative or ethnomethodological understandings and methods is required.

The paucity of research at both the local and the national level is symptomatic of the marginal social position that museums have occupied for the greater part of this century. The resurgence of museums in the last few years, with new museums opening at the rate of roughly one a week, and long-established museums taking on new roles, means that the need is now very pressing for qualitative information to justify new ambitions, to attract new forms of support, and to account for the spending of often large sums of money.

Attitudes to museums

Museum visitor surveys convey information only about those people who visit the museum. A museum whose visitor numbers are falling and who rushes therefore to 'do a survey' is in fact looking at the wrong thing. A visitor survey will not, however hard it tries, reveal the opinions of those who have not come to the museum. It will show those who come, and if this is compared with local population studies, the gaps will become clear. To obtain a truer picture of why the figures are falling or, even better, to see what people think about the museum anyway, it is necessary to do a general population study, and to talk to both those who do visit museums, and those who don't. This will entail leaving the museum building! Two studies from North America provide both useful methodology and useful findings.

The Museum and the Canadian Public suggests that the image of the museum is a positive one in the minds of many people, but that this does not mean that they visit them.[19] More significantly, in comparing the museum with five other leisure activities, both in-home and outside, the image of the museum is more ambiguous. Whereas reading, visiting a movie, or attending a concert or a play had fairly clearly defined images, with the in-home activity having the clearest definitions, visiting a museum was not clearly perceived across a number of dimensions. Compared to other activities, visiting a museum is not clearly defined as either 'relaxing' or 'exciting', nor as either 'modern' or 'old-fashioned'. Although a majority of Canadians found the experience 'valuable to me', 'sociable', and 'easy on the brain', the museum was less likely than the other activities to receive any of these designators. The only ways in which museum visits were really distinguished from other activities were in being perceived as 'inconvenient', 'something I don't do very often', and 'educational' rather than 'entertaining'. Non-visitors felt that they would need a prior knowledge about the collections and subject matter of the museum that they knew they·

did not have. Both visitors and non-visitors are likely to perceive the museum as an institution that did not live up to its promise, that did not deliver a full, enriching active experience, that was difficult, needing a high level of knowledge about the collections, and that was physically uncomfortable.

A second study from North America is useful in pursuing the attiudes of both the visitor and the non-visitor to museums.[20] Work on visitor research is more firmly established in the USA than in Britain, and this study was able to start from the premise that demographic descriptions are not in themselves explanatory. We may know who comes, but we do not know why. Marilyn Hood, working with the Museum of Art in Toledo, focused on how individuals made use of their leisure time and energy, and considered psychographic characteristics, looking at attitudes, values, perceptions, interests. Hood identified six major attributes underlying the choices adults made of leisure time. These are listed in alphabetical order as follows:

1 being with people,
2 doing something worthwhile,
3 feeling comfortable and at ease in one's surroundings,
4 having a challenge of new experiences,
5 having an opportunity to learn,
6 participating actively.

These attributes are perceived and valued differently by individuals but all are of fundamental importance in how the choice was made to visit the museum. Using these criteria, Hood proposes that attendance patterns can be identified by leisure values and attributes.

Hood identified three distinctly different audience segments; frequent participants, occasional participants, and non-participants. Frequent visitors to museums (who visited at least three times a year) were likely to value highly all of the six leisure attributes and perceive all of them to be present in museums. The attributes that this group valued most were: having an opportunity to learn, having the challenge of new experiences, and doing something worthwhile in leisure time. This group made up a minority of the community of Toledo, about 14 per cent, but accounted for about 40–50 per cent of the museum's visits.

Non-participants, who represented 46 per cent of the Toledo metropolitan community, tended to value those leisure attributes that were least highly valued by the frequent visitors: being with people, participating actively, and feeling comfortable and at ease in their surroundings. These were not perceived as being part of the experience of the museum, and other choices were made for their leisure time. Museums were perceived as difficult and requiring special skills to read the 'museum code' that this group did not think were available to them. Museums were also perceived as places that impose restrictions on group behaviour. Activities that emphasize active participation, with casual and familiar surroundings and the chance to interact socially with people, were chosen instead of the museum visit.

Most striking were the findings in relation to the occasional participants, those people who visited the museum once or twice a year, and who made up 40 per cent of the community, and 50–60 per cent of the museum visits. This group tended to be more like the non-participants than the frequent visitors. As a group they tended to have been socialized as children into activities that emphasized active participation, and as adults they tended to be active not only in outdoor activities and sports, but also in playing musical instruments and engaging in arts and crafts. Family-centred activities were seen as important, in contrast to the frequent visitors who were more likely to visit the museum alone. Occasional participants valued comfort in their leisure activities, and meant by this not only physical comfort, but also a feeling of being at ease, of belonging. These people did not feel at ease in the museum, and tended to visit on special occasions only, often with a support group to provide social validation.

This study showed that the museum was perceived very differently by different groups. Those who visit frequently are those to whom the museum is experienced as appropriate, comfortable, and familiar. They made up a very small proportion of the community in Toledo. The vast majority of the community, 86 per cent, perceived the museum either as offering barely enough of those valued attributes that determine choice to merit a visit, or as being an inappropriate place in which to spend leisure time. The curatorial reaction to the study was to understand that planning must go beyond the internal concerns of the museum and should consider the public that is being provided for. 'We now realize that we should plan more on their terms, not just on our own terms.'[21]

This study focused on a specific type of museum in a particular area. The Canadian report took a broader stance. Both point to the conclusion that the museum offers a satisfactory experience to only a small proportion of its visitors, and to an even smaller proportion of the community that it serves. How far can we relate these studies to the British experience? From the limited information that is available it seems highly likely that in Britain too, museums have satisfied only a very small proportion of their communities. Let us critically examine the experience of the museum in relation to the visitor, to find out why this might be the case, and also, to find out how this experience might be changing for the better.

The museum experience

The museum experience is made up of many different aspects that operate in relation to each other. These aspects will include the role, status, and perceptions of all the people involved in the museum (security staff, administrators, academic staff, user groups, voluntary workers, trustees, councillors); the institutional and architectural site; and the material collected, stored, and displayed. These elements may act to reinforce or contradict each other, and there is likely to be substantial variation between one museum and another. Museums vary from the enormous national museums that may have many miles of floor space and some hundreds of specialist staff, to the small one-room museum attached to the local library with only one person to act as curator, warder, desk-staff, and teacher. Sites for museums vary from boats to barns, from entire parts of the countryside to prisons.

One of the most crucial elements in influencing the museum experience is the attitude of the museum worker. One museum director once told me that he understood 'his' audience in relation to a ladder, with those who knew least about the intellectual areas and the collections of the museum at the bottom. The educational task of the museum was to enable the ignorant to climb the ladder to reach the top. He pointed out that he was not making a value judgement about the quality of the view from each of the rung of the ladder; each might be equally fine. None the less the task of the museum was to enable a steady climb that would thus offer improved perspectives. This anecdote reveals many of the attitudes that can be found in museums, attitudes which position the curator firmly as expert in 'his' subject, and the visitor equally firmly as 'below' this level of knowledge. Once this hierarchical position is established, the curator is free to adopt a stance of pastoral care, both patriarchal and evangelical, that offers opportunities to the visitor to improve and reach up to the higher levels of knowledge and virtue that the museum (and the curator) represents.

The exercise of social control through the meting out of learning, mediated and identified with the achievement of worth, is very deeply embedded in the museum. It was explicit and overt during the nineteenth century when many museums were founded, and still underpins much of museum thinking today. An example will draw this out. Palmerston, prime minister in 1856, during the discussion in Parliament as to whether or not to set up a National Portrait Gallery, made the following remarks:

'There cannot, I feel convinced, be a greater incentive to mental exertion, to noble actions, to good conduct on the part of the living, than for them to see before them the features of those who have done things which are worthy of our admiration and whose example we are more induced to imitate when they are brought before us in the visible and tangible shape of portraits.'[22]

This statement shows how the aim of the museum was not merely the collection of portraits, or even the construction of a national past with specific dimensions. The objects themselves were to be used to construct a moral imperative, through a specific view of the past, that would shape social behaviour. The representation of the past (and therefore the present) was to act on the individual at both a mental and a physical level, a shaping of both mind and body.[23] Museum curators were given a role as moral custodian that ran parallel to the role of custodian of things. Through the collection and display of objects and artefacts, not only was the visitor to be controlled, but also dominant social images were to be constructed that would have far-reaching effects. This historic role of moral guardian still influences the perceptions of many curators.

The power of the curator

Curators speak from the security of institutions that are sanctioned within society as places of worth and value. Their words and deeds have a legitimation and a power that is accorded them by this institutional context. The institutional context of the museum enmeshes with other institutions within society. Museums operate in a linked network with other agencies that organize and control social life. These operate at both the local and the national level. The discourse of the museum reinforces and is reinforced by governmental, educational, and cultural agencies. In some cases the same individuals that sit on elected boards for museums perform the same function for other bodies. In fact, they are chosen for exactly this power network that will then accrue to the museum. Thus the words of the curator enmesh with the power and control networks of society and have a resonance beyond the power of the individual worker. This resonance is felt by those who enter the museum as an authority effect.[24]

The authority of the curator is reinforced by the architectural aspect of the site. Many museums occupy buildings that were specifically built to convey a cultural message, often one about the value of classical culture, about which only some groups within society have any knowledge.

The museum building may sometimes be one that relates architecturally to the law courts, the police station, and other repressive agents of social control. These large dominant buildings convey messages about the power of the state and its institutions within a society. The museum may take its place alongside. Sometimes museum buildings are old, valued to the locality because of their links back to the past. Here again that message of value, of social worth, is conveyed, though it may well in this specific instance not be as exclusive or repressive as in other examples. However, that after image of the other museum forms will linger on the mental retina of the observer. In many cases the messages of the buildings may be enough to deter those who don't know about classical culture, who do know about the power of the law and who have not found many images of the past that have served them well.

The authority of the curator and the site is reinforced by the guards at the door of the museum. The door is often closed and guarded. On entry to the museum the visitor must pass the warders, those security men that protect the objects from theft or harm. This is no small matter. The visitor is assessed on entry and reprimanded and ultimately expelled if not thought to be behaving quietly and docilely. A visitor survey carried out at a Midlands museum recently found that both visitors and potential visitors were discouraged by the uniformed male guards at the entrance. These have now been replaced by non-uniformed women.

The secure aspect of the building is often unconsciously emphasized in such a way as to make people feel uncomfortable. The objects within the museum are valuable, and the building operates as a secure area. It is alarmed, surveyed, and patrolled. Visitors are watched as they look at the objects, sometimes by guards in uniforms like those of the police (and indeed 'security' staff are often recruited from either the armed forces or the police), sometimes by closed-circuit camera. Spaces are arranged so that surveillance can be put into effect. Spaces are also arranged so that in the event of theft, they can be isolated and closed. The need for security means that all exits and entrances – breaks in the boundary defences – are scrutinized by the curators in planning the use of the building, and by the security guards in the operation of their duties. The museum is in fact a prison for objects. The visitor walks through the prison under close watch, maintaining a decorous and quiet conduct. Some visitors, particularly the young or the untidy, will be watched with extra care.

This aspect of museums has been tackled differently in at least one museum in America. The Children's Museum at Boston works with the concept of floor staff, and uses interpreters as part of these. Floor managers oversee the well-being of both interpreters and visitors as they chat together to enliven, humanize, and extend the displays. The floor staff are often youngsters from school, or young adults on their way from school to employment. They work on placements at the museum for a few months, taking part in a training scheme that explores working with people in many different ways. The training programme might include elements of teaching theory, films about working with mentally retarded children or adults, and discussions with trained and experienced people about the presentation of self and the interpretation of body language. The development of the interpreters is regarded as part of the educational work of the museum, and staff members, time, and resources are put aside to resource this programme.[25] This way of using staff members as facilitators of informal learning rather than as guardians of cultural property is being promoted by some of the more thoughtful British museum professionals.[26]

Museum buildings are environmentally controlled for the benefit of the objects stored there. The light, heat, air, and humidity are closely monitored and set at levels that are suitable for the objects they envelop. An ideal environment from the museum point of view is one in which every aspect of the physical climate in which the objects are held is controlled in order to arrest their decay. Thus light is not permitted to enter until damaging rays have been excluded, illumination levels are set, air is cleaned, temperature is moderated. The environment in which the visitor moves is ideally controlled in all its aspects to arrest time and its effects, to prevent death and decay. In practice there are many reasons why such a thing does not happen, but museum workers constantly strive towards this. Visitors are part of the problem as they bring dirt and damp from an uncontrolled, polluted atmosphere into the purified space of the museum. The heat generated by their bodies and the breath that visitors expel add to the traces of impurity which will have to be eradicated after they have left the building.[27] The housekeeping tasks of the curator are to efface the effects of the visitor, to preserve the pure and ordered space, much as in the home the task of the housewife is to restore the damage that living inflicts on the environment of the home. Although one is not perhaps aware of this control of the environment as such, doesn't it partly account for that feeling of walking surrounded by cotton-wool, of being an interloper, allowed in on sufferance?

When the British Museum was first set up it was established in a very grand and elaborate private house. The keepers lived on the job, and much of the early work of the museum seems to have taken the form of squabbles over who had the most coal. Reading up the history of the museum, this domestic atmosphere and this feeling on the part of the staff of being part of a family has been valued very highly. In fact, it is only fairly recently that the staff have not come from an extended family circle. This was written in 1973:

> No longer is it true, as it was until quite recently, that many in the museum have had a father, an uncle or a grandfather in the Trustees' service and had spent or were prepared to spend a lifetime in the same service.

The same writer also writes:

> Hitherto the Museum has retained something of the spirit of the private house in which it once lodged and of the intimacy and essential friendliness that that entails – and sometimes of the bitter feeling that now and then breaks out within a family. We still have a housekeeper and housemaids and not just cleaners; we still carry house-keys; our names and ranks are recorded in a house-list and we enter and leave the Museum by the Front Hall, as did our predecessors in the days of the old Montagu House.[28]

Museums have in the past formed very closed and insular 'family' communities. How far does this go to explain that feeling of being in the wrong place at the wrong time that can sometimes befall those who are not part of the family and who thought they had the right to view their possessions?

The power of the object

Objects form the *raison d'être* for most museums and this is rarely questioned. The structures of privilege that guide the principles of collection in the museum are rarely clearly articulated. Objects will be acquired because they relate to existing collections. Thus the history of the institution and the decisions made over collection policies by former curators will deeply influence what is possible in the present and the future.

This often results in a display of objects that is out of joint with current values. Where collections were established within a nineteenth-century world view, and have maintained this momentum some curious ruptures can be noted. For example one of the first women to be represented in the National Portrait Gallery, collecting to stir people to mental exertion and noble actions, was Nell Gwyn.

Within the museum there will be a series of imperatives at various levels that will result in some objects being made visible, and others being concealed. It is rare that the perceptions of visitors, their interests, are consulted. Decisions are made according to structures of relevance that relate to the internal concerns of the museum and its immediate context, including its political network.

Changes are being made to this way of working in the area of multicultural provision. Some museums have recognized the fact that Britain is a plural society and that the museum has a duty both to collect and to exhibit artefacts that relate to all sections of the community. Leicester Museum was one of the first to appoint specialist staff to develop relevant collecting and communicating policies. Work has been undertaken with many different sections of the local multi-ethnic population, including Asian, Afro-Caribbean, and Chinese groups. The work has proceeded slowly and with care, with advice and collaboration from community leaders.[29] In one sense it might be posited that the museum is neutral territory for all groups and, in maintaining this, is able to work with them all without being identified as belonging to a particular section. This, at any rate, is very much part of the complexities that multicultural workers are encountering. This is certainly felt to be the case at the museum in Boston, which has a long and successful history of networking and collaborating with different ethnic groups. The staff have set up advisory boards made up of members of the different communities, and will always confer with the relevant board when doing either display or outreach work.[30]

This aspect of multicultural work in Britain is innovatory. There are few other instances where particular groups are targeted and where the potential audience is co-opted to act as advisers to the displays. In most other circumstances it is rare that curators concern themselves with the way in which people interact with their displays. The opinions of visitors are not taken into account in their planning, and as a result the intellectual level of the displays are often too high, and the texts and labels are often incomprehensible to a majority of visitors. A simple readability test reveals that the bulk of museum labels are written in such a way that a reading level of 17 or higher is required to begin to understand them.[31] Putting this together with the often erudite content of museum exhibitions and the fact that texts are read while standing, even while moving, and it soon becomes clear why museums are so exhausting, and why most visits do not last longer than ninety minutes.

After installation it is a rare curator that spends time evaluating the effects.[32] During the entire exhibition process the museum staff (except for the security staff) and the visitors remain invisible to each other. There is no contact or communication. From the visitor's point of view the displays present a closed system. They are seen as a finished, completed form, the makers are anonymous and unidentified, and there is no possibility of influencing or changing the existing cases or panels. Evaluation of displays is a much more common practice in North America, where exhibits are designed and tested in a cheap mock-up form, with brown paper and felt-tip pens, before the expensive production process begins. This try-out period often results in dramatic changes as curators discover that the display that they thought was self-evident did not in fact convey the message.[33]

The work of the new multicultural appointments in museums has demonstrated that specific attention given to the needs and interests of clearly defined target groups has changed not only the closed and self-referential method of museums, but also the nature of the audiences. Working closely with ethnic community groups and their leaders, new relevances have been found for the museum. To achieve this, changes have been made. These have entailed a review of collecting policies, to identify which objects are important and why; a review of modes of transmission, often entailing a move away from a static display to more active methods; and a review of priorities, to incorporate those of the audience as well as those of the curator. The workers in this field are very few, only about half a dozen, and significantly, most of them have been working in fields outside museums. They are all working in local authority museums, and are beginning to formulate a coherent work methodology. As this develops, it will become even more obvious that these methods are of enormous relevance to museums in general, and that if museums can become valuable, and new audiences can be recruited in this way from specific ethnic communities, then new links can be made with other groups too. The traditional élitist pattern of museum visiting could be broken down, and the museum, which is after all supported by the population in general, could perhaps be of use to the population in general.

Museums are very various indeed. Those that are beginning to expand and cherish their audiences, redefine their objectives and re-evaluate long-standing work practices are those that are visited and revisited with pleasure. Those that cling to irrelevant and insular activities will find (as some are already finding) that their visitor numbers are falling, and that they are left as residual cultural forms. Museums must demonstrate their relevance and recruit their audiences in a new aggressive leisure market. It is no longer (if it ever was) merely enough to exist.

Acknowledgements

My thanks are due to John Reeve, British Museum, and David Anderson, National Maritime Museum, for their helpful comments on an earlier draft of this paper.

Notes and references

1 Cumming, V. (1985) 'The role of training in managing change', in N. Cossons (ed.) *The Management of Change in Museums*, proceedings of a seminar held at the National Maritime Museum, Greenwich, 22 November 1984, London: National Maritime Museum.

2 Burrett, G. (1985) 'After Rayner', in N. Cossons (ed.) *The Management of Change in Museums*, London: National Maritime Museum, 5–7.

3 Sekers, D. (1985) 'Independence stimulates', in N. Cossons (ed.) *The Management of Change in Museums*, London: National Maritime Museum, 37–8.

4 *Leisure Futures* (1986), London: Henley Centre for Leisure Forecasting.

5 American Association of Museums, Commission on Museums for a New Century (1984) *Museums for a New Century*, Washington, DC: American Association of Museums.

6 See for example Arber, A. J. N. (1975) 'A survey of visitors to the Roualt exhibition at Manchester City Art Gallery', *Museums Journal* 75(1): 5–8; and Doughty, P. S. (1968) 'The public of the Ulster Museum: a statistical survey'; *Museums Journal* 68(1): 19–25; 68(2): 47–53.

7 See Heady, P. (1984) *Visiting Museums*, OPCS, London: HMSO; Mann, P. (1986) *A Survey of Visitors to the British Museum (1982–1983)*, British Museum occasional paper 64; *A Survey of Visitors to the Scottish National Museums and Galleries* (1981) Central Research Unit Papers, Scottish Office, June.

8 Dixon, B., Courtney, A. E., and Bailey, R. H. (1974) *The Museum and the Canadian Public*, Toronto: Arts and Culture Branch, Department of the Secretary of State.

9 *General Household Survey*, produced annually by the Office of Population Censuses and Surveys, Social Survey Division, London: HMSO.

10 *Social Trends*, produced annually by the Central Statistical Office, London: HMSO.

11 English Tourist Board (1982) *Visitors to Museums Survey 1982*, London: English Tourist Board.

12 'Pressing the charges', *Sunday Times*, 20 October 1985.

13 Henley Centre for Leisure Forecasting (1983) *Leisure Futures – fact pack, 1983/4*, Henley Centre.

14 Arnell, V., Hammer, I., and Nylöf, G. (1976) *Going to Exhibitions*, Riksutstallningar/Swedish Travelling Exhibitions, Sweden.

15 Mann, P. (1986) *A Survey of Visitors to the British Museum (1982–1983)*, British Museum occasional paper 64: 9.

16 Heady, P. (1984) *Visiting Museums*, OPCS, London: HMSO, p. 14.

17 Mann, P. (1986) *A Survey of Visitors to the British Museum (1982–1983)*, British Museum occasional paper 64: 9.

18 Coles, P. (1983) *Please Touch; An Evaluation of the Please Touch Exhibition at the British Museum*, London: Committee of Inquiry into the Arts and Disabled People/Carnegie UK Trust.

19 Dixon, B., Courtney, A. E., and Bailey, R. H. (1974) *The Museum and the Canadian Public*, Toronto: Arts and Culture Branch, Department of the Secretary of State, pp. 44–5.

20 Hood, M. G. (1983) 'Staying away – why people choose not to visit museums', *Museum News* 61(4): 50–7. See also Hood, M. G. (1981) 'Adult attitudes toward leisure choices in relation to museum participation', PhD thesis, Ohio State University.

21 ibid., p. 57.

22 Hooper-Greenhill, E. (1980) 'The National Portrait Gallery; a case-study in cultural reproduction', MA thesis, University of London.

23 For an analysis of the effects of space in the control and construction of minds and bodies see Foucault, M. (1977) *Discipline and Punish*, Harmondsworth: Penguin.

24 The authority effect in its operation in the behaviour of museum visitors has been investigated at the Natural History Museum by Paulette Macmanus, postgraduate research student at the Centre for Science and Mathematics Education, London.

25 Gurian, E. (1981) 'Adult learning at Children's Museum of Boston', in Z. Collins (ed.) *Museums, Adults and the Humanities*, Washington, DC: American Association of Museums.

26 Feber, S. (1987) 'New approaches to science: in the museum or out with

the museum', in T. Ambrose (ed.) *Education in Museums; Museums in Education*, 85–93.

27 Wilson, D. (1982) 'Public interest versus Conservation', *Museum* 34(1): 65–7.

28 Miller, E. (1973) *That Noble Cabinet*, London: André Deutsch, p. 17.

29 Nicholson, J. (1985) 'The museum and the Indian community: findings and orientation of the Leicestershire Museum Service', *Museum Ethnographers Group Newsletter* 19: 3–14.

30 Gurian, E. (1981) 'Adult learning at Children's Museum of Boston', in Z. Collins (ed.) *Museums, Adults and the Humanities*, Washington, DC: American Association of Museums, pp. 291–2.

31 Sorsby, B. D. and Horne, S. D. (1980) 'The readability of museum labels', *Museums Journal* 80(3): 157–9.

32 The exception to this is the pioneering work carried out under the direction of Roger Miles at the British Museum (Natural History) which has been extensively documented. See in particular Miles, R. (ed.) (1982) *The Design of Educational Exhibits*, London: Allen & Unwin.

33 The literature on evaluation is extensive, but see in particular Patten, L. H. (1982/3) 'Education by design', *Education* 10, ICOM, Unesco.

Index

Note: museums in London are entered directly under their name. Those outside London can be found under place. Page numbers in italics refer to illustrations.

Index

realism, and museums 12–13, 57–9, 121

reality effect 12, 30

'real thing', romance of 12, 15, 130

recorded sound: access to 178–80, 181, 182–3; archives 7, 199, 180–5; attitudes to 172–3, 177, 192; cataloguing process 178–9; control over 176; copyright 171, 184; and critical discourse 173–5; as cultural documents 171, 177–8; intrusive 173; preservation 180; professional or untrained voices 65, 188; transcription of 185–6; *see also* audio technology

representations 3, 6, 84; alternative 107, 119; of the people 4, 5; of women 6, 106–7, 119, 121

restitution of artefacts 13, 148–50

Rivière, Georges-Henri 32

rural life, conceptions of 69

St Fagans, Welsh Folk Museum 70, 182

sale of collections 94–5

Scandinavia, folk revival 4, 12, 63, 70

Science Museum 16, 24; admission charges 92; household appliances, display 6, 115–19; Nuclear Physics/Nuclear Power Gallery 96–7, 132; origins 129–30; pressures on 5–6

science and technology museums: nationalist ideology 132–3, 138; new initiatives 128–9, 139–42

security arrangements 225–6

Seeger, Peggy 186

Segaud, Marion 7, 170

selection, principles of 104

sentimentality and the past 64, 65, 67, 74, 77–8

servants, female 109

Shepherd, R. 174

SHIC system 111, 114

Silver, Jeremy 7, 14

Skansen folk museum 70

skill, demonstrations 140

Sloane, Sir Hans 90

Smith, Stuart *41*

social class culture, and museums 63–4, 73, 82–3, 99, 104

Social History Curators Group 106

Social History and Industrial Classification *see* SHIC

social history museums 99–100; and contemporary industrial society 156; material culture and women's invisibility 106–10

Social Trends 217

Somerset Rural Life, Museum of 110

sound *see* recorded sound

South Kensington Museum 129

South London Art Gallery, Peckham 94

Southwark, London Borough 94

Spanish Armada, defeat 100

Special Temporary Employment Programme (STEP) 44

sponsorship 95–8, 190; and bias 96–8; multinational companies 133, 149–50

staff: accountability 104; bias 99; employment structure 44–5; female 105–6; 'floor staff' 226; housekeeping tasks 227; and local authority members 98–9; as moral guardians 224; MSC-funded 43–4, 45; and multicultural provision 228–9; new initiatives in 99, 228–30; and political interference 5, 98; power of 224–7; relations with visitors 214–15, 223–4; types of 11; volunteer labour 42–3

STEP *see* Special Temporary Employment Programme

stereotyping 150

Sullivan, Sir Arthur 172

surveillance, and security 225–6

surveys of visitors 216–20

Sweden, classification system 114